Chechen Blues

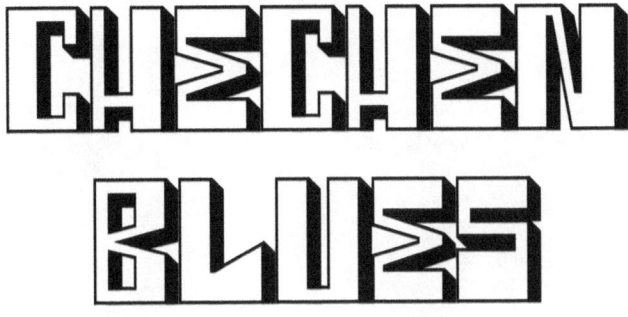

CHECHEN BLUES

BY

ALEXANDER PROKHANOV

TRANSLATED BY

ANNA IVANOVA

ANTELOPE HILL PUBLISHING

Translation Copyright © 2022 Antelope Hill Publishing

First printing 2022.

Originally published in Russian as Чеченский блюз by Moskva: Centrkniga, 1998. Translated with permissions.

Translated by Anna Ivanova 2022.

Cover art by Swifty.
Edited and formatted by Margaret Bauer.

Antelope Hill Publishing
www.antelopehillpublishing.com

Paperback ISBN-13: 978-1-953730-35-0
EPUB ISBN-13: 978-1-953730-36-7

"He wore a cloak that had been dipped in blood…"
Revelation 19:13

1

It was winter, with a pale sun and barely noticeable sparkle of frost. Under this chilly illumination there were protrusions and figures of armor, turrets of tanks with long, black cannons, APCs, columns of honed infantry war machines, cargo vans, and KUNGS,[1] with lattice dishes of antenna arrays, pins, crosshairs and masts, canvas tents spewing smoke from iron pipes, artillery tractors, and ambulances with stretchers. In its midst, a black pothole in the road that was hastily repaired caused a tank to break down and slip, unable to escape. And behind this road was a brown Chechen steppe with rusty hills and confused withered weeds, a reddish village with brick houses and a spindle-shaped prickly mosque.

Beyond this in the distant fog was a white-pink city with smoke, neighborhoods, indistinct flickers, waving steam, and mysterious, indistinct life. These sights were separated from Kudryavtsev's eyes by a thick, icy blue air punctuated with a rare flight of sparkling, multi-colored snowflakes. Captain Kudryavtsev, the company commander, was looking at Grozny, where the brigade was aiming. The city seemed like an illusion, ready to disappear that day on New Year's Eve. He was watching the flying sparks in the distance. The soles of his boots rested on dry, frozen ground, under which a liquid, unhardened mud stirred.

The combination of winter light through a blurred, silvery cloud and flashing, colored snowflakes had suddenly shaken him, as if an invisible particle had flown in and hit his temple. It punched a tiny hole, like a needle prick, and he flew into another space and time through this

---

[1] KUNG was a Soviet and then Russian term for a standardized military vehicle module/trailer system.

puncture. Their house was surrounded by a fence. There was frozen mud by the porch and a goose that acted like it was important and sleek. It was standing on its pink leg with its neck pulled in and its orange beak resting on its chest. A Christmas tree could be seen through the window. Anyone who saw it would feel a nostalgic sadness, a feeling that the last moments of the year were disappearing, and a premonition of something huge awaiting them as if it were a flight of sparkling snowflakes.

It lasted for just a second, and then he came back to reality. He was standing on the Chechen hills among tanks, antennas, and tents. The oil truck was driving slowly out of the muddy clay that covered the road. It was roaring loudly and sliding in the muddy tracks.

A messenger came running up, splashing through the puddles with his soiled boots. From afar he put his hand to his spotted cap for a salute and loudly cried out, "Comrade Captain! You must go to the brigade commander! It's urgent!"

He thought of the goose with the orange beak and the Christmas tree decorated with ornaments as he passed through an infantry square made up of armored personnel carriers and tanks, half-sunk in the mud. He went around the communication vehicles with squealing and screeching radios and the command tent covered with a camouflage net. He approached the KUNG where the brigade commander lived. In front of the KUNG, the chief of staff, the chief of artillery, a deputy for the rear, the chief of intelligence, and a special officer had already gathered.

The whole Great Khural, Kudryavtsev thought in awe, stopping a little further away so as not to mingle with the senior officers. *And why me, I wonder?* The officers impatiently rocked back and forth while glancing at the iron doors, from where the brigade commander was expected to appear.

The chief of staff was a thin man, with a dull, yellowish face. He also had a duck nose and painful, anxiously shifting eyes. He was feverishly coughing into his bony fist.

"Tell me the situation first! Give me the location of the enemy! Give me a line to the artillery! And only then push me into the city! We've been here for a week; have you been there, Scout? I'm asking you, can you show me the location of the strongholds?"

"Never mind where the strongholds are located!" The chief of intelligence dismissed him. "The trolleybuses are running, and the shops are open. Let's go in, look around, and I'll even take you out to a restaurant."

"They'll take you to a restaurant with a grenade launcher to the balls!" snapped the chief of staff and immediately started to hoarsely cough into his unwashed fist. Everyone watched how painfully his shoulder blades moved on his bent back.

The chief of staff was a smart and meticulous person. He was annoyed with the eternal ailments, disorder, lack of equipment and personnel, worn out engines, lack of shells, confusion, and haste in which this host convened. The engines were somehow loaded onto the transport. They were dragging them for a week across the Central Russian plains and landed them in the damp winter foothills, moving straight ahead, bypassing roads and highways. It was at dusk, on the very first encounter with the enemy from the neighboring hills, that the Grad rocket launchers struck the column. It destroyed a truck and overturned two APCs. Red tracers flew thickly in the darkness. White dotted lines of machine guns were crossing and flashing. A truck was burning with thick smoke, and the company commander, Kudryavtsev, came under fire for the first time. He stood there, watching perplexed at the chaotic dance of the multi-colored lights that filled the sky.

"Does anyone know why the brigade commander called us? Maybe to drink in honor of his new star?" the special officer bantered as he snapped his finger on his neck, as if he had already seen a soldier in a white apron, carrying fresh pastries and a pot of potatoes with green, poisonous-colored tomatoes, ready to be served on the table accompanied by their favorite bottle of booze.

"Lucky commander! He achieved colonel on New Year's Eve! That's what it means to be friends with Santa Claus!"

Everybody started laughing. The special officer's joke hinted at the commander's connections in Moscow, and the joker himself looked like the town drunk who knew where to drink.

The brigade was like a big village, where instead of houses and buildings, there were APCs and tanks lined up in formation. Any incident or rumor traveled from car to car, from crew to crew as quickly as rumors spread within a village. The order to bestow the rank of colonel had not yet come through officially, but only through word of mouth as it became common knowledge to every ensign and conscripted soldier, which excited them and made them happy. It seemed as if it touched them personally and promised good changes. The officers were happy, but also envious, because they knew that with the brigade commander's new rank, the way to Moscow was opened to him, toward the elegant, sugar-colored building of the General Staff Military Academy, away from the Chechen fields, away from the frosty cars in the city square and the foggy, dirty-white, and hostile city.

"The commander made it clear that in the evening we are to wash the star," said the deputy from the rear. He was a plump, loose major, whose uniform sat awkwardly, as if damp, whose cheeks turned a deep red crimson when in stressful situations. "I got a calf for the occasion. Let's taste some fresh veal."

"Whose is it? Dudaevsk's?" asked the special officer, wafting at the air, as if hoping to catch the smell of hot meat aromatizing around the cold armor and exhaust of the tank.

"Where, dare I ask, did you get it?"

"He surrendered himself as a prisoner of war!" the deputy at the rear chuckled and looked over at the towers and cannons in the distant rusty hills, where the village was turning red in the evening sunlight frost with a mosque in plain view. "He voluntarily came over to our side!"

Kudryavtsev stood at a distance, listening to the officers joking. He was uncomfortable and anxious in the winter wind, which carried away the bluish exhaust of the tank. Under the low sky was the pointed mosque, and the white sun peaked through the camouflage net. There were many prints of soldiers' boots in the viscous, frost-stuck mud. Everything was so fragile, but it all gets lost in time. It was the last day of the year, and it was already ending.

The metal door of the KUNG opened with a screech, and the brigade commander appeared. He knew that they were waiting for him; he had heard some of the conversations.

His pink, shaven face displayed health and freshness. It was not affected by the difficult and dangerous crossings along the muddy Chechen roads under the sullen looks of the residents who watched the movement of the armored columns. His black, cheeky mustache over his luscious lips was trimmed, and in his dark, shiny eyes, mocking and imperious, he was anticipating the officer's holiday at the New Year's celebration. His dense body, deftly and well-drawn into a clean, ironed shape, enjoyed the opportunity to move, as he balanced on the wobbly steps of the KUNG. In the frosty wind it smelled of expensive cologne from his wet, smoothly-combed hair, from his vest that turned blue at the unbuttoned collar, and from his washed hands and pink nails. An oval mirror shined through the open door, in the illuminated space of the KUNG, along with a small, green, faux Christmas tree with glass ornaments.

"Hello, comrade officers!" the brigade commander said cheerfully, benevolently and contentedly looking around at his companions who were waiting for him. They were a close-knit circle of people who knew and respected each other, among whom he sat at the head of the table.

"Allow me to congratulate, Comrade Lieutenant Colonel!" the chief of artillery cheerfully and loudly exclaimed, capturing the mood of the commander, and playing along with him.

"What should I congratulate you with?" the commander raised a thick eyebrow, feigning surprise. "It seems that half a day is left before the New Year!"

"Congratulations on your promotion to colonel!" the chief of artillery reported loudly, as if conducting the ceremony himself. "And if you're ready, Comrade Brigade Commander, we are ready to toast your star!"

"What do you mean!? Where did you hear that? There is no such promotion!" the brigade commander was dismissing superstitiously, pretending to be angry while shaking his beautifully-combed head. But the smile that ran over his ruddy lips could not hide the fact that he already knew about his promotion. He was happy and thankful to the officers who congratulated him on the good news.

"I'll give you the star, comrade Brigade Commander," said the special officer, squinting his eyes at his own field shoulder strap with the green star for the rank of major. "Let's drink a toast! And the army surplus will arrive and join us. Larisa will open her tent, where you can buy a star from her and give it to me."

Everyone smiled and winked faintly. Of course, they did not believe that the special officer did not already have a couple of new stars to pin on the commander. Before going on the campaign while waiting on their orders, the special officer took care and bought them in town. In the military shop, behind the counter, among the piled copper buttons, gilded cockades, chevrons, field and ceremonial shoulder straps, stood the regal, magnificent, and lazy saleswoman Larisa with wet, shimmering eyes, a white, open neck, and fragrant hair that fell to her shoulders. She was constantly smiling at something, absent-mindedly listening to customers. Everyone knew that she was not indifferent to the brigade commander. Now, lagging behind the brigade, she moved with the rear in the van of the military surplus. The brigade commander hung an oval mirror in his KUNG, decorated a Christmas tree, trimmed his mustache, and sprayed himself with cologne, expecting from hour to hour the appearance of the long-awaited rear column.

"As you all know, we have deployed a task force to the district," said the brigade commander, becoming serious. "The general is recalling us to his location. I believe there will be a brigade review. Each of you, I am sure, will be able to competently answer the deputy commander's questions. Do not overestimate our capabilities, and do not try to show off. But do not underestimate, and do not groan and cry... Do I make myself clear, Scout?"

"Yes sir, comrade Colonel!" the scout leaped to attention with his dashing, hussar mustache. His bulging, blue eyes laughed.

Everyone appreciated this appeal to the brigade commander as an accomplished colonel. The brigade commander did not correct him. An expression of undisguised pleasure arose and lasted for a moment on his cheerful face.

"Comrade Brigade Commander, did you call me?" Kudryavtsev reminded the commander that he was there, standing aside, not mingling with the senior officers invited to report to the general.

"You will come with us," the brigade commander said sternly. "We will show him your company as being the most effective in terms of combat and political training." He said the last words with irritation, making it clear that he was talking about the most recent incident. Two warrant officers, drunk, opened fire from their Grad and damaged a roof in the Chechen village, causing some indignant old men from the village to protest the brigade commander.

"And in the evening, we'll have a festive dinner! Deputy for the rear, get four bottles from the emergency rations!"

He jumped off the steps of the KUNG. The officers parted, letting him in, and followed their commander. Kudryavtsev, closing the procession, saw the polished boots of the brigade commander shine and the frozen, viscous mud crumble under them.

The headquarters tent, into which the officers entered, was intensely heated. The iron stove crackled with wood, and the crimson coals could be seen. Lamps hung from the ceiling under tin visors. A huge map of Grozny lay on the floor under a blinding light. Around it, trying not to step on the blocks, neighborhoods, and streets, the officers stood. The large map showed neighboring units scattered across the steppe from consolidated regiments to artillery batteries and Marine Corps brigades. They looked enchanted at the city, which had arrows dismembering it. The general walked on the map, advancing on crisp paper with leather boots. He was clean-shaven, with a big elbow and stubbornly-knitted eyebrows. Heavy eyes glanced sternly at the officers. The general was in striped pants that were tucked into his socks. He wore leather slippers that were pointed upwards and a red brace over his uniform as he walked across the map's urban landscape, which gave him resemblance to General Yermolov, who, as Kudryavtsev read about, also walked in slippers on a map spread like a carpet in a camping tent. Kudryavtsev was amazed at the coincidence. And then he guessed that the general deliberately wanted to be like Yermolov, and he wanted the audience to discover this similarity.

"I gathered you here to bring orders from the minister of defense. The orders arrived at the task force last night. It is not open for discussion, and we will do our best to immediately fulfill it."

He looked around at the officers with heavy eyes peering out from under their bulging foreheads, and Kudryavtsev could not tell whether these expressions were connected to their new orders or with the irony in the general's resemblance to Yermolov. Kudryavtsev noticed the brigade commander of the Marine Corps also perceived the subtle irony. He grinned and said something quickly to his neighbor, an officer in a black Marine uniform.

"The orders from the minister of defense read as follows: Parts of the brigade stationed within the vicinity of Grozny must enter the city. Move toward the administrative center, from the Presidential Palace to the post office, to the train station, to the main government administrative buildings. Stand in blocks along the main street and, indicating presence, take up defensive positions. Do not engage the enemy, which will give them the opportunity to leave the city in groups along the abandoned corridors.

"Enemies that will leave the city become targets for our aviation and artillery and will be defeated and scattered outside residential areas of the densely populated city, which is fraught with great destruction and casualties among the civilian population. Due to being unprepared and small in number, the enemy cannot offer serious resistance to the regular army. The regiments and brigades are scheduled to perform today, at 1600 hours. I invite everyone to listen to the plan for entering the city that was developed by the task force…"

It became so quiet that one could distinctly hear the humming vibration of the crimson stove and the crunch of the paper map, on which the general's pointed shoes stepped over. The officers were silent, assimilating what they heard. The general was also silent, giving some time for surprise, disagreement, misunderstanding, and murmurings to slowly and steadily turn into readiness for carrying out the military order.

"Now the details about the routes, the individual tasks assigned to each military unit, and the rules of engagement," the general broke the silence, believing that the order was imprinted under the skullcaps of the commanders where it fit tightly and meaningfully behind their foreheads, at the bottom of their eyeballs. The order was also imprinted on the bridges of their noses and in dark wrinkles. "Our orders are as follows…"

His pointing stick looked like a billiard cue and was inlaid with bone and pearl pieces. Copper rings were placed onto the mahogany along its entire length.

He used the pointing stick like a cue, as if preparing to break the pyramid of pool balls. And one of these balls represented Kudryavtsev's company, as well as his life.

"There are three routes offered. The Motorized Rifle brigade, another consolidated regiment, and separately, the Marine Corps brigades. The routes should allow all brigades to reach their destinations at the same time at 2200 hours and take up defensive positions…"

Kudryavtsev watched the general's pointer move around the map. He tried to learn the plan by heart. He tried to remember the streets along which the armored vehicles and tanks would pass, the names of squares and parks where ambushes and mine explosions were possible, crossroads from which shelling and raids were possible. He knew his company would be in the vanguard. His company was supposed to be the first to go to the station square, put up obstacles in front of the train stations and warehouses, and wait for the Marines to come out on the flank along the railroad tracks.

The arc will close, and like a compressed spring, the armed groups of Chechens will begin to retreat. The company commander stood up to his waist in the hatch of the tank and looked at the stucco building of the station and the platform of the shiny track which reflected the night's light.

He saw the track and the building of the station as if looking at a color photograph, even though he had never seen or been there before. The distant city dragged him into its gravity, with excitement and a sweet anxiety generating in his soul. But there were also premonitions and fears that were akin to knowledge. Flexible steel columns deployed turret machine guns and cannons on two sides into a sort of herringbone, led ready to attack the lighted windows, facades, and night lamps in lilac rings. This sweet anxiety atoned for all hardships and tribulations and made his military profession attractive and desirable.

"Unit commanders and chiefs of staff will receive city maps with route markings. You will have time to explain and brief these orders to the commanders of the units," the general explained. He threw his pointer into the air and deftly caught it by the thick end, as experienced billiard players do before bending down and placing their spread fingers on the green cloth of the billiard table. "I must add that tomorrow is the minister of defense's birthday. Accomplishing this task he has assigned us will be the best birthday present. And he, I know," the general smiled, showing his strong, yellowish teeth that made him look like an elderly yard dog, "will make sure there is proper compensation and rewards! Any questions?"

The general twisted his bobbed head impatiently, looking at the commanders, artillerymen, scouts, signalmen, and air gunners. Not expecting inappropriate and ridiculous questions, he was preparing to release them from the heated tent out into the damp space where tanks and combat vehicles hunched over.

"Questions?" he repeated, glancing at the table lined with telephones and walkie-talkies, near which the signalman was on duty.

Kudryavtsev observed the officers and saw how differently they took the minister's order. Some, and among them the brigade commander of the Marines, did not discuss the order. Concerned and stern, they were already thinking about how to fulfill it. The officers were among the armored columns, assigning the crews to their vehicles and making sure that nobody was lagging behind. The vehicles entered the filling stations, along with the ammunition trucks and the ambulances. Others, and among them Kudryavtsev's commander, were upset and annoyed and complained about the disrupted New Year's dinner, silently hating the general and the minister of defense, who decided to drag troops into the city on New Year's Eve, dooming them to a sad night in iron cars, making it impossible to sit by the hot stoves, in a smoky KUNG for a roast, for a bottle, for anecdotes and songs with a guitar. Still others, who are younger, such as the chief of intelligence, whipping in different directions with his gallant golden mustache, rejoiced at the unexpected throw, the opportunity to distinguish themselves, to be in full view of their superiors, to earn awards and titles. A few, such as the chief of staff, were tormented by disagreement but did not dare express it to the general.

They were ready to remain silent, and to carry their disagreement with them.

The chief of staff looked at the brigade commander and tried to catch his eye. With a suffering and dissenting look, he urged the brigade commander to speak on behalf of the brigade officers. But the brigade commander was silent.

"Can I ask a question, Comrade General?" the chief of staff turned to the general with a thin, yellow face, plagued by malaise and insomnia.

"Speak!" the general said with displeasure, annoyed at the delay.

"I have several remarks on the outlined plan of the operation," the chief of staff greedily gulped the hot, smoke-filled air, as if preparing to rush into fluid-like airless depths, gathering all his remaining energy for a fatal leap. "I must report that there is not enough intel about the enemy at the brigade headquarters: their numbers, weapons, places of deployment, methods of ambush. The team, due to lack of time, was deprived of the opportunity to carry out reconnaissance on their own, but the task force did not receive information from our intelligence agents..."

The general rolled his eyes, swelling with anger in surprise. His feet in woolen socks and shoes were in a stable position, as if he was preparing to strike a boxing punch into the ugly, duck-nosed face of the chief of staff, who no longer wanted to notice the danger.

"It seems to me that our armored columns' advance through city blocks without any support from infantry and without first setting up roadblocks on the routes contradicts the classic tactics of combat in urban areas. In the academies we were taught to use the experience of recent wars. There is danger in exposing military hardware and personnel under attacks of grenade launchers and snipers..."

The officers were ready to disperse, to take with them an unexpected plan of operation full of absurdities and contradictions, in order to proceed at their own peril and risk, filling in the gaps with their own experience, with the skills and diligence of their soldiers and the hope of military success. The officers whispered, trampled underfoot, and shook their heads, supporting the brave chief of staff, who, like some sort of suicidal person, objected to the minister's order.

"In addition, the backlog of rear units and the lack of fuel and ammunition can lead to complications during the fighting. Insufficient subunits, incoordination of consolidated regiments, poor training of personnel, who are mostly first year soldiers, can lead to significant casualties in such difficult urban battlefields..."

The general blushed, as if a red lantern had been pointed at him. His cheeks were becoming crimson, like a red-hot stove wall. He felt the mood of the officers, who had grown bolder after the speech of the chief of staff. They were ready to bombard the general with a barrage of questions, remarks, and doubts. Blushing, he was gripping his cue with his white bone fist.

"Therefore," the chief of staff concluded his speech, looking not just into the general's face, but also at his shoes, which were trampling on the map of the city, "it seems appropriate to postpone the operation into the city for a week. Conduct intensive reconnaissance along traffic routes. Draw up detailed schematic maps showing us each checkpoint's location, every street name and every building number. Bind artillery targets at every intersection and obstructions that the enemy can use as strong points. Use the delay time for accelerating coordination, training the personnel of the subunits. That's all, Comrade General."

He stopped talking, feeling amazement at his courage. For a moment, a void formed around him, like around a stone that had fallen into the water. In a second, the irritability and impatience of the officers should have poured into this awkward silence. And anticipating them, the general stepped toward the chief of staff, crunching the map of the city, stepping on the Presidential Palace, on the central street, on the station building under purple winter lanterns, and on the black-and-white steel track reflecting lights.

"Who are you to question the order of the minister of defense!?" the general raised his voice, in almost a shout, giving his voice a deliberate scream and wheeze. "You talk like a self-taught soldier, who was allowed to participate in regimental exercises! Did you know that the plan was developed in the Main Operations Directorate, using all the data from space and from all the intelligence at our disposal?! It is fully agreed upon with the political leaders of the country! It had been finalized at the headquarters of the district! It was brought to you after dozens of the best staff officers worked on it!"

The general established himself in his superiority. He saw the chief of staff cringing, pressing his narrow head into his shoulders. Pale, white spots appeared on his yellowish, haggard face.

"The operation is bloodless and purely demonstrative," the general continued. "It will not require large-scale street battles like in Berlin in 1945. According to operational data, the enemy is already leaving the city, seeping out of it in small groups. You just need to push, make some noise, rattle the cage, and he will retreat. Chechens are all bandits and thieves who are only capable of robbing trains and store counters. They will scatter at the sight of such a show of force. Therefore, I repeat, the plan assumes organization in solid columns and placement in open areas of the city!"

The general, large, strong, crimson, felt his moral and physical superiority over the stunted and sickly chief of staff. He bent him over and continued to bend and break him, and along with him the silent, retreating officers, who gave over the unlucky comrade to the general's reprisal. Kudryavtsev alone felt their torment, cowardice, and inability to support. The brigade commander averted his eyes. He did not want them to meet with the general's, the chief of staff's, or anyone else's who was looking for a commanding gaze.

"Maybe you're just afraid?" the general scoffed. "Maybe you just don't want to tear your ass off the warm stove? Maybe you prefer to get spoiled on New Year's Eve? In recent years, there are too many officers who are accustomed to the rear's chow and are afraid of combat like a devil running away from incense. If you are a coward, write a report and I will dismiss you from the operation! Your comrades will go without you, and then we will deal with you personally!"

Kudryavtsev saw how the chief of staff was insulted, how the cowardly brigade commander was not saying a word, how the suppressed officers slumped. He felt shame and disgust for the general and contempt for the brigade commander. He was ready to speak from behind the officers and throw furious words in the face of the offender, but the phone rang out loudly, with a special ringing, and the signalman hastily grabbed the receiver and reported, "The First is in touch, Comrade General!" the general's expression changed from an imperious, merciless one into another, helpful and respectful.

He gripped the phone tightly and said, "I can hear you, Comrade Minister… That's right, Comrade Minister… The order has been given to the troops, Comrade Minister… The attitude is fighting, cheerful, Comrade Minister! And where else should they go? Just forward… Happy birthday and a Happy New Year… We will be glad to see you in Grozny, and, as they say, clink glasses with you in the Presidential Palace… Thank you… Thank you for everything… Everything will be done, Comrade Minister!"

Kudryavtsev heard the conversation. He was imagining Moscow's white marble ministry building, a huge office with portraits of tsars and generals and huge globes, in front of several colored telephones where a festive, energetic minister with the cheerful eyes of a paratrooper stood. The minister puts a gold star onto his shoulder strap and sends greetings to the Chechen hills and foothills.

The general hung up the telephone with a loud slam. For another moment he kept a solemn expression on his weathered, crimson face.

"The meeting is over, comrade officers! Prepare the troops for the march. At midnight, I will personally arrive to the city to check on the execution of our orders and wish the commanders and personnel a happy New Year!"

He turned away and went into the depths of the tent, crossing the crisp map. The officers left, silently and gloomily dispersing. Kudryavtsev saw how the brigade commander was nervously fiddling his trimmed mustache, like a stooped, old man stepping toward the chief of staff. He felt embarrassment for his commanders. He lagged behind them in order to not hear the scout's inappropriate, awkward jokes.

2

The brigade's headquarters was just a canvas tent with a hot iron stove. Next to the oven was a soldier whose thin face and tips of his tenacious fingers were illuminated as he threw pine into the fire. The brigade commander assigned the required tasks for each battalion and company commander. Young officers dressed in gray-green uniforms with faded field shoulder straps, on which major's and captain's stars were barely distinguishable, took the order with excitement. They were discussing the problem loudly, nudging with their elbows, looking at the map, poking their fingers at the marked dotted line of the route, taking note of the radio frequencies and call signs, clarifying the width of the alleys and streets, the possibility of quick delivery of fuel, shells, ambulances. There was also light-hearted banter.

"Comrade Major, you didn't get an opportunity to drink. You won't have another chance for a whole year!"

"And you said there wouldn't be any champagne! Now look, we'll enter the city and buy some from the first store we see!

"Klimuk, you were dying to find a woman! Consider yourself lucky. We'll get to crash the New Year's celebrations!"

"Kudryavtsev, as always, you've got the armored columns in mind! Let us know on the radio which restaurants are open. We can book a table in the train station's restaurant!"

Kudryavtsev almost forgot the ugly circumstances surrounding them. Like everyone else, he was excited and anxious. His body, mind, and soul were searching for a meaningful goal. For this purpose, he endured the hardships of engaging in routine work, helplessly shaken on the liquid mud roads, hitting his chest against the edge of the steel hatch, cursing when the engine stalled and needed to be towed out of the mud. The city was waiting for him ahead, the huge, bustling city, inhabited by many lives he was not acquainted with, some of which were scared and did not want him to appear, while others were impatiently waiting. He would enter this fallen, agitated city, which had broken apart into several fields of battle. He would have to pull it together with iron braces and restore peace and order to this place. The city promised an unpredictable, desirable future, which would reveal courage, luck, and heroism.

The chief of staff, still crumpled and shaken, was gradually moving past the shame inflicted upon him. He explained to the young officers the subtleties of the mission ahead, "Keep the armor close to the buildings, okay? Don't block the roadway; we need the reinforcements to be able to get through, understood? Troopers! Get to your assignments! If something goes wrong, focus all your firepower on their grenade launchers!"

The brigade commander felt bad for the chief of staff, for he was experiencing his own cowardice. He kept repeating to himself, "Do not think that this will be a walk in the park! We don't have any verified information about the enemy! You've never been taught how to fight in urban battles! Besides, the city is ours; it is Russian. Russian citizens live there! Remember, your guns will be aimed at Russian citizens!"

The officers were listening, nodding, and not believing they would have to use their weapons. They wanted to get out of this boring, drab steppe as soon as possible and move into the city. They had already memorized their roles and were rushing to their battalions and companies to prepare everyone for the attack.

Kudryavtsev's company was integrated into the defensive infantry square of the brigade. Around them were the trenches, fortifications, APCs, tents, soldiers' outhouses, drinking water tanks, smoking kitchens, sentries, an invisible network of land mines, heaps of empty cans, all the iron, explosives, plowed red earth, and human flesh that exuded the transparent haze of life into the cold air. The gray weeds were cut as the sappers dug into the ground, revealing the cone of fire. The fresh, unfrozen opening of the fortification was dark.

The combat vehicle plunged its camouflaged compact body into the opening and directed its cannon onto the steppe. Soldiers were sitting around the car on ammo crates, wooden panels, and canvas raincoats. The sounds of laughter and whistles rang out.

There was a pine branch at the back of the IFV where it was fixed in place. Instead of Christmas tree ornaments, it was decorated with colored cigarette wrappers, foil, and polished can lids. At the top of the tree there was a bright brass shell from one of the cannons. In front of the decorated branch, two soldiers dressed up as Santa Claus and the Snow Maiden were putting on a show, whistling and dancing. Santa Claus had no shirt, his pumped muscles shaking, with a thick, gold bracelet glittering on his wrist. He wore a dirty Chechen hat with a makeshift beard made from a ruffled rag. Santa Claus was shaking his hips, puffing out his biceps, and hugging the Snow Maiden's waist. The soldier dressed as the Snow Maiden was also shirtless, wearing a homemade bra stuffed with rags. He also wore a short skirt that was falling from his belly, from under which crooked, hairy legs could be seen. From his belly button up under the bra, a blue tattoo snake was seen too. As the two soldiers put on a show, the others were bursting into laughter, hitting their plates with spoons, whistling, throwing woodchips, lumps of dirt, and crumpled newspapers at the dancing couple.

Kudryavtsev approached them, taking a deep breath of cold air, preparing to exhale it with a commander's roar, to interrupt the laughter and whistling, crush the naive soldiers' celebration, and send them to work into their assigned roles and places. As he grew near, he inexplicably hesitated and could not find the right timing nor the right step and rhythm. He did not want to interrupt the soldiers' holiday and laughter.

"Comrade Captain!" The platoon commander jumped up to meet him, a young pink-cheeked lieutenant with a delicate porcelain face, shining with transparent, blue eyes that made him look like Cupid. When Kudryavtsev saw him, the lieutenant reminded him of an old painting on the ceiling in one of those old museums: plump, fresh, with wings and a wreath of roses. The lieutenant didn't have any roses, but instead, a mug of hot tea. His nails were dirty, and he had a crumpled, green cap that was pulled over his head, covering his blond hair. But he still had a sort of youthful freshness in his appearance, preserved against the cold winds, sleeping on armor and with the tough conditions of camp life.

"Second platoon will be…"

"Belay that!" Kudryavtsev interrupted him, seeing how the soldiers turned around, disappointed by his appearance. Santa Claus and the Snow Maiden reluctantly uncoiled their arms.

"At ease!"

Kudryavtsev did not understand why he allowed them to continue celebrating. The lieutenant sat him down on the ammo crates, shaking off the lumps of dirt. The soldiers returned to their festivities, not wishing to disappoint the commander.

Santa Claus puffed out his biceps with a blue vein, glittering with the gold bracelet. He grabbed the Snow Maiden's rag breasts and danced in front of her, singing folk songs and staring at the soldiers' bulging eyes. He sang:

"With the little Snow Maiden,
"I was playing hide-and-seek!
"I shoved her off the tree,
"And planted my needle in her...!
"Ho-ho-ho-ho-ho-ho-ho!"

He was tapping the armor with his shoes, while obscenely thrusting his hips into the air and pointing to his groin. The soldiers put their hands to their sides and sang along. The little cherub lieutenant was also laughing with the group. Kudryavtsev was not happy to hear such a vulgar song sung in the thug's voice.

In Kudryavtsev's eyes, the lieutenant looked just as repulsive as the other soldiers, and it make him feel uneasy. These troops were recruited quickly and from the many different regions of the country, from different garrisons, and they didn't have the time to transform into a well-coordinated combat unit.

The Snow Maiden was dancing with his crooked, hairy legs, fanning himself with a torn piece of newspaper instead of a handkerchief and answered his partner:

"Our commander is as handsome
"As a scarlet flower.
"He says to each of us: 'F— you'
"But has too small a tool for that!
"Ho-ho-ho-ho-ho-ho-ho!"

Everyone was chuckling, looking back at the red-faced lieutenant. The man blushed, not knowing how to react to this insolence. He decided not to show how offended he was and laughed with everybody, red with resentment.

And this behavior unpleasantly struck Kudryavtsev, the debauchery and insolence of these mercenaries who flew into the brigade from God knows which barracks and drunk tanks. The platoon commander was weak and inexperienced and did not know how to properly show these scoundrels their place.

Santa Claus bounced off the Snow Maiden, almost knocking over the

Christmas tree with the polished shell. He started dancing in a squat while thundering on the stern of the vehicle and singing in the same ragged, hysterical voice:

"One day a Chechen came to me,

"Flashing his one-meter dick.

"Quickly I took TNT,

"And shortened it immediately!

"Wow, oh-oh!"

He was dancing, holding his hand with the bracelet above his head, and the Snow Maiden, wagging his hips, twitched with his sunken belly, on which the blue, prickled snake wriggled among the pimples and scratches.

Everyone was giggling in unison, making a beat with whatever they could bang on. One soldier in unlaced boots folded some newspaper that held an air pocket, popped it loudly, and then threw the torn newspaper into the crowd.

Kudryavtsev chuckled and caught himself thinking that he might have thought the display amusing. He, like the other soldiers, were sick and tired of these rusty, frost-covered hills, which from behind them was a possibility that a lone whistling bullet would fly toward the group. Kudryavtsev felt bitterness toward the red-bricked, wealthy Chechen villages, with green iron gates and pointed mosques, in front of which were silent, stern people in hats and flat-topped leather caps. But, having caught this bitterness in himself, he immediately drove it away. The city they were to enter was inhabited by Chechens, Tatars, and Russians. This was the bond that all the soldiers shared, a common experience of living so far from home, near factory chimneys and power transmission towers in the foggy remote districts.

The Snow Maiden could not think of a good duet, so he missed his turn. All he did was squeal, kick, and made some more obscene dances. Santa Claus slapped his butt and sang:

"I've been digging a latrine all day,

"Because I am not a banker.

"Come to us, bankers,

"And christen the toilet."

Everyone was falling over with delight and whistling loudly. The young lieutenant forgot his grievance and gave them a thumbs up, encouraging the performance. And once again, Kudryavtsev caught himself enjoying the display, for he, like everyone else, had a dislike for the mysterious inaccessible bankers who scheme in their mansions and glass towers, sending troops to this winter steppe, supplying stale stewed meat, patched up tents, and thin mattresses thrown onto the bottom of the cars. He has not seen a single banker. There were no bank employees among his friends and acquaintances, either. But, like many other officers he had a strong dislike for the bankers' unknown, newly born tribe, with which many troubles were associated.

"And now Santa Clause will give us gifts!" the Snow Maiden announced. Kudryavtsev saw a cloud of hot steam erupt out of his open, gaping mouth. "Santa Claus, what did you bring for us?"

He fluttered his rag beard and bent awkwardly over the hatch, reached inside, and pulled out a cardboard beer box. He took out a present from the box, a polished red and yellow submachine gun cartridge. He held it with two fingers, turned it in all directions, and showed the soldiers as if it were a diamond.

"Come here in a single file line before I change my mind!"

The soldiers were jumping up and reaching for the gifts, and Santa Claus was bending over the armor, distributing them. Then they happily returned to their places and examined the cartridge, on which the year "1995" was neatly inscribed in black paint.

Kudryavtsev felt a vague, superstitious excitement as he was watching the soldiers. They all were venturing into the unknown, pushing their limits, with outstretched hands, stained with dirt and machine lubricant, accepting bullets as gifts.

Santa Claus, sarcastic and taunting, passed out bullets to everyone, as if he were inducting them into the brotherhood. He gave them the one and only thing he could give to them in the winter Chechen steppe.

"Comrade Captain, take one too!" the platoon commander said smiling happily with fresh crimson lips, holding his small souvenir in his palm. "There's enough for everyone!"

Kudryavtsev hesitated. He was struggling with premonitions and was overwhelmed by superstition. He arrived at the combat vehicle. Santa Claus, playfully grinning and winking, stretched out his hand with the gold bracelet. He dropped an acorn-heavy cartridge with the neat, black numbers into his palm.

"Happy New Year, Comrade Captain! Save the gift! You'll remember this day until the day you die!" And he laughed, while the steam and bad smell of fumes hit him.

"Comrade Captain, let me continue the concert!" the lieutenant turned to him, naively believing that he had pleased the commander. "Many more great numbers!"

Kudryavtsev was swept up in the moment, looking at the man giving gifts, the crooked pine branch decorated with cigarette foil, and the time in which he lived, like water flowing into a small spinning funnel.

He dove through this tiny vortex to another time, to another New Year...

The school was built from dry, warm timber. There was a small hall with the portraits of writers and scientists, and a hot tile stove. Reaching up to the swarthy wooden ceiling was a tree, with a sparkling glass top, resting against it with a fragile gold point: fresh, oily, thawed, in trickles of silver threads. In the hot gloom among the music, flashing faces, crackling firecrackers, fountains of confetti, he danced a waltz. He danced with the teacher, a young and lovely woman whom he adored! He looked straight into her eyes, smelled her perfume, and bent over the tracks of her boots printed in white snow, kissing the grade she wrote down in his notebook. Now, at the New Year's ball, he is dancing with her. He can feel her breath, wrapping his arm around her waist, feeling her flexible body moving through the dress. Whirling, almost losing consciousness, falling, seeing a silver ornament on the tree, he pressed himself to her chest, experiencing a sweet sensation, a fiery romantic excitement. He saw her laughing green eyes that reflected the tree.

Then, he woke up in the IFV with a pine branch decorated in foil, and in the palm of his hand: a brass cartridge.

"Comrade Captain, let me continue the concert!" the lieutenant said while looking at him with anticipation.

Kudryavtsev took in a deep, cold breath of air from the steppe. He turned to the soldiers. The angry shout exhaled with a hot stream, which interrupted their fun and celebration, "This concert is over! Platoon!"

And with his command, the soldiers rushed to their stations from car to car, from caponier to caponier, from one troop compartment to another; this was music to his ears. Engines started roaring, and the curly blue haze was gathered. Armored cars came to life slowly, twisting in their tracks, throwing out clods of earth, and crawling out of the fortifications. And everywhere, among the trucks, vans and tanks, young, excited people ran, hurried while shouting. Kudryavtsev was walking, urging them to act livelier and harmoniously with his commands and shouts.

He peered behind the vans of the field bakery, where the field kitchens were located, where split boards lay, and where empty cans that did not have time to rust sparkled. He saw three ensigns; they were standing in front of a birch block, on which an open bottle of vodka gleamed. One was bringing a glass to his lips, while the other two were chewing, holding slices of stewed bread. Hanging from the side of the van, suspended by the legs, was a half-skinned veal carcass with pearly tendons and golden, cut skin. Blood had accumulated under it, black and sticky, not absorbing into the wet earth. Between the drooping legs with dark hooves was a stump of a neck with a sugar-pink vertebra visible. On the ground lay a severed calf's head with a rough, pink nose, velvet ears, and hazy, blue eyes with whitish eyelashes. The lips were parted, and the tip of the tongue was visible, clenched by its teeth. The head was looking in the distance, through the vans, cooking pots, piles of cans, into the twilight steppe, where the blurred city lay.

"What is going on?" asked Kudryavtsev, stepping back from the pool of blood, which was now black as oil.

"Well, we've slaughtered the calf," one of the ensigns answered lazily, showing his yellow teeth and continuing to chew. "The deputy for the rear wanted to cook dinner, and now, you see, we have orders to attack! So, we decided to take it to the city with us where we will cook it. Otherwise, the soldiers will just feast like vultures here."

"And in the city, we'll chop it into pieces and cook it in the cauldrons," added the man who had just taken a drink of vodka. He grimaced, sniffled, and broke off a piece of meat. "We'll even have enough to cook some aspic!"

The head of the calf, with its spread out, golden, suede ears, looked aloof into the distance, and it reminded Kudryavtsev of someone. Someone very familiar and alive. But he could not understand who. The sight of this dead, sad-looking head, warm, enveloped in wet steam, pressed against the iron side of the van struck Kudryavtsev. He kept trying to remember who the head that had been cut off and placed on the vertebrae reminded him of.

"Maybe you can join us for a drink, Comrade Captain?" the ensign suggested, pointing to an open bottle and a used, wet glass. "To warm up!"

"No," replied Kudryavtsev, and he walked away, feeling the insolent warrant officers watching him. He just could not think of who it was that reminded him of the severed head.

3

The brigade moved sullenly. The straining, huge, steel body breathed and squelched. The soldiers woke up, angrily and grumpily shaking off the dirt and litter. It was a difficult task to get everything ready as they crawled out of their dens and into the light. And in this cold light their bulging muscles began to glow dimly, their eye sockets flickered, and sharp, metal claws scraped the ground. And where an invisible creature had recently been snoozing, there was a steamy black rut, an imprint of a huge body, a damp, sweaty bed, from which a disturbed beast rose and walked on its mighty crooked paws.

Kudryavtsev was standing in the hatch of his IFV, squeezing the walkie-talkie, sending commands to the platoon commanders. He directed the vehicles to the nearest path while dodging the movement of oncoming vehicles and clumsy tanks. They moved into a single, slowly assembled column, into which platoons and companies, communications vehicles, ammo trucks, and support trucks were driven in with shouts and obscenities on battalion radio frequencies. The marshallers were being splashed in mud and choking on the caustic burning fumes as they signaled to the tank drivers with their wands. As angry drivers shouted, they waved their sticks to direct the stupid, clumsy herd in one direction to the black, earthen path onto which they were organized into a marching column.

In the opposite hatch, separated from Kudryavtsev by the barrel of the cannon, was the platoon commander. His soft, flaming face, transfixed into a filthy tank helmet, was blushing in the wind like a rosehip. He leaned into the hatch, shouting something angrily and rudely to the driver. But, looking out over the vast space filled with smoke, delight

23

shone in his eyes as he opened his crimson lips. It was obvious that he was rejoicing, feeling that his small, insignificant life had a purpose in this mighty armada and that anyone who joined it became invincible and omnipotent.

The brigade slowly lined up, and the tanks moved like a careful predator, lightly touching the ground. The brigade stretched across the steppe among the gray hills. Scaly, swollen iron flesh cluttered the tops of the hills. As they lowered into the valley like a big-eyed head with an armored forehead, the tail wriggled listlessly among the potholes, fortifications, abandoned sanitary facilities, and dumps. The head was tense, meaningful, and fixed on a tight, swollen neck as it rushed forward to an invisible but desired goal.

Kudryavtsev placed himself at the head of the column in front of a platoon of heavy tanks that threw mud bricks toward him.

The steel tracks glittered in the black thick. The taillights of the tanks turned red, the call signs and codes sounded on the air, and through the wheezing and whistling he recognized the voices of the battalion and company commanders and the rare, intermittent commands of the brigade commander and the chief of staff, who, as the column lined up, became calmer and more restrained, intertwined with the haunting rumble and clank that shook the steppe.

They went down from the hills to the lowlands. The village stretched among the empty, frosty pastures, dark green fields, and leafless gray gardens. Pinkish foggy houses lay flat, with reflections off their iron roofs of a fragile spindle of a mosque. Kudryavtsev was peering into the village, trying to find signs of life—cattle, men, carts, anything. But the village seemed like an empty shell that slammed all its doors at the smallest hint of danger.

"There are Chechens hiding!" the platoon commander shouted over the clanging and wheezing of the engines, grabbing at the wet, frosty cannon. He pointed to the village with bulging, shining eyes and rejoiced at the mighty movement of the machinery that bypassed the outskirts.

A rocket took off over the village, cutting through the fog in a white trickle. It hung on a bent stem, shimmering in a pink, milky cloud. When it flew to the mosque, it swayed, lowered, and died out, leaving a faded disappearing curl. Its silent, lonely appearance followed by its slow, sad disappearance gave rise to an alarm. Kudryavtsev peered into the outlines of the village, into the empty, trampled pastures, into the soft, blurred outlines of the surrounding hills, expecting to see the source of the alarm.

But it was not there. The rocket announced to someone that he, Kudryavtsev, was moving past the village, in a tank helmet and pea jacket, with a machine gun on a canvas belt, resting against the back of the seat on which the shooter could fit. The blue optics captured shimmering off the roofs, iron gates, and brick walls of the mosque. This message ascended as a pink cloud high into the air, where it was carried by the wind into the foggy steppe. There was someone, somewhere, invisible behind ditches or leafless gardens in the blurred distance who received the signal. Whoever it was learned the armored column was on its way.

"They are sending a message!" The platoon commander, who a minute ago, was joyful and playful, now looked at Kudryavtsev warily, skeptically, as if expecting confirmation of what this alarm means. He reached down into the hatch. He took out a machine gun. He put the belt over his shoulder and the barrel toward the village, which was floating away over the red hillock.

The brigade swayed through the hills, pushing them apart with the cold steel of the column. They rushed up to the rounded peaks and from there, looked over the undulating steppe. The column became stretched and broke, while its head went forward, and then, pulsing like a snake, it shrank, crawled, and bent around the hills. If any of the engines died, the entire convoy froze, resting on the stalled vehicle. They would have to pull it out of the mud with a cable and tractor and move it to the side, so that the bulk of the column, clanking and thundering, continued to move, catching up with the detached head.

Kudryavtsev saw in front of him a stack of burning, ruby taillights of the tanks ahead, with a heavy cannon facing the hills. The guns of combat vehicles and tanks were deployed in different directions to the tops of the hills. The eyes of the shooters and the commanders of the vehicles fumbled along the soft, blurred edges, waiting for a white machine-gun flash, like an electric short-circuit spark, to hammer on it with all the power of their focused barrels.

The city was approaching, and the outskirts sent out their messengers to meet them. High-voltage lines hung their copper conductors over the armored column and covered them with weaving metal towers. There were abandoned buildings without windows and doors, as if burnt out from the inside. The rusty railway with rusty reservoirs sticking out among the weeds seemed to have fallen from the sky. The column encountered the stench from a huge landfill that leaked a greenish vapor, strewn with prickly metal, rotting garbage, and loose lumps of shapeless substances chewed up and spit out by the city and haunted from the croaking of crows.

The flocks of crows in all the corners of the landfill grazed the ground, sometimes flying up and scaring off other flocks. They were all screaming, muffling the sounds of the engines, and eventually merged into a black cloud, filling the sky with their black spread wings, bowed heads, and clawed feet. Obscuring the sunlight, they circled their magnificent merry-go-round above the column, all the while diving with their angry beaks and small, furious eyes. Steel vehicles, machine guns, cannons, all stuck in this viscous, screaming, and flapping cloud. The crows did not let the column go untouched and sprinkled them with litter, excrement, and black, shaggy feathers.

The young lieutenant descended into the hatch, as if expecting a blow from a sharpened beak, and put up a machine gun barrel. Kudryavtsev turned away from the landfill, from the poisonous fumes, from the stench flying from the earth into the sky. He saw a crow with spread feathers fall onto the vehicle. An elastic jet flew out of its rear end, collided with the vehicle, and splashed a warm drop on his face.

He wiped himself off with disgust and shielded himself from further punishment with his elbow. He bowed his head as if he were driving under a low, dangerous vault. The landfill remained behind them, where it subsided and eventually fell from view. The birds lagged, perched on the warm, rotting garbage, basking in it, and pecked at the decayed substances thrown out of the city.

When they came close to the city and moved onto the concrete road, it started to snow. Where there had just been a black, bird-strewn, perforated, tattered sky, there was now a soft, sowing whiteness. The snow was thick and evenly falling. It chilled their faces with a fragrant coolness, tickling eyebrows and cheeks. It was melting on their lips. It collected on the armor and roads and surrounded the ruby taillights of the tanks.

The snow was sudden and abundant. It hid everything in sight, as if it had been sent down by someone's command. It seemed that a cover was thrown over the highway and on the nearby town, a blanket of snow. However, it also blinded the eyes of the drivers, blocked the hot engine grilles, clouded the windshields and sights, and clogged the cannon barrels.

Kudryavtsev found himself in the weightless, airy whiteness and was almost frightened by this sign from heaven. A multitude of fragile particles rested on his head, which begged him for something, then disappeared and perished into the white void under the steel treads.

Nature was trying to tell them something, talking to people in an inarticulate language. But they did not understand it. They continued, squeezed their weapons, cursed, and spoke in hoarse voices. The crew, turning on the headlights, commanding the transmissions and propeller shafts, made their way through the snow, leaving a black, sticky mark on the white ground underneath.

Kudryavtsev felt the mystery of this sudden snowfall. He tried to unravel the message hidden within it. He reached out with his palm to reach for the snow, caught snowflakes with his lips, and took a moment to look around at the countless snowflakes falling from the sky.

He remembered an old snowfall from childhood, which covered their town with a wet, white robe. It was when the snow suddenly began to fall on the wet ground, in the front garden, on the black water of the river, on the fences, on the dead awns of the sunflowers, on the pink flabby asters, on the rotten bench, on the handkerchief that was forgotten outside. It was thick, moist, sweet-smelling, as if it had come from a fragrant, heavenly garden. Kudryavtsev stood in the front garden, amazingly happy, alone, in an impenetrable whiteness that separated him from the rest of the world. This falling, pure cold, wonderful, weightless matter, was for him, in his honor. It gave him a nameless precious miracle that made him different from everyone else. To him alone it communicated the silent, wordless message of something heavenly and wonderful. He suddenly felt excitement with such childish tenderness that he knelt down and, hidden from sight, pressed his face to the ground, melting the snow to the wet, slushy grass. On the ground was the imprint of his face. It made his cheeks burn. There were melted, cold drops on his eyelashes. In the snow, there was a rose bush with hard red berries.

Kudryavtsev was looking at the ruby taillights of the front tank, which were fogging up, and at the snowflakes melting on the polished barrel of the machine gun.

The column was drawn into the suburbs, barracks, factory buildings, and into a heap of fences and warehouses. The snow stopped and was replaced by the blue twilight of the sky. In this twilight above the railway tracks, above the oil tanks, above the elevator tower, was a high, radiant fire burning on the mast, as if a cruel star had descended from the sky.

The radio commands sounded off more often and angrier. The column lined up, and the spacing was set. Machine guns and cannons were turning toward half-dark buildings. The soldiers climbed out of the hatches, perched on the armor near the towers and cannons, and looked at the city with curiosity. Kudryavtsev, squeezing the walkie-talkie, ordered them off the armor and pushed them into a secure depth under the protection of steel shells.

They passed a gloomy, dilapidated building with a huge, bald wall, which was illuminated by a weak, white spotlight. In this beam, a slogan lined with bricks could be seen: "We are building Communism!" Their appearance gave Kudryavtsev a strange feeling, as if they were lost, going off on the wrong map, and fell into a different, wasted, and decayed time, and the soot of this time lies on the slogan, on the armor of the machines, on the face of the platoon commander, and on Kudryavtsev himself.

He felt nostalgia mixed with a sickening anxiety that disappeared as they entered the city.

It was dark, but the streets were brightly lit. There were lights coming from many places like the windows of houses, spacious shop windows, and neon signs. The fresh snow gleamed elegantly. It showed the tracks where a car had recently driven. There were footprints scattered in the shape of a black fan along entrances and gateways. But all the people and cars were missing. The streets were empty. In the illuminated shop windows, goods flaunted, advertisements flared, and traffic lights blinked. Christmas trees were displayed in the windows in different colors. But there were no passersby and no tenants standing near the windows. The snow under the lanterns was an untouched white, and an alarming thought came to mind: the people have turned invisible. There were still the signs and signals that people were still present: leaving footprints, looking out of windows at the passing troops, but they could not be seen through scopes and windshields, nor seen through night vision devices.

"Has everybody died or what?" the platoon commander looked around anxiously, staring at the signs that floated by that were so tempting after occupying the wild steppe: "Restaurant"; "Shop"; "Movie Theatre."

They were now moving through a long main street with large, elegant houses, ornate, stucco facades, arches, and walkways. Off to the side in an opening flashed a river with black, shiny water, a snow-covered bridge, and an embankment illuminated by lanterns, each of which was surrounded by a transparent, bluish flame and reflected in the water with a golden brushstroke. There were no people or cars on the bridge, just a thin, black trail of a stray car making its mark in the snow.

Through the trees of the park there were merry-go-rounds with horses, camels, spaceships, carts, and sleds, which were prepared for a festival. It seemed if you were to go to the carousel and investigate one of the carts, you would see a candy wrapper or some other sign of use.

This complete lack of people seemed incredible. At any moment, it could turn into noisy crowds energized with festive glee. Or turn into something completely different, unpredictable, and terrible.

"Point, slow down! Do not break away from the column! Rear, what the hell are you doing so far behind? Pull up, close the gap!" the brigade commander's voice sounded on the radio, in prickly static.

The leading tanks slowed down, slowly thrashing snow onto the roadway. The column swelled, filling the street with armor, heavy cannons, and caustic, bluish exhaust.

They passed the square with the illuminated Presidential Palace. All the windows were lit, as if there was a reception. Faceted lanterns on patterned, cast-iron pillars illuminated the square, but no lacquered limousines, guards, or attendants could be seen, as if everyone invited to the reception heard about the approach of the column, felt the earth shake from the movement, dropped their crystal glasses and plates with delicious snacks and ran away, hiding from the vehicles, guns, and soldiers.

The front tanks stopped. The IFV where Kudryavtsev was sitting advanced and almost rested against the taillights of the tank in front of them. A tanker stepped out of the hatch ahead, turned around, and waved.

A man stood in the snow in front of the tank in the beams of the searchlight among the sparkling snowflakes. He was small, wearing a ragged earflap, tattered fur coat, and crooked, broken shoes. He laughed as he was blinded from the light, turned his bearded little head, and uttered something joyful through the roar of the tank.

Kudryavtsev, picking up a machine gun, jumped off the armor and, feeling how softly the snow was being pressed, approached the man. He smiled blissfully with a gap-toothed mouth, blinked his blue eyes, and said in slurred and tongue-tied speech, "Someone heard you! Aida let's go to the store! Klanka shouts, 'Wait!' And he said to her, 'What the fuck?!'"

He laughed, twisted his little head, and told Kudryavtsev some funny story about what happened to him. He sniffled his sunken nose.

"We are going to the train station, right?" Kudryavtsev peered at a dancing face, in wrinkles and cracks, similar to the shaggy face of a cheerful animal.

"Arslanka calls, 'Aida!' I told him, 'You jump so high!' And he ran away without saying anything…. We have bread, so I can live!"

"Who are you?" Kudryavtsev peered at the strange peasant who appeared in the path of the column. "Where is everyone?"

"He is Arslanka, nonsense! Thousand, not a million!"

This peasant was crazy, tongue-tied, and speaking nonsense. In his head, under the torn earflaps, under the whitish braids of hair, merriment splashed like a puddle full of spring frogs. To Kudryavtsev, it seemed to be an opportunity to get some answers about what was going on in the city. An answer to the noiseless rocket flying over the sleepy village, an answer to the embittered black clouds of birds, the sudden magical snowfall that covered the city, the seemingly invisible populace of the city and palace. The blessed peasant was explaining something to Kudryavtsev, who listened attentively to his gurgling, but was unable to understand.

"I should be able to get them in! And the Klan-ku will come afterwards!" He turned his head, mocking Kudryavtsev, who did not know how to understand his simple and straightforward language. He waved his hand, hit himself on his rear-end, as if he was about to take off, and then, jumped up, stomped, pretended to be either a chicken or an airplane, spread his arms, and ran, leaving a path of footprints in the snow. He just disappeared, as if he had taken off, dissolved in the lilac flame of the lantern.

The column moved on, clanking iron, rustling ether, making its way through the enchanted city.

From afar, through the roar of motors, Kudryavtsev heard music. At first it was indistinct, obscured by buildings, which seemed to be a deception, but then turned into loud, fresh sounds carried in the cold air, as if in front of the square, among the white snow, there was a grand piano being played by a pianist in a tailcoat, pressing the copper pedals with lacquered boots, hitting the keys, shaking his long hair, while a bouquet of red roses lay in the mirror lid of the black instrument.

The tanks drove out onto the square, onto its white oval, in the middle of which was a tall tree. It twinkled, shimmered, permeated with running multicolored lights, decorated with ornaments, powdered by the snow, and with a large golden star on top.

Music poured from the loudspeaker. The Christmas tree in combination with energetic, vigorous sounds seemed to be prepared especially for them, who had arrived from the wild steppe, yearning for the holiday.

Tanks and combat vehicles surrounded the tree with dark armor, towers, boxes, and guns, and enveloped it in exhaust. Heads in helmets, "caps," and knitted hats protruded from the hatches. The soldiers stared in amazement at the shimmering marvel displayed for them in the middle of the square.

"Now that's what I call a warm greeting!" the platoon commander gasped, widening his joyful eyes with arms wide open, as if he wanted to hug the green tree and snuggle up to the multicolored flags and ornaments.

"Do you think the residents will leave us any gifts?"

Kudryavtsev was amazed, not by the tree, not by the magnificent sounds of the piano, but by the view of the station building, which was old-fashioned with stucco moldings, columns, and semicircular windows. This is how he imagined this building when the general described the mission. It was greenish white and surrounded by bare trees, with a sticky platform and purple lights like the eyes of a bewildered animal, with a dull blue stretch of steel track that the general says the Marines would approach.

The square was packed with vehicles where they all drove up, blocking all entrances and exits. Soldiers crowded on top of the armor. They did not dare jump to the ground. They simply looked around, laughed, and waved to each other.

While this was happening, the decorated spruce sparkled and flickered, and the crystal music rushed from the loudspeaker.

Kudryavtsev saw how people began to come out of the neighboring streets and into the illuminated square. Their appearance brought relief. The city was not deserted, bewitched, or abandoned by its inhabitants. Men and women in groups approached the cars. From a distance they could see their smiles, colored handkerchiefs, and hands raised in greeting. They approached the tanks, bowed, and held out dishes with grapes, apples, and white towels with bread. Kudryavtsev saw how the woman who approached her had white teeth gleaming in a smile, a beautiful, elongated, and black-browed face, and a handkerchief patterned in a mica sheen.

"Welcome, dear comrades!" said a tall, dark-skinned Chechen without a hat, showing his lush shoulder-length hair, who pressed his strong arms to his chest, bowed, and raised his face to Kudryavtsev, who was standing in the hatch. "We've been waiting for you! We welcome you into our city as defenders and liberators!" The women had prepared trays of fruit in outstretched hands. The platoon commander looked back at the tree and laughed happily. He imagined that the fruits and bread in the hands of women were the very gifts they were expecting. He took a pear and took a bite. You could see how his strong teeth plunged into the juicy pulp, how juice splashed on his chin. His face expressed pleasure, from which he closed his eyes like a child.

"Take some bread, have a bite!" a young Chechen woman said in Russian, with a slight accent, holding out a towel with bread to Kudryavtsev. "It's still warm! I just took it out of the oven!" She smiled and nodded. The bread was a rich white and lush. Kudryavtsev hesitated, reached out of the hatch, and touched the bread. He pinched off a pliable, soft hunk. He then put it in his mouth, feeling its warm, springy softness.

"More! More!" the woman said smiling. The appearance of these beautiful, friendly people with their abundance of fruits, aromas of bread, and a subtle, barely passing scent of female perfume suddenly cooled Kudryavtsev's head. All the anxieties he had endured, the exhausting suspicion, the expectation of a trap, an ambush—all of this suddenly vanished, and he found himself in a New Year's festival among beautiful, hospitable people.

"Where is Dudayev?" Kudryavtsev jumped to the ground and was now standing in front of the thick-haired man with a swarthy face, who was wearing a white shirt under a long-brimmed leather coat and had a gold chain around his round neck. "Where are the militants?"

"They left this afternoon. They learned that troops were approaching and left. They abandoned the Palace ministries and fled as best they could on foot or in cars. We are from the public consent committee. They sent their people to occupy the Presidential Palace. Tomorrow morning, we will hold a meeting in the square in honor of our liberators, where our people's leaders will speak."

Soldiers were jumping out of the cars and tanks. They accepted the gifts and tore and divided grapes among themselves. An old Chechen man took out a bottle of dark wine from under the floor and poured it into a glass. The soldiers, looking around to see if the commanders were watching, drank hastily and ate the pears and apples.

And all this was familiar to Kudryavtsev, reminiscent of front-line newsreels, when grateful residents met the troops on the squares of the liberated cities.

"You can come with us, dear comrades! You can warm up!" invited the man. "We have a house nearby where we have food for a New Year's Eve dinner. We would love to have you!"

Kudryavtsev was listening to the broadcast, waiting for orders from the battalion commander, instructions on where to place the cars, which checkpoints into the station to take control of. But there was no order. It was noisy and crowded all around. Soldiers' helmets and caps mingled with women's scarves and astrakhan hats. Laughter rang out, engines rumbled at idle, and loud music played. And he yearned for the warmth and comfort of a home and a delicious feast. He wanted a New Year's holiday.

Kudryavtsev, succumbing to irresistible temptation, justifying it as his desire to look around the area, chose convenient positions for the vehicles and called for the platoon officer and a couple of soldiers. They shoved the machine guns behind their backs, feeling they were welcome guests, and set off from the square after their cordial, hospitable host.

4

They left the illuminated square filled with tanks, combat vehicles, and a noisy crowd of soldiers into a quiet nearby street, where there were small one-story houses made of brick and surrounded by fences with iron gates painted in green and blue. One of the gates was cracked open, and Kudryavtsev followed the Chechen into the courtyard. In the snow on the ground, streaks of light fell from the windows of the house. A table was laid under a canopy, under a roof that was interwoven with vines. Freshly cooked meat with piles of fragrant vegetables and huge, round tomatoes were steaming in a porcelain bowl on the long tablecloth. Pears and apples glowed in the glass bowls; dark bunches of grapes hung down from the canvas. There were bottles of red and black homemade wine. Young women were busy setting the table and sweeping the damp, sticky snow from the benches. When they saw the guests, they were embarrassed. They smiled and disappeared into the shadows.

"Welcome, my dear guests! Sit down and eat with us!" invited the dark-haired owner, with a broad gesture to the feast and long benches, on which two nimble, little boys with troubled eyes were laying thick woolen pillows embroidered with black and red patterns. "We hope you enjoy the food!" he said while smiling, wishing to please his guests.

Off to the side, in a dark corner of the snow-covered garden, a stove was smoking and flashing. The reflections showed young, male faces, dark mustaches, quick eyes, dexterous, strong hands, and skewers with bunches of hissing meat on the coals. Young people bowed from afar and gestured to come join them. Kudryavtsev noticed how the watch on the bracelet flashed over the fire.

They sat under the vines on warm, comfortable pillows. The platoon commander looked cheerfully and greedily at the hot food. He also noticed the curved, black vines breathing the cold, dark sky and the open lit door, where laughing feminine faces appeared for a moment. The embarrassed soldiers clambered to put their submachine guns at their feet under the table. Their eyes, open mouths, and sensitive noses were aimed at the abundant, pungent-smelling food.

Two teenagers led an old man out of the house. The man was in a sheepskin hat, a long, kaftan-like quilted jacket, and quilted boots shod with galoshes. The old man had a white beard and moustache. A strong, humped nose stood out on his wrinkled face. His half-blind eyes were covered with shaggy gray eyebrows. They took the old man to Kudryavtsev, and the elder shook the captain's hand with his cold, bony fingers.

"Who is Dudayev? He is a fool! He took a swing at Russia! They asked him, 'Dzhokhar, are you mad? We must be friends with Moscow! Moscow gave everything to Chechnya: oil, cities, scientists! How long will you taunt Moscow? They suffer and put up with this and then hit. I am done waiting! Chechens and Russians are brothers forever.' I told Ismail, 'Go and bring the Russians!' ...We thank all of you for coming!"

While the old man was speaking, his trembling cold fingers squeezed Kudryavtsev's hot palm. It was as if he wanted to share the thoughts that were overwhelming him through touch for greater persuasiveness. The one the old man called Ismail was a thick-haired, dark-skinned Chechen who nodded respectfully.

"He went to see Dudayev," Ismail said when the old man stopped talking and the teenagers took him to the table where they gently sat him on a patterned pillow. "He said all of this to his face. We thought he was going to be killed. Dzhokhar does not like the truth. But the old man was brought home in a Mercedes with great respect."

Kudryavtsev, who had been gathering troops in Chechnya a month ago, had extraordinarily little idea of who General Dzhokhar Dudayev was. Looking at his portrait, he was dressed in a dapper garrison cap with a thin mustache and wearing gold general's shoulder straps, which did not cause Kudryavtsev hostility, but only irritation, like most things that occurred outside of the garrison, like watching it on a television set. Shown on the television were incessant scandals, tedious squabbles, countless deaths, grueling elections, pointless debates, performances by annoying artists and tired unfunny pranksters, talkative, sexless ugly creatures, flaunting their flabby body. And amidst this multicolored slurry of oil spills, among the bright and poisonous streaks, the rebellious Chechen general was one of many who represented rot and decay.

Kudryavtsev, an officer who devoted himself to service, did not understand the reasons for this decay, nor could he find its deep roots. He was almost indifferent to the Chechen general, who seemed neither better nor worse than others who are Russian, Ukrainian, Kazakh, who had fallen away from the great army or broke off a juicy chunk of it and eagerly feasted.

Standing in the steppe on the outskirts of Grozny, looking through foggy neighborhoods with binoculars, listening to intelligence reports and radio intercepts, Kudryavtsev changed his opinion about the rebellious Dudayev. The general gradually turned into an enemy with an army. However, this army was not able to withstand the onslaught of the countless regiments and brigades of the Russian Army and would inevitably crumble, like a clay dish covered with cracks crumbling when hit with a hammer.

Now, in the gloom of the winter garden, surrounded by lights, piles of bluish snow, looking at the nearby vines, each of which glowed with a small golden spark, Kudryavtsev thought of Dudayev as something that had already passed, disappeared, and melted as soon as the mighty armored column entered the city.

All of them sat down. Many beautiful and friendly people were at the table. Each of them tried to express their favor to the guests by words, looks, or gestures. They passed out knives and forks. They poured wine into faceted glasses. They put boiled meat blanketed in steam encasing white, slippery bones on a plate. Others simply smiled from afar, pressed their hands to their chest, and bowed if they met Kudryavtsev's eyes.

"Dear guests, soldiers of our army!" black-haired Ismail got up, holding a glass filled with wine. He was courageous, handsome with his resinous curls, white shirt, and a gold chain around his strong, round neck. He looked like a movie actor. His speech, solemnly friendly and at the same time imperious, set him apart from the rest. He was in charge, the master of the house, and as such, he was instantly obeyed. At his glance and gesture, young people rushed and brought him a clean towel, a bowl with pieces of meat, and another pillow embroidered with colored wool. "Dear brothers! I greet you at this New Year's table in a simple Chechen house! You are far from your families, from your mothers and sisters. We are your brothers, your closest relatives. Happy New Year!"

He raised the glass to his lips and drank the dark wine shrinking in the glass, moving his strong, swarthy Adam's apple while the chain around his neck trembled. Kudryavtsev drank his wine, enjoying the tart, fragrant sweetness. A soft, warm stream poured into his throat, and in a moment he felt the slightest sweet intoxication touch his eyes.

"Please help yourself," said Kudryavtsev's neighbor, an amiable elderly Chechen with a graying mustache, who took a piece of meat out of a bowl with his hands. He shook off the drops of fat and juice and, holding it by the bone, carefully put it on Kudryavtsev's plate. "Try the lamb; it's very tasty!"

He smiled embarrassedly, as if asking Kudryavtsev for forgiveness for this straightforward, common method among close friends of giving meat directly with their hands. Kudryavtsev smiled back, accepting his gesture. He ate the hot, tasty, rich meat, and washed it down with tart wine.

The soldiers he had brought along with him pounced on the delicious looking food. When the solders came back, they started quickly eating porridge with canned stewed meat and vegetables along with drinking wine. They laughed, loosened up their tense muscles, shook their heads, and got lost in conversations. One of them was the same skinny contract soldier who a few hours ago portrayed the Snow Maiden, danced shirtless on the stern of the IFV, and sang explicit verses. Now the soldier was stuffing his mouth with meat, swallowing unchewed pieces like a dog, gagging, all the while not able to take himself away from the food. He stuffed his cheeks again, as if he was afraid that this miracle would end and he would run out of time to satisfy his hunger before being taken away from the table.

The other soldier was a chubby Mordovian from the village, serious and reserved. He ate slowly and calmly. He cut off chunks of meat, chewed it thoroughly, and washed it down with small sips of wine. He smiled politely and nodded his head to the person next to him who was talking.

Kudryavtsev had a fleeting thought: wasn't he getting too carried away by this feast? Wouldn't it be better to get up, thank the hospitable hosts, and go on reconnaissance along the surrounding streets? Outline the locations for placing combat vehicles? Place "blocks" with cannons and machine guns, in half-dark alleys with dim lights, defending the city square, station, and railway track, along which the Marines will come to rendezvous with them? Several times he tried to get up and return to the square where the fighting column had accumulated and huddled. But the food was so tasty, and the owners were so friendly that he stayed every time while grabbing bunches of leeks and sipping wine from a glass.

"I am a teacher at the academic institute," said a specious elderly man as he leaned toward Kudryavtsev. "I carefully studied the historical relations between Chechnya and Russia. Imam Shamil, in the end, signed a peace treaty with the tsar and recognized the entry of the Caucasus into Russia. It was for the good of Chechnya. All who are trying to create discord between us are enemies of the Chechens. They must be judged as enemies of the people!" He firmly put his hand on the tablecloth, and his wedding ring flashed on his finger.

Kudryavtsev tried to understand of whom this crowded family consisted. Who are the grandfathers, fathers, and children, who are the uncles and nephews, and who are just neighbors invited to the dinner party?

"Did Dudayev really commit atrocities here?" asked Kudryavtsev, to support the conversation with this question, for his thoughts were about something else. He felt good and calm. Leafless vines with black knots and clumsy buds with sharp bends thoroughly covered the tent. The snow melted slowly and smelled like a fresh cut watermelon. Through the hedge, a small, illuminated section of the city square could be seen shining. They could hear music, voices and see the sparkling of a Christmas tree. It seemed like the edge of a shining crystal chandelier, under which the incessant celebration continued.

"People disappeared without a trace!" the neighbor shook his head woefully. His gray brushed mustache moved sadly. "Last week, a Russian girl was killed and abandoned on the street. Everybody in the area was afraid to say anything about it or risk being killed themselves. They detained me for a day. We are grateful you arrived to end the horror. They say Dudayev fled to the mountains, or even to Turkey. With him gone, peace and order will come."

Kudryavtsev liked the feeling that he was a sort of savior to these kind, peaceful people. The wine he drank and the lamb that melted on his lips, these were things he had earned. He deserved these things for all the hardship, sickness, shelling, endless labor, and worries that fell to the soldiers and officers of the brigade. The rebel general with the thin mustache and his radical supporters, wearing machine gun belts and ram hats, were now making their way out of the city in the dark. They avoided highways and exposed military posts. They crept along country roads and dirt paths like hunted fearful animals.

He was tipsy, but not drunk, in a way that the lights in the distance were shrouded in the lightest mist. He didn't want to talk about politics. He wanted to be invited into the house, through the bright, open door, where an elegant curtain dazzled and every now and then a laughing feminine face appeared. He wanted to examine the decorations in the house and their unfamiliar way of life, the carpets on the wall, next to a silver dagger in a sheath and some silk-embroidered capes. He would compare the decoration of a Caucasian house with his own home which was neat and tidy.

Mother invited the family, which included her two brothers, who were both railroad workers, and their wives, for the holidays. She also invited her sister, who was unmarried and childless, thin, mocking, and a cashier in a store. Kudryavtsev's father died early from a fleeting illness that set him on fire with fever. But his father's aunts and uncles did not forget their nephew. At the feast, the table was crowded and cheerful. It was so nice to sit and watch the adults celebrate and drink. There were many tasty dishes served, such as sauerkraut with chunks of ice, alongside spicy pickles with currant leaves, and a fat jellied meat trembling on a knife. They poured the vodka into shot glasses and drank. And the eldest of the uncles, with a mighty, red face and thick lips, somewhat like a bull, lifted his glass with a huge, slightly trembling hand.

The Chechen gathering reminded Kudryavtsev of such memories that touched his soul. Kudryavtsev felt hot and tender. These two feasts took shape, were shifted, and then intermixed by Russian and Chechen people. He felt gratitude to these hosts who were recently strangers, but accepted him into this foreign city and warmed him up and caressed him in the foreign land.

"Comrade Captain, allow me to say a toast!" the platoon commander smiled blissfully. He was overwhelmed with enthusiastic thoughts and feelings. He had to share them immediately.

A young Chechen, the same age as the lieutenant, shaved bald with handsome black eyebrows spread out, was cutting a piece of mutton with a knife. When the lieutenant got up, the Chechen stopped wielding the knife and placed the fat, dull blade on the piece of meat patiently waiting to listen to the lieutenant with a smile.

"Friends!" the platoon commander turned to face everyone with his pretty, pale, pink, cherub-like face, and everyone there watched him and encouraged him by returning a smile. "I am so pleased to be in your house! So suddenly everything turned out! And honestly, I feel as if we have known each other for a long time! I would like with all my heart..."

Kudryavtsev listened with a smile and condescendingly forgave the sentimental, slightly intoxicated lieutenant. But as the paused lieutenant gathered his thoughts, intending to say something fancy and unusual, Kudryavtsev suddenly felt that something around him was rapidly and imperceptibly changing, as if this was the precipice to a daunting event, ready to be unleashed. It was enough to send a silent, flashing alarm through his head.

The curtain in the open doors of the house were still fluttering, and a girl's face flickered. In the far corner of the garden, in the darkness, red sparks rained down; someone was waving a fan, fanning the coals, and again a hand with a watch flashed. An old man in a cap was chewing something listlessly, looking with dull eyes on the food of his plate. Ismail threw back the curls that hindered his face and patiently waited for the lieutenant to continue speaking. And in this brief, ensuing hitch, it became especially quiet. The festive music rushing from the city square was silent. In the silence came separate jarring screams and the roar of engines. The lighted crystal chandelier, without this festive music coming from the loudspeakers, seemed to have faded away. And everyone who was at the table perked up, listening to this sudden eerie silence.

In this void, as if screeching out to some mountain tops and creating an avalanche, a loud roar poured out. "Allahu Akbar! Allahu Akbar!" the invisible crowd roared. "Allahu Akbar!" answered the low, black sky, answered the earth filled with houses and the snow-covered weaving of trees, as if a dense, dark crowd rushed into the square, surrounding it like a ring. The Chechens at the dinner table exhaled threateningly, "Allahu Akbar!" This roar was like the fall of huge sheet of iron, the bubbling of a stadium filled with passion and hate. The shouts hit at the feast, overturning the unstable world fortified on a thin axis, turning it upside down.

The lieutenant, who was making a toast, was still picturesquely raising his elbow like an officer, holding a glass of wine, smiling sentimentally. But this smile turned into a grimace of pain and horror. His transparent blue eyes rolled and bulged, for in his throat, sunk up to the hilt, stuck a knife. The bone handle of the knife, soiled with mutton fat, was gripped by the strong hand of a young Chechen, who had recently smiled shyly and was ready to serve and help. The knife stuck in the lieutenant's throat, with blood protruding from under the blade, which was immediately absorbed again into his throat. The lieutenant froze, put his chin on the knife and slowly sagged, his eyes black with incomprehension and pain.

As in slow motion, the glass fell out of his hands, and the splashed wine, as if in weightlessness, floated to the ground in large red drops.

The Chechen dropped the knife, and the lieutenant collapsed at once, falling under the table. The head with a protruding bone handle was thrown back next to Kudryavtsev on an embroidered pillow.

"Allahu Akbar!" roared through the trees, as if a huge damp sack full of rotting gizzards had burst out into the open.

The Mordovian, chewing meat, froze with full cheeks, with a swollen mouth filled with food. He tilted his head forward, like a choking dog, and Ismail, holding out his hand with a pistol, fired at his exposed white forehead. Kudryavtsev, dumbfounded, saw how the hand with the pistol jerked up, the heavy, beautiful hair of the Chechen threw back, and the bullet, separated from the barrel, burst out of the feathered flame, plunged into the sergeant's broad forehead, drilled a hole into it, and went into his brain, mixing blood vessels with the spongy substance of gray matter. The bullet hit the back of his skull, where it flattened and flowed like a molten drop out of a hole in the back of his skull. A black-red ooze dripped from the hole, and the Mordovian fell headlong into his plate, mixing mutton flesh with his raw, hot, blood-mixed brain.

The spray scattered across the table, and Kudryavtsev turned into a stone pillar, unable to move, and felt a smear on his cheek.

"Allahu Akbar!" a black landslide fell from above, capturing trees and houses in its fall, upturning the city by the roots, leaving in its place a black steaming hole.

A soldier squealed shrilly and thinly, like a shot hare. He jumped up, grabbed a machine gun leaning against the bench, and tried to get out because of the close quarters. Continuing to squeal, he rushed along the table and rolled over on his shoulder as he walked in order to shoot a burst into the table, sweeping away plates, vases, and crushing Chechens who had stood up. But the old man in the fur hat stretched out his shiny boot, and the soldier stumbled head over heels, spreading his arms, and began to fall. A short burst of bullets struck into the soldier with outstretched arms trying to catch himself near the open fire pit, filling him with holes. Then, the perforated body, with pierced entrails, collapsed. He became silent, stirring among the soggy, fallen leaves, wet snow, and water that was black as oil.

All of this happened in a split second. Kudryavtsev witnessed these three instant deaths that occurred in an inverted world that fell off its axis. He survived the numbness when his eyes, glazed, dropped out of their sockets and gained panoramic vision. He was alone, and the lens of his eyes suddenly felt the air begin to change, tremble, and lose transparency. Death had begun to approach him, penetrating through the lens. He suddenly went blind, and his whole life, at which death was aiming, turned into a blind desire to get as far away from death as possible, which made him act passionately and recklessly.

The Chechen next to him, a gray-haired old-timer was digging around, trying to pull out a clumsy, uncomfortable pistol from his belt. He understood that he was hesitating and became angry, while raising his eyes to Kudryavtsev. Kudryavtsev struck with the crushing blow of his fist into the old man's eyes, and again in his mouth with the push of a pointed, ramming shoulder. This knocked out his dinner partner, and he fell back. First, Kudryavtsev ran to the house and its brick wall, to the open, through its seemingly salutary doors. Pistol shots rang out, just nearly missing under his elbow, over his shoulder, and near his cheek. They struck the wall, ejecting dust from the holes.

Dodging more shots, he drew back from the house. He rushed to the gate and hit his head on it. He heard a gong, and then noticed that the gate was locked. Bullets clattered on the gate and the bolt, producing blinding sparks. An illuminated snowy street flashed outside through a tiny hole in the punctured gate.

Kudryavtsev rushed along the high hedge, breaking bushes, overturning wooden planks, tangling and tearing rags and clothes. A long, inaccurate burst of machine gun fire shot holes in the wall above his head, overtaking him with the sound of the rifle, the sparks of the bullets missing their mark, and the bright, prickly flashes from the muzzle.

Ahead, at the end of the wall, was a barn. It was a dead end, a black corner, where death was trying to overtake him. He felt weak, almost resigning himself to its inevitability, but at the last second before dying, he gathered all the strength he could muster into a final push. All that he had experienced, all the crunching of bones, the groaning, the torn muscles—all this with his pushing and struggling was able to rise over the obstacle in front of him. He flew over the hedge, facing the sky, seeing flashes of light in his vision.

He rolled over in the air and fell like a cat on four limbs. He then ran on all fours like an animal, loosening the snow with his face, hands, and knees. He jumped up when he thought it was clear and ran as fast as he could away from the house and toward the rest of the brigade in the city square, where the crowd's wheezing roared out into the air. He could already hear rumbling, gunfire, and explosions, which had whipped up in chaotic vortices. Behind him, his pursuers chased and shot at him down the street. They followed him as they howled and shouted, as if a flock of black, stunted dogs were chasing something along the fence. And in front, where the square was approaching, a roaring, shaggy monster stood up to meet him. This monster was breathing red smoke and out rang, "Allahu Akbar!" as if roaring from one hundred combatants.

He ran into the square, and he felt a wave of heat, as if from an open stove. He blew out a white, blinding draft into the open air. Overcoming the pressure of wind and light, Kudryavtsev jumped out into the open and immediately disappeared from his pursuers. They lost him in the mix of screams, whirlwinds, and the massive moving masses of iron that whistled and clanged. Surveying the situation, Kudryavtsev pressed himself against the wall of the nearest house, surrounded by explosions and bullets.

The square trembled and clanked, billowing in clouds of soot, where dazzling balls of fire exploded. The explosion displayed sparkling fountains and threw jets of flame. The square erupted into chaos and was stitched with dotted lines of gunfire. Out of the chaos, people scattered about looking for order and safety. People stumbled around, going in different directions, and fell, then turned around and ran back into the fire, into the smoke, and the whirling of steel.

Kudryavtsev saw a tank crawl out of the fire and piles of tracks and turrets. It was engulfed in a tall, raging flame along its treads and rear. It blindly drove right into a nearby house. A burst of fire shot out of its cannon, the shell bluntly piercing the wall, exploding, while a turret stuck into the opened hole filled with brick dust and fumes. The tank exploded, scattering spinning wheels, rollers, and scraps of its tracks. The dilapidated wall of the house crumbled onto the burning tank that was stuck in the building.

Kudryavtsev pressed himself against the wall, searching with his eyes for his company with their IFV's lined up, which he recklessly abandoned, succumbing to the faux hospitality of the Chechens. He wanted to get through to the vehicles, to the abandoned soldiers, looking for the numbers on the tanks for his company. But there was no company to be found, no vehicles built in a column. The fiery merry-go-round spun, clanking, colliding, and splashing in all directions in a multi-colored slurry with poisonous smoke. People were being pushed out from the fight but then immediately sucked back in. Trails of long, curly smoke from the rocket-propelled grenades flew into this carousel from all directions.

They pounded into it, blew it up, and threw fiery debris, thorny bouquets of red-hot wire, and coal-red flowers from the burning cars.

Kudryavtsev saw grenade launchers firing out of the surrounding houses in groups of two or three. Standing and kneeling, they guided steel pipes with pointed, root-like pomegranates to the center of the square. They were shooting, driving stinging, smoky wedges into the cluster of equipment. The grenades pierced the armor, exploding inside with heavy blows, ripping and throwing open hatches, throwing out bursts of light, torn flesh, and sticky tongues flying through the air.

The grenade launchers retreated as soon as they fired their volley while others ran out in their place. They fell to their knees, fired their salvo into the square, driving sharp wedges into the armor. This was being done from all the surrounding rooftops and open windows. Curly, smoky arcs flew, hung in the air and dug into the sides of the armor, into the cabins and turrets, tearing the stupid, frozen equipment to shreds.

From the speakers in the square, through the explosions and machine-gun crackles, shrieked "Allahu Akbar!" With each exhale and cry of the hundred-man crowd, the square became brighter and brighter. The explosions pushed layers of light into the sky, and the square lit up, raising huge moving arches of fire. In the middle of the encircled, dying people, burning fuel and tanks, a Christmas tree glimmered with firecrackers, painted drums, pipes, and other ornaments visible through the smoke.

Kudryavtsev understood that a huge blunder had occurred, an irreparable blunder. In this catastrophe, his company and his brigade perished, his soldiers and commanders were exterminated, and he, unarmed, thrown out to the outskirts of the square, was unable to help them. He stood there with wide eyes, full of tears, in which men were burning, turning into fire and light, and then into nothing.

An IFV emerged from the smoke, pushing the burning equipment aside, hitting and knocking down trucks. It rushed along the square in an arc, gliding on bends, spinning around with a machine gun, shooting out at random. It began to drive into the next street. And toward it, illuminated, full-length, without fear of a machine gun, a grenadier stepped forward and fired straight into it with complete accuracy. The troops that were inside fell from the doors as they were thrown open by the explosion. They rolled to the ground, stunned, but as they began to get up and try to escape, they were shot point-blank by submachine gunners holding trembling barrels at their stomachs.

His horror and madness were so great that they drove him not away from the square, nor away from hell, but, on the contrary, into hell itself, into the center, into a red-hot focus, where existence itself melted and where the sharp fragments of the exploding grenades flew, feeding into his focus. He was forced into emptiness, into a molten hole, and, tearing himself away from the wall with a darkened consciousness, he rushed to the square. But someone invisible stopped him, pressed him back with a blow of hot air and wordlessly ordered, *look!* So, he remained, pressed against the wall, with dilated pupils. He watched as ashes swept past his face.

Explosions and flares went from the square and traveled to the base of the central street. They plunged into the surrounding alleys where the equipment was gathered and cars stood beside them. From there rose crimson clouds, where the facades and roofs lit up and explosions burst, as if the city had squeezed the brigade in its arms, along with the facades. But in this embrace, the captured brigade was torn, poking into the walls and bursting, unable to withstand the pressure of the embrace that squeezed it. In this open hearth, among the bubbles and molten steel, one could hear howls and groans. Crews, troops, confused commanders, and truck drivers were killed. From where they died, the turret flew up like a hat torn off by the wind. Slowly, turning over, the cannon fell into a white fury of fire.

Look! continued to ring in his mind, and this imperious order kept Kudryavtsev against the wall.

From the fire, separated from the wrecked cars, two of his comrades jumped out. Embracing each other, engulfed in flames, they fled. Weaving their legs in a stumbled run, they supported each other. Their flaming overalls and trousers seemed puffy, with flesh bubbling and boiling under the fabric. Burning while on the run, they could not collect themselves. They fell, lying in the fire, continuing to move, and it was unclear if they were still alive or if it was post-mortem spasms, with their dead, burning tendons bulging.

A Chechen dressed in a leather jacket, camouflage pants, and a thin, bearded face ran past Kudryavtsev. The Chechen had a machine gun in his hands. As he ran, he met Kudryavtsev's gaze and started to raise his machine gun, directing it to the wall, but did not bring it. He shouted something hoarsely, hatefully, and continued to run where the tankers jumped out of the hatches and where his bullets, his machine gun, and his black evil eyes were required.

The tree was emitting smoke, engulfed in flames from below. The lights continued to flash. Fleeing from death, a man climbed along the trunk. Nearby, a liquid bottle exploded with a mushroom of fire which spilled onto the tree and onto the climbing man like a sort of sticky rain, turning the tree into a white candle.

Everything was sintered, fused, and turned into solid red coal. In the slag, in the poisonous ash, screams slowly went silent. Bursts of cannon shots were heard less often. Above the square was like an ugly, multi-winged creature among hovering clouds of smoke, spitting red saliva from above, spitting white mucus, and with staring bulging eyes in all directions. Over the dying brigade, turning its own death into someone's victory and jubilation, was the incessant "Allahu Akbar!"

Kudryavtsev came back to reality. He looked at his empty, unarmed hands. He looked around the square, where everything roared and disappeared in the fire. The distant edge of the square was dark; there were no tracks flying around, no red-hot grenade fires flashing. Instead, there lay a heavy layered smoke. There, toward this smoke, away from the carnage, Kudryavtsev ran, feeling a soul-crushing fear that pushed him and kicked his back, forcing him to spew out from his lungs a continuous silent shout.

5

In a Moscow mansion in a business club, among the fluffy snowdrifts, amethyst lanterns, silent varnished limousines that whipped the street like a feather bed, New Year's Eve was in full gear. In the dining room, which was lined with dark bog oak, were tables under white tablecloths. Candles were burning in silver candlesticks. The fireplace was burning bright and hot, throwing smoky coals. The Christmas tree, tucked away from bottom to the top of the fragile glass star, shimmered and shuddered when the fast, half-naked dancers darted too close to the elegant branches strewn with ornaments. It smelled of tar, sweet smoke, and women's perfume. They were mixed with expensive tobacco, and the hot food that was placed on the tables. There was a steady continuous hum of voices, the clink of glasses and dishes. In the background was radiant, bright music. Young, pretty women were dancing in the multicolored beams of light. It seemed that their bare shoulders, exposed cleavage, and slender legs swept in the snow as they danced, falling into the beams of light that were reflected from the glass, mirror-like ball.

Not far from the fireplace was a table between the tree and a white piano decorated with golden heraldry. At the table was the famous banker and influential businessman, Yakov Vladimirovich Berner. He dominated the scene. Advertisements for his bank were displayed on huge street billboards. Signs of his corporation shined on the rooftops of Moscow buildings, burning the blue night with their neon hieroglyphs.

Berner was youthful and thin, with bright, black eyes and fresh, red lips on his pale, cleanly-shaven face. He was sitting half-turned on a carved chair. He joyfully and keenly watched as a dancer in a transparent leotard lifted a long, strong leg to a right angle. Her skin-tight clothing perfectly accentuating her thigh had aroused him. He wanted to take and squeeze her tightly, to feel her hot, wet body beating, trembling in his arms.

"Tell me, dear, is it true that you personally selected this ensemble, examined each ballerina like a horse? Looked into their teeth and measured their calves?"

His wife, Marina, beautiful and sarcastic, caught his greedy gaze and stuck out her lower lip in displeasure. They had been married for a year and a half, she was pregnant, entering the second trimester, her belly tightly wrapped in the greenish fabric of an English evening dress, and no one noticed her pregnancy. But Berner felt how her temper had changed for the worse, how often she was irritated and could hardly stand the smell of fragrant sauces and fish.

"Yes, honey," she joked. "Just like a herd of horses. But believe me, I never tried to saddle any of them. I only have you, my dear horse!"

Yakov Vladimirovich invited guests to the New Year's table. Some guests were invited by accident, having turned up on someone's arm just before the holiday. Others by all rights could be called a friend, some for reasons of utility, being one of Yakov's business partners. Several toasts were made with drinks of vodka, whiskey, Italian wine, and French champagne that made the guests drunk. Softened and complacent, feeling comfortable with the drinks and music, their lips became loose in such a way that the owner of the table would certainly hear them, and Berner gave them a smile or an approving look. He chuckled inwardly, not skimping on smiles and glances.

A guest from France, who happened to be a Russian princess related to the Russian imperial house, spoke. "August," Marina whispered to her husband sarcastically. The princess was old, her skin dry, like the skin of a snake thrown on the sand. Her hair was gray and lush, with a bluish tinge, which resembled whipped cream. Her lips, surrounded by many wrinkles, resembled the lamellar underside of a mushroom. On her wrinkled, sclerotic hand was a pale, green emerald.

"I particularly like Moscow on this visit," said the princess, keeping herself very erect, pulling her turtleneck out of the lace collar. "There are a lot of beautiful, well-dressed people. Such bright and cheerful faces. This is what it means to free yourself from Bolshevik oppression! And, of course, there are many beautiful, renovated mansions. You know, I visited the mansion in Polyanka, which belonged to my family before the revolution. I was amazed at how well they preserved the rooms. Even the copper chandelier that I remember from my childhood still hangs in the hallway."

"It is possible," Berner smiled, encouraging her somewhat parchment rustling speech, "it is possible that soon there will be a law that will return ownership of all the buildings seized from the royal family during the revolution. My MP friends are working out a new bill. Who knows, maybe you will soon be able to return to your ancestral home!"

"Oh, that would be a miracle!" The princess quietly shook her head, closing her yellow eyelids, which looked like those of an owl. She seemed to recall hazy images of her childhood.

"Is it true," Marina mimicked the princess with a barely noticeable accent, "is it true that if the monarchy is restored in Russia, then the monarchists will be granted the titles of counts, princes, and barons? Can my husband and I become counts?"

"Oh, certainly!" smiled the princess, showing her porcelain teeth, which looked like the edge of a plate. "Your wonderful husband is doing so much to restore the Russian monarchy!"

"Baron von Berner!" Segal, the merry fellow sitting at the table, laughed. He had a porous, pink nose, a shining, bald head that was tanned under sauna quartz, and hair white as dandelion fluff. "A Baltic German!"

Berner looked sternly in his direction, and he fell silent with a weak giggle. The princess came to Moscow with funds and at the invitation of Berner. In a few days he will send her to Yekaterinburg, where the princess wanted to visit the burial place of the royals. There, she wanted to take a handful of earth, which, as she said, contains "a particle of the relics of the emperor." Berner had already booked her a hotel, a car, a guide, and spoke on the phone with the governor. In return, he hoped for the princess' protection, who was in kinship and friendship with influential politicians in France, where Berner was going to open a network of gas stations. Nikolai—this was his thought to name the company that sells gasoline abroad, in honor of the murdered emperor.

A waiter in a white frock coat, which was narrow at the waist, and a lace shirt with a bow, making him look like a bullfighter, presented a silver platter with sliced sturgeon. Not long before this, a whole sturgeon, scaly, wavy, and with a bunch of paper flowers in the shape of a pointed beak, was demonstrated at the feast. Now, cut into even slices, the fish lay on the platter. The waiter gracefully waved a pearly spatula, took portions, and put them on fresh plates, not forgetting to put a silver spoonful of fragrant horseradish.

"Gentlemen, the food is so wonderful! Unbelievably delicious!" Segal got up, dropping his napkin while holding a crystal glass. "I propose a toast to the health of our friend, and I'm not afraid to say, the benefactor who gathered us at this wonderful table! To Yakov Vladimirovich, for whom, I dare to hope, the new year will not only be a year of great wealth, but literally a year of fortune! By the way, so as not to forget..." he quickly changed his pompous, pathetic speech to a funny one, with the hoarseness of an Odessan accent. "Time for an anecdote! Two Jews terrorized a village with their two sawed-off shotguns!" and, not waiting for others to laugh, he laughed, violently shaking his stomach. He clinked glasses with Berner across the table.

Berner was not angry with him, but mockingly watched as he plunged his thick lips into a crystal glass and then sloppily thrust a large piece of sturgeon into his mouth.

"Tell me why," Marina asked sarcastically, "when a Jew tells such stories, it's called an anecdote, but when members of the Pamyat Society say it, it is an anti-Semitic trick?"

Marina did not like Segal, nor did she understand why her husband put up with this untidy and stupid jester beside him. Berner appreciated his wife's witty remark but did not explain to her that he valued Segal as a reminder of the past when he, an inexperienced young engineer, took his first timid steps in business while Segal, a seasoned lawyer, saved him from criminal prosecution.

He turned to where there was a small table at the white grand piano. Without wine, and instead with bottles of mineral water and sandwiches, his bodyguards sat at the table, sturdy, tough guys in green, swollen jackets, and along with them was Akhmet, the head of the Ingush security service, who was reddish, wiry, and had a trimmed stubble. Akhmet caught the owner's glance, looked at his phone lying in front of him, and shook his head. Berner understood that the call he was expecting had not come. The long-awaited news was late.

This news he pursued concerned the assault on Grozny, which was set to occur on New Year's Eve. The minister of defense explained that his troops will quickly enter the city and oust Dudayev into the rural areas, where air strikes will attack the fleeing general. The army will then establish control over the oil fields. Berner was interested in those fields. These would be untouched by war along with the mothballed factories with shining steel towers and fat chimneys stretching out into the steppe—all of them were to become Berner's property. His business would take advantage of the situation and the support of the government to take possession of the property. This military operation calling for the "Pacification of rebellious Chechnya" was dictated by oil.

The supply lines have already been drawn on the maps, hanging in the offices of oil traders and refineries. The lines go through Chechnya's territory to Russia, Azerbaijan, and Kazakhstan. They looked like multi-colored beams, reminiscent of battle plans. They were plans and strategies for dominance in the twenty-first century.

Akhmet needed to bring news of the troops' movements in Chechnya. Berner waited for the phone on his desk to gently ring like a black octopus strewn with suction cups on its tentacles.

Another guest that Berner invited entertained the feast with his conversation. He was a well-known figure of the Russian patriotic wing of the party, who made himself known back in the days of communism. He advocated the revival of Orthodoxy, the renaming of streets, the restoration of churches, and for the Russian people to call each other "sir" or "madam." He was criticized in the Soviet press and was almost known as a dissident, even though he published articles and books and traveled abroad.

Nikita Stanislavovich Zagrebelsky, ruddy and white-mustached, with Skobelev's style of perfumed whiskers, gazed like an eagle at the crystal and silver jewelry on the necks and fingers of the ladies. He put down his fork which he had just used to bring a bit of fish to his mouth and, still chewing, said, "Dear sir Yakov Vladimirovich, unlike the new rulers of Russia, you understand the role and importance of the Church in building the Russian state. The Bolsheviks, as you know, built their paradise without God, and all hell broke loose. They built their church without God, and the GULAG was the result. They were building an eternal 'Internationale,' but it turned out to be an empire of dust, which the wind blew away!"

Zagrebelsky spoke edifyingly, but also with a slight sneer. He was as instructive as a shepherd, but with a slight irony to what he was talking about. His old wife, who looked like a white mouse, was chewing and grinding something, moving her little nose, which tugged at her ruddy cheeks, and dimly scrutinizing the remains of food on the plate.

"But a new Russia, which again they want to build without God, on only one economy and American common sense—God will destroy it again! That is why you, my dear sir Yakov Vladimirovich, spoke very correctly at our meeting with the Patriarch that it was time for them to enter politics. It is time to take it upon themselves, not yielding to its soulless little people, among whom, many zealots of the Comintern are hiding and lying-in wait. The Church must, finally, proclaim its divine word from the pulpit!"

Berner needed Zagrebelsky as a representative of that "lordly" eloquent layer of the Moscow intelligentsia, which dreamed of creating a conservative patriotic party. Such a party was conceived by Berner as a counterbalance to the radical liberals, to whom many also ranked him, as well as to the red revenge-seekers, who seemed to be the most dangerous in Berner's opinion. He began investing in the creation of an "Orthodox patriotic party" and recently attended a reception with an influential metropolitan, where he presented his views. Before the visit, he rehearsed in front of a mirror for a long time the bows and gestures befitting such a blessing. The reception went wonderfully. The metropolitan was pleased with the gift—an old Easter egg covered with tiny rubies. He promised to assist in the creation of the party.

"Do you really want to appoint him as the head of the Russian Idea?" Marina whispered. "His wife looks like a guinea pig. This is the company we have at our party!"

"There's nothing we can do, my dear," Berner sighed, kissing her warm, diamond studded earlobe. "All politics are reminiscent of the nature documentaries *In the World of Animals*."

The young bullfighter appeared again, in lace, with a crimson bow. On a silver tray was a turkey, glazed and carefully plucked, as if shaven with a Gillette razor. The waiter, like a dancer, gracefully pivoted around on an axis, carrying a dish to the table, demonstrating the next meal. Berner imagined a bullfighter with a red matador cloth and red cloak, fighting a turkey. Having defeated the turkey in a bloody battle, he demonstrated his trophy.

Marina guessed his thoughts and smiled, saying, "A month ago we were at a bullfight. You forbade me from looking, and you said that the baby didn't need to see it," she put his hand on her stomach, and he felt an emanating warmth, a swollen elastic bulge.

"I'll order an artist to commission a fabulous, magical painting for you," said Berner, feeling moved. "You will look at the painting and adore it. In the future, our child will likewise look at the painting in adoration."

The turkey, cut into chunks of white and dark meat, was already on the plates. Sauces were poured over the meat, which was soon ground into soft fibers and washed down with wine and vodka.

"My dear Donald," Berner turned to the thin American secretary of the embassy in heavy horn-rimmed glasses, who was benevolently watching the Russian table as a nanny watches children playing in the sandbox. His young wife, who did not understand Russian well, and had a horse-like head, got a little drunk and suddenly began to laugh loudly with a strange, also horse-like snort.

"My dear Donald, tell me, how do you think the American public would react to a small victorious war unleashed by our federal center against one of the rebellious outskirts? Would you protest, as usual, or turn a blind eye to it?"

The diplomat was engaged in the collection of strategic information from Moscow. Berner needed to carry out a small but important operation related to his financial interests in America. Berner provided services to the American, reporting confidential information from the "corridors of power," acquainting him with influential officials, and in return receiving patronage from the US State Department and Wall Street's financial circles.

"Which outskirts do you mean?" asked Donald, sharply enlarging his eyes in the horn-rimmed eyepieces, as if somewhere he had tightened an invisible screw. "Tatarstan or Chechnya?"

"No, no, not Tatarstan!" Berner waved his hands. "Let's say it's Chechnya!"

"I think everything will depend on the duration and level of the conflict." The American became serious, and his horn-rimmed eyes shrank again by a half turn of the screw. "If the war is short-lived and victorious, with few casualties, then, I suppose, the Americans will turn a blind eye to it. It is important whether a proper informational background will be provided to them, as it was in Moscow during the storming of your parliament. Americans, sympathetic to any duly elected parliament, were then on the side of your president, not parliament."

The answer was neat and accurate. It seemed that the diplomat had long foreseen the possibility of a war in Chechnya. An analytical note had already been sent to the State Department, data already collected on separatism in Russia.

"Donald, can I ask you a favor?" Berner turned the conversation from big to small, from general to personal. "My companion, a great friend of America, must urgently fly to the States. But your consular department denies him a visa based on information about his criminal past, allegedly available in the computer. The Communist past was criminal for all anti-communists. One should not consider the conflicts and difficulties that arose between the totalitarian regime and the most capable part of society. Help him get a visa, and we, in turn, will return the favor."

"What is the name of your companion?" he asked with his glazed eyes focused on Berner. "I'll try to talk to our consulate."

Berner took out a business card with a tiny holographic logo that flashed like a snowflake. He wrote the client's name with a small gold pen and handed it to the diplomat. The snowflake flashed once more in the diplomat's thin, painful fingers and disappeared into his pocket. His wife, not understanding the meaning of the conversation, gave a loud, horse-like snort. Her pink nostrils fluttered with the hot masses of exhaled air.

"I would like to put a kopeck worth of hay in front of her!" Marina snapped.

Berner glanced toward the white, gold-decorated piano, where the bodyguards stood motionless, like dummies in a shop window. Akhmet instantly caught his gaze and shook his head. There was still no news, and it irritated and worried Berner.

He looked around the crowded, oak hall. He was the master here. He glanced over and gave an imperceptible nodding gesture which was expected by the head waiter, who was a large, noble man, like a heraldic lion. The waiters in modest postures stood against the wall like candelabras, ready at the first sign to rush and fulfill the whims and impulses of the guests. The guests themselves, noisily clinging to the tables, popped confetti, lit sparklers, laughed, and talked loudly, while constantly and imperceptibly glancing at Berner. They wanted to catch his eye, smile at him if possible, then come up, shake hands, and exchange a couple of insignificant words.

Berner was used to these expressions of attention and implication. He listened to the hum of the celebration he created, reminiscent of the work of a weaving machine with many multicolored silk threads.

"Well, Andrei Fyodorovich, do you regret being in our modest society? Would you like to be sitting now, on New Year's Eve, in front of a forest den, wasting away without any food?" With these humorous words, Berner turned to another guest, the deputy minister of fuel, who looked rustic with a rough chipped face and many cuts and scars. It was as if this face had once boiled and then froze in place like a piece of volcanic pumice. The deputy minister was going to fly to Siberia on a bear hunt to a den, which the oil workers had prepared for him. He also invited Berner, but Berner wished to remain and wait for the important news.

His wife, a small, chubby Bashkir woman with cheeks like ripe apples, babbled merrily, amusing Segal. The old Casanova was kissing her hands as he tilted his pink, shining, bald head, and the frivolous, mischievous woman laughed as it seemed that she was going to flick his bald head with her varnished nail.

"Do not regret this, Andrei Fyodorovich. The hunt will still be there. We may need you at any moment." Berner looked at the oil man with sympathy, for he needed constant effort and zeal for the seizure of the Chechen oil complex. The deputy minister was supposed to ensure Berner's victory over competitors, to achieve a favorable government decision. At the same time, the minister reserved a place for his brother on the board of directors of the newly created conglomerate.

"No, I don't regret it, Yakov Vladimirovich," the deputy minister replied, sparkling with small, bead-like, rogue eyes. "The bear is asleep. Well, he will sleep for another week until we wake him up. With you, our business does not sleep nor does it let us sleep!"

"That is correct, Andrei Fyodorovich. We will be here for the first week of the New Year, before the first meeting of the government. And only then, God willing, will we travel to Siberia and slay the bear!"

"We will do everything in the best possible way, Yakov Vladimirovich. The rifle is already prepared for you, and you will have your huntsman. Not only that, but we will give you the best place near the den. Let the bear sleep and wait for us." The beads inserted into the dark meteorite glittered merrily. They both understood each other perfectly. They were ready to provide each other with services related to long-standing interests, dangers, gambling, and lots of money.

"Is it true, Andrei Fyodorovich, that our venerable prime minister was recently on a bear hunt and shot a bear, who left behind four cubs? So, he, a great lover of nature, ordered the cubs to be stabbed and made into stuffed animals and gave them away to his German friends. Is it true?"

"All the same, the cubs would have died, Yakov Vladimirovich. Without a mother in winter, they would have died from cold and hunger!"

"I always said that Russia was lucky with their prime minister!" Marina stuck out her lower lip with disgust. "After the incident with the bear, no one dares to accuse him of being heartless!"

Through the music, laughter, clinking of dishes, and shuffling of feet, through the hot, thick air, Berner heard the phone ring. It was not a sound, but a silvery V-shaped web, stretching from the white piano to his sensitive ear.

He looked around; Akhmet was talking on his phone. Just a few words. He then put the phone aside and went to Berner.

"It has begun, Yakov Vladimirovich, a few hours ago. The troops went in. The officer of the general staff has reported it."

And within himself, Berner felt joy, cheerfulness, and a surge of energy. Like the sun had risen. He felt a surge of warm, pulsating blood rush into his cheeks, eyes, and muscles, as if he had joined the mighty conflict, which he himself had caused.

His efforts, invisible to the world, were of painstaking work with the military, intelligence agencies, members of the presidential family, his friendship with ministers, editors of newspapers and television programs, many aides and experts, each working separately but with his coordination, all working together. The impact of persuasion and money, evenly applying pressure across the entire frontlines—this was all a result of his work.

The troops entered the city, and the entire plan, which existed as a project and blueprint, as an abstract dream and opportunity, came to life and began to move. It turned into the endeavor of armored columns, into the rattle of motors, into the energy of young, active people who, unknowingly, were carrying out his, Berner's, will. This will, materialized and reified, immediately turned into abstraction again, into numbers, into stock quotes, into fluctuations of currency rates, into the volatility of the world economy, instantly and delicately reacting to the first shots.

All of this spun like a wheel of fire in Berner's mind with lightning speed. Turning away from his wife's questioning eyes, he said to Akhmet, "Put me in touch with the minister of defense. He's celebrating, so dial his backup home number."

The security chief's fingers, cleanly washed, with red hair, ran over the buttons. They lit up like transparent eggs. Akhmet held out the phone, and Berner heard the cold, restrained voice of the colonel's assistant.

"This is Berner. Happy New Year! If possible, ask the minister… Yes, he is at the table, Yakov Vladimirovich. There are guests… I'm sure he will be pleased to hear me…"

A minute later, the familiar, hoarse, warmed-up voice of the minister said, "Yasha, my dear friend, hello!"

"Happy New Year, Comrade Minister, with happiness! And, of

course, happy birthday!"

"Thank you, my friend! Will I see you today?"

"If you haven't changed your mind, then as you requested. In the morning I'll come over and we can go to the banya."[2]

"I've got everything warmed up! The branches are soaked, and the beer is chilled!"

"Is it true that the troops went? After all, there was a different date set for the operation!"

"That was overturned... There were new orders, from the very top. Come, I'll tell you..."

"You also promised that the infrastructure would not be damaged. The factories and oil storage facilities must be preserved. You gave the order to your falcons to bomb far away."

"Don't worry, they are my jewelers. Sixty miles away in only the periphery of their left eye! Come and talk. I'll keep my word, and you better keep yours!"

The phone buttons went out. The small device passed a beam of information through its labyrinths and closed, like a snail that hides in its shell, leaving the sensitive horn of the antenna on the outside.

Berner returned to the table cheerful, confident, and hospitable to the guests.

"Have you brought good news?" The ubiquitous Segal noticed his temperamental conversation on the phone. "Is it the growth of your shares on the London Stock Exchange? Or perhaps falling property prices in the Canary Islands?

The question was clownish, but Berner was not angry with him. "Great news! We're already living very well! So now we'll live even better!"

He turned to the orchestra, which shone mysteriously through the fir branches with its saxophones and electric guitars. The orchestra caught sight of his gesture, the snap of his fingers, and reckless dazzling music burst out, as if pouring a bunch of gold coins out of a bag. A drunken couple galloped over these coins and danced. A plump young man hooked his thumbs on his vest, pulled it off in an extravagant way, and flashed it into the air.

A cameraman with a TV camera and a young journalist in a noticeably short skirt made their way across the hall through the dancing crowd to

---

[2] A Russian sauna

Berner. While she was approaching, Berner had time to voraciously inspect her open legs and the deep neckline of the dress, in which her breasts, free from the bodice, swayed and swayed. The TV camera arrived according to his plan. This holiday was to be shown on the TV channel that he controlled. Food, musical numbers, eminent guests, their jokes, New Year's jokes and wishes all to be broadcast.

The journalist approached the table and came directly to Berner first. She smiled with luscious lips in pearl lipstick. She leaned her plump, hot shoulders toward him and held out her microphone.

"Mr. Berner, you are the main organizer of our wonderful holiday. The viewers would like to know what you are experiencing in these wonderful moments. What words do you have for them?"

The camera slowly, intently examined the table: silver candlesticks; distended wax; expensive crystal; a porcelain dish with steaming pale pink shrimps; porcelain tureen with red lobster spreading its claws; chrome plated tools for cracking the shells. His guests looked into the camera and smiled: a Russian princess with bluish artificial teeth; an American diplomat with telescopic eyes; a gray-haired, well-fed leader of the Conservative Party. Berner, preparing to answer, could smell the perfume emanating from the journalist, and the exciting fragrant heat of her close, young body. He experienced acute excitement, the desire to kiss her pearly lips, pull them in, suck them in, grab her back with his palm, and feel her moving muscles through the dress.

This sudden, blinding passion was familiar to him. It was his reaction to overstimulation, protection against excess nervous energy that saved him from overload and stress.

His pregnant wife, whom he continued to love and desire, had taken on subtle new qualities in recent weeks that had alienated her from Berner. Now, looking at her dense, silk-covered belly, Berner wanted not her, but this young, accessible woman, whose white forehead, covered with golden shining hair, was so close that it was possible to press his lips to it.

"So, a few words to our viewers, Mr. Berner!"

"I wish all Russians to feel warmth and love on this New Year's Eve!" Berner looked through the peephole of the TV camera and smiled, squinting his dark, radiant eyes. He knew he was charismatic, energetic, and convincing. The words he uttered will be carefully transferred like jewels to Ostankino and from the huge bell tower up to the clouds, where it will then fall onto the world, splashing with strength and freshness.[3]

"Our difficulties and worries are temporary. They will soon pass. Resolute, courageous people are at the helm of the Russian state. We know how to act, how to make Russia great! Happy New Year, my friends!"

He uttered the last phrase especially sincerely and earnestly, knowing that he would be heard in every home, by every family, on their TV set. He nourished people with his love of life and confidence. Suddenly, he felt a silent blow to the chest. It was like a bullet came and hit him. It penetrated his body, where it sank lower into his stomach, and there it turned into a tiny living embryo. This embryo stirred, began to grow, turning from a small embryo, into a mobile, pulsating worm. It stunned and frightened him. He was pregnant, and the sperm that flew into him like a bullet was released from space, flew over vast distances, and found him here, in a stuffy room, at the New Year's table.

"You spoke very well, Herr Berner!" the journalist smiled at him, holding out the microphone to the neighboring princess.

He was silent, not understanding what had happened to him. Someone burst into him and nestled among his heated entrails.

---

[3] Ostankino is a television studio and technical center in Moscow

6

Kudryavtsev, driven by fear, ran to the corner of a dark three-story building. He wanted to go around, to go deep into the darkness of the unlit buildings near the station, but he imagined that people were moving along the platform. Then there was the light of a cigarette that flashed and went out. He stumbled back, began to go around the building to the other side, breaking through bushes, stumbling over children's sandboxes and benches. It seemed that snipers were lurking behind every bush and that they would hit at close range with a string of bursts. He turned and ran along the wall, back to where the city square was blazing, but a terrible rumble and the pressure of the hot light stopped him. Unconsciously, fleeing from the fiery, perilous square, he ran into the entrance, into complete darkness. Stumbling over the steps, grabbing the handrails, he ran upstairs, and after finally achieving night vision, saw in the dusk of the stairwells the numbers on the apartment doors. It seemed to him that one of the apartments had an open door. Frightened, he ran upstairs, poked at the locked attic door and froze. He sank to the floor, breathing heavily, powerlessly burying his face in the dusty rags, so as not to see the crimson reflections splashing in all directions of the tracers.

Clenching his burned eyelids, he did not see them, but he heard how his swollen heart was filled with boiling blood as it pumped, while outside the machine guns were firing and ammunition was exploding from the destroyed tanks.

He was sitting and holding his head, feeling paralyzed, wanting to disappear, become invisible, and shrink to the size of a cricket, shrink into a single cage and in this state survive and endure this catastrophe. But this primitive type of horror began to give way to conscious fear. His darkened consciousness began to gradually clear up, and in this, still twilight, deafened consciousness, the first glimpses of will arose. Danger came from everywhere. From an area filled with enemies looking for new targets for their grenades and machine guns. From the dark buildings surrounding the house, where an ambush lurked and sharp-sighted evil eyes watched. From the house where he was and whose half-closed doors and unlit windows could suddenly open and catch fire and angry people would jump out of them, grab him, and lead him to the square.

He was sitting huddled against the attic door, hiding under an old, dirty cloth. His mind was throbbing and felt hot, as if a blood vessel had burst and sought salvation.

If they didn't grab him right away, if they allowed him to run to the staircase, heard him stomping up the stairs, and no one chased after him, turned on the light or flashlight, this meant that either the tenants were scared to death, hiding in their apartments, or there simply was no one at all. Thus, staying in an empty, abandoned house was not as dangerous as staying near the fiery square.

He got up and, trying not to make a noise, went down to the lower platform where he put his ear to the door. He was listening, hoping to catch the sounds of life: footsteps, talking, the clinking of dishes. But it was quiet. The smell of a smoldering, burnt dwelling emanated from the doors.

He approached the doors, first on the top floor, then the floor below, listening for a human voice, or the barking of a dog, or the clatter of chairs being moved. But there was only the clatter of machine guns and the thunder of battle. Through the window overlooking the stairwell, fireballs appeared, which rolled and jumped across the square.

The door on the second floor was open. Without looking into it, he felt that the apartment was empty. He did not go into it, but went to the window, and on the windowsill, there was an empty tin can with cigarette butts, left there by the tenants, men who went out onto the stairs to smoke. He clung to the windowsill and began to look out.

The square looked like a huge frying pan lit with red coals. In this frying pan, the coals hissed while being swollen with fuel and sprinkled with shapeless burning debris. These slices were the brigade. Tanks with heavy guns, pointed IFV's, hunchbacked clumsy trucks, thick-sided tanks with fuel—everything turned into flattened burnt piles, among which poisonous smoke wandered, with blushing wicks of burning machinery and gears. Among this roast, with streams of boiling water, grease, and mucus, was his company with inexperienced, understaffed crews, naive soldiers decorating consoles and airborne compartments of the vehicles with magazine clippings, photographs of brides, and handmade plastic gnomes.

During the persistent fear that prompted him to carefully peer about, to flee cowardly and save himself, a painful amazement arose, not connected with his own life and the danger that threatened it. He tried to figure out what had happened, where the misfortune came from, whose senseless and stupid will, whose mediocre mistake pushed the brigade into a trap. Where did these furious and confident shooters come from, these brave and ruthless fighters who exterminated the brigade? What does this defeat mean? How far along the streets of burning equipment and burnt, shot soldiers did the torn, fiery crack of destruction stretch? To the outskirts? To the suburbs? To the surrounding villages and towns? Or further, to the steppe, to the foothills, to Russian cities, to distant garrisons, to the Kremlin itself with its palaces and cathedrals?

In this defeat, his company, his brigade, perished, and he, the company commander, was still alive. He left behind a stabbed lieutenant in the garden of a Chechen house. He left behind a company column in the square, where the soldiers burned alive. What should he do, standing at the window of a deserted house? Alone, without weapons, without will, without strength, looking out at the slaughter?

He had to leave. He had to break out of the hostile city, through ambushes and traps, into the cold night steppe, where there are no roads or villages. Navigating empty fields and pastures, hiding from the eyes of the enemy, moving only at night, like beasts, this was his only option. To get out of this cruel land and go to friendly native towns and villages, where there are Russian faces and speech, where there are still airfields with front-line aviation, parks with self-propelled howitzers, and an undisturbed, non-disintegrated Russian army. There, somewhere in Russia, he will arrive and inform them of the defeat of his brigade.

He was in a hurry to get ready. He looked around the staircase, around the blind doors of the apartments and the windowsill with the tin can. He had a feeling of gratitude for being sheltered here.

"Thanks to this house, I'm still alive. Now let's go to another one," he repeated mechanically, going down toward the exit.

He looked out along the facade, intending to slip out and disappear like a shadow. He wanted to sneak to the railway tracks, hide in the wayside, and then leave the city. He was about to leave the house but saw two people approaching in the glow of the burning cars, bending over. He did not see their faces, but by their frightened, mincing run, their hunched over backs, their heads squeezed into their shoulders for cover, he guessed they were his people. These could not be Chechens, who would have fled with the free, strong gallop of persecutors, but his own fearful, persecuted solders.

Two ran past the entrance, shuffling hard. Kudryavtsev whistled softly to them and called, "Hey, guys!"

They stopped, trampled in a daze, not knowing whether to run away or heed this whistle and shout, without waiting for a burst of automatic fire to hit them from the darkness.

"Come here, I said! To me! Friendlies!" They approached hesitantly, peering into the black entrance, not seeing Kudryavtsev and still fearing of shots. He let them into the house and here, in the windless entrance, he noticed how pungent their clothes smelled of smoke and hot iron. This smoky, iron stench, together with the sweat of a frightened hot body, was the smell of the many recent deaths from which they fled.

"Which battalion?" asked Kudryavtsev, peering into the faces of the fugitives. These were the young faces of soldiers, driven and frightened, with darting, stunned eyes, and their noses sharpened from suffering. "From which battalion are you, I asked."

"From the second one," one said exasperated in a half-whisper, thin and awkward. And in this exhale, there was a scream of tears, a wheeze of burnt lungs, the complaint of an abandoned, useless child.

"Where is your battalion commander? Where is the company commander?"

"Killed," answered the second, and in his answer there was more firmness. Short, strong, he was sullen and angry. Along with fear, there was a feeling of resistance, the unused excitement of the recent battle.

"Don't go there!" Kudryavtsev pointed toward the one-story houses where the soldiers were heading. "They will intercept you there. We need to go to the station and go along the embankment. Less housing and less people..."

They saw among the wavy lights, running away from them, another shadow was moving past the house, all in the same direction, toward the low houses near the station. A shadow was approaching with a heavy crunching of soles and harsh breathing.

"Hey!" Kudryavtsev shouted and whistled softly. "Come here!" The man stopped, and Kudryavtsev quietly, imperiously, trying not to frighten him off, firmly and demandingly called, "Come here, I say... Friendlies."

The man approached. He was a strong, tall soldier in an unbuttoned peacoat, with a round, shaved head. Peering into the mouth of the entrance, from where he was called, he said, "There are many Chechens in the side streets. You'll be caught."

Kudryavtsev let the soldier into the entrance, where he, finding himself among friendlies, immediately stopped hurrying and, like a donkey, went limp.

"Which military unit are you from?" asked Kudryavtsev.

"From an anti-aircraft missile battery. I'm a driver," the soldier replied.

Kudryavtsev didn't ask him why, being in a battalion of anti-aircraft missiles following in close proximity, he found himself on the square among the leading vehicles, burned along with the leading tanks and IFV's.

They were standing in the entrance, and Kudryavtsev, who had recently been seized by the horror of being a lone survivor of a massacre, suddenly felt relief. These frightened soldiers that suddenly appeared were a burden for him, but a welcome, saving burden. They returned him to a commanding role and demanded meaningful, responsible behavior. And although he was silent and the soldiers were silent, they also sensed a commander in him. They pressed close to him, expecting orders from him that would save their lives.

None of them had any firearms. Kudryavtsev lost his machine gun in the garden during the chase. The anti-aircraft gunner had only a bayonet-knife, and his comrade had a pocket torch. Weapons were nearby in abundance in the square, but that was not a safe area, being on fire, where the fire set off whirlwinds of tracers, and none of them thought to return to where the nameless combatants had just carried them out.

They were sitting on the steps of the empty entrance, smoking a cigarette, only one for all of them, covering the red bead with their palms. They took a drag and then passed it on to a neighbor. Kudryavtsev took the burning cigarette butt and shone the light on his watch. A thin, fragile arrow was running under the red glow of the tobacco, indicating that midnight had already fluttered, the New Year already arrived. Kudryavtsev met this New Year in the icy entrance of an unfamiliar house, in a strange, terrible city, in the city square, where the brigade had just died. The sides of the cannons, transparent from the fire, were slowly cooling down. The tanks with their fallen cannons clumped together in an ugly formation like dead rhinos that gored each other. Something was pouring and burning with a white, magnesium-like light in the cabs of the trucks. And he suddenly thought of the general posing as Yermolov, whose Eastern, bent, leather shoes stepped on the map of Grozny. He felt an instant hatred for the general that cut through him like a razor.

"Now let's go one by one, with an interval of ten meters. If there is an ambush, we all run in different directions..." said Kudryavtsev, smearing his cigarette butt on the steps. He was about to get up and go outside, where the railway track glowed dimly, but suddenly he saw two headlights on at the station in the dark, moving forward. A truck rolled into the square, previously invisible, lurking in the shadows. In the back were a crowd of armed people. The truck rolled through, highlighting white snow with its headlights first, and then, approaching the carnage, spreading water and greasy fumes. Another truck lit its headlights and rolled away from the other wing of the station. Kudryavtsev staggered back, into the depths of the entrance, hiding in fear within the darkness, thanks to someone who detained him for a moment, who did not substitute the shooters for bullets.

"Thanks to this house..." he repeated the phrase again and watched the truck pass by slowly. People with machine guns held onto the sides of the truck, and they all looked in one direction at the square, at the crackling inferno.

People began to come out onto the square from different sides, from different angles, from behind fences, from under the ground, from tree branches, one at a time, in small and in large groups, carefully aiming from machine guns and grenade launchers at the burning husks. Sometimes short bursts were fired. They surrounded the square. Others approached it on foot, on motorcycles, and in cars and trucks. They looked like dark figures, flatly imprinting on the wall in the glow, reminiscent of cave paintings of cavemen with spears and harpoons that would surround a huge mammoth they had killed. They warmed themselves by the fire, contemplating their prey, as if pondering how best to approach it. They did not yet know whether the slain beast was dead or if it would strike with a sharpened tusk in its dying throes.

Some took an open position around the perimeter, holding at gunpoint the remnants of damaged equipment. Others, holding their weapons in the air, began to seep in from different directions into the accumulation of dead vehicles, disappearing and reappearing among fire and smoke. They jumped onto the armor, jumped onto the turrets, and hid in the hatches. Fire illuminated them as they scurried among the destroyed columns. Where they appeared, single shots were heard from time to time, and Kudryavtsev realized that they were finishing off the wounded there.

Saved from death but unarmed, he fearfully hid in a dark entrance. In the troop compartments and in the cockpits, the enemy was finishing off his soldiers, who were burned, stunned and in death did not release their triggers.

It was quiet. The speakers, which had recently spewed a bubbling roar, were now silent. The lanterns, recently surrounded by a transparent blue glow, were off. The flashing tree was gone. But there was light from the many fires, the burning spilled fuel, and the smoldering rubber. And in the silence, there were screams from the winners and the rare claps of shots.

The street along which the armor column arrived and stood on the square, though obscured by houses, also shone through. Raspberry flames and thick, jam-like smoke billowed from the facades and reflected in the windows. There, on an invisible street, a halted, destroyed column was also burning. Among the shops, trolleybus stops, and kiosks, black skeletons with smoldering with foul innards.

Kudryavtsev looked at the red smoke and sticky balls of fire. It seemed that the wind blowing from the square together with the stench of oil, burnt rubber, and iron armor carried a sweet, sickening smell of burnt meat.

Due to this stench on the fat smoke of burnt flesh, birds began to flock. Awakened by the battle and disturbed from the surrounding landfills by explosions and fires, they circled over the city, afraid to approach the tracers, white flashes, and streams of metal sparks in the sky. Now when the explosions had subsided, crows swirled in the red sky with countless shadows and strokes like slanted wedges. They went down, sat on the roofs, and filled the sky with eager, impatient cries.

Kudryavtsev listened with fright and disgust to the growing, ringing rumble of the approaching flocks of crows. The same birds that saw the column approach during the day looked down from the sky and into the hatches, aiming with their black beaks, marking the cars with putrid, white blotches. It was as if they knew about the imminent battle, so they chose their prey and counted on it with their small, evil eyes.

The cries of crows, intermittent machine gun bursts, sluggish waving smoke, and scurrying dexterous figures of enemies were all before him, and he, Kudryavtsev, was powerless and humiliated, as though saved from the carnage for some sort of purpose, put in this dark entrance to see and survey all of it.

He saw that it was possible to slip out of the entrance, merge with the facades, and dive into the darkness. Furthermore, he could go through the bushes and sandboxes, through the backyards at random, into alleys and streets, to the railway track, and, while meandering among warehouses, abandoned carriages, and uninhabited factory outskirts, be able to lead all of them out of the city to the steppes where they would be safe. But fear held him back. Chechens, who were keen on victory, will not notice four fugitives. But the birds, being angry and sensitive, will rush after them, screaming their heart-rending screams and diving in the dark, where they will strike with their sharp beaks. They will lead the pursuit, while the Chechens, having surrounded the fugitives, will shoot them while they're cornered. This crazy thought kept Kudryavtsev at the house. He did not let the soldiers go. All of them remained in the building.

He saw two cars pull up onto the square. They stopped at the edge of the fire. People with TV cameras came out of them in a hurry and recklessly ran around. They impatiently filmed the burning tanks alongside the armed riflemen. They scanned the sky with their cameras, taking pictures of the birds, and then, having gotten enough with the first random shots, they began to slowly, at choice, remove the damaged equipment. Militants were placed in the background. They made them run and shoot on the move. They tilted the lenses to the ground, fixating the scene with scattered, shapeless clods. They went into the depths of the burning column, disappeared, and then returned from the fire. And you could see how their sweaty faces shined, how the fire reflected on their glistening foreheads and cheeks.

The Chechens, who had gone deep into the arrangement of vehicles, came back. They brought back with them bundles of assault rifles and machine guns over their shoulders. They then began to pile them up in the street. The TV crew filmed the trophies and posed the winners next to their spoils. They began to disassemble the weapons that were laid out on the ground, and then threw the parts onto the asphalt. Many of them willingly posed for the camera and giggled at the sound of clinking on the ground. Kudryavtsev was disgusted with himself; he felt cowardly, hidden, and powerless. He could not interfere in the victors' celebration, in the mockery of the weapons torn from his dead comrades, whose bodies had not even gone cold yet.

An entourage of cars drove out onto the square, skirting around the smoldering debris, without approaching the clumped tanks. A long, shiny limousine, followed by a few Zhiguli vehicles stopped in the light. Guards jumped out of the cars, bristled with trunks, forming a ring around the limousine. Out of the car came a man, who stepped forward, thin, casual, and domineering. He turned to face the raging fire, and from afar it seemed to Kudryavtsev that he could distinguish the spiky hair on his narrow, thin face. This was General Dudayev.

The rebellious general, who until recently seemed almost non-existent, unreal, and causing only slight annoyance and irritation, suddenly appeared before him as the embodiment of his defeat and shame, as the main culprit of the irreparable misfortune that had happened. The entire wreckage of vehicles, with the remains of an incinerated brigade, was personified by a single man standing in the distance, whose face, turned to the fire, reddened like a small drop of juice. And there was no sniper rifle with a smooth butt and blue enlightened optics through which to view his spiky, thin mustache and thin cartilage nose.

People were running up to the man from all sides. They raised their fists with machine guns. They shouted as they shot tracer rounds into the sky. The general turned to this salute and raised his hand.

The crew was spinning their cameras, filming the enthusiastic people shooting at the smoldering vehicles. Everything was moving, getting in the way, swirling in chaos. A circular dance spontaneously appeared from the noisy, disorganized tangle of people as if a rigid spring had begun to decompress.

People, clinging to one another, ran in a circle with an uneven, leaning run. They raised their fists and exhaled indistinct, moaning sounds. The crowd grew as more and more soldiers became a part of it, in a hurry to take part in the victory dance. They glorified a being who looked at them from heaven. They glorified the commander standing among them. They glorified their victory, which crushed a formidable enemy who found death.

Kudryavtsev looked at the ancient victory dance, at the crows flashing in red clouds, and at the remnants of the brigade. He felt like howling and wailing in despair. He then saw a cloud of steam flying out of the general's mouth.

7

The climax of the New Year's celebration had come, the time when the guests were not yet completely drunk and tired but were enjoying themselves in excitement, demanded spectacles, and intense experiences. Berner prepared a surprise on this occasion. He looked around the room. He found a waiter standing at the door with a thick head of hair, looking like a British lion. When he made a signal with his hand, the waiter bowed respectfully and disappeared through the doorway. The orchestra, which had stopped playing earlier, now began to play a bravura march from the *Aida* opera.

The oak doors opened wide, and four porters appeared: black, half naked, in loincloths, and with rings in their noses and ears. In their muscular arms they held a stretcher, in which there was a semblance of a nest built from spruce branches, cotton wool, and golden rain. A huge egg was laid in the nest with a milky radiance mysteriously pouring out through the translucent shell. It seemed that the egg was alive, magical, and concealing an embryo inside.

The porters, students from African countries hired by Berner for this exotic role, placed the egg on the ground. Then they each stood at a distance with their arms crossing their chest.

The music began to pick up. The shell of the egg pulsated and shuddered, as if it was being opened by a living, growing chick begging for freedom. The beams of the searchlights focused on the egg, and it suddenly burst, shattered into fragments, and from it, shimmering, blinding, flew out a magical feathered woman dressed as a firebird covered with peacock feathers and a diamond tuft, a black woman, half naked, with round hips, velvety-moist breasts, and strong, lilac nipples like plums. She was white-toothed, with bulging, porcelain eyes as she jumped to the floor, shaking her pelvis, to which a fabulous, beautiful wavy tail was attached.

As the orchestra began to play a rumba, the dancer in high gold heels began to passionately swing her strong arms and wet, oily chest in a dance. From her every movement, the huge peacock's tail fluttered and shimmered like a fluorescent sea. The diamonds on the tuft radiated a multicolored magic ray in the entire room.

The guests were blinded and amazed as they gazed at the dance of the bird-woman. They reached out to her and grabbed the hot air flying away with their lips and nostrils. They swam in the air in a fiery ball of music, beauty, and passion.

Berner was glad that his surprise was a success. This mulatto woman, a famous cabaret dancer, winner of the Brazilian Carnival, and imported from Rio de Janeiro, was here, in the frosty New Year of Moscow, stomping on golden heels and dancing a red-hot rumba.

There was a pause after the magnificent performance, when the bird-woman, accompanied by her black guards, flew out of the hall. The guests got up from their seats and strolled along the tables. During this break, many wanted to approach Berner and express their respect for him and wish him a Happy New Year, but there were several others whom he himself intended to approach and sit down for a short conversation at a table. One of these guests was sitting in the distance under a Gothic stained-glass window, behind which, it seemed, a crimson-blue dawn was pouring in. Berner never lost sight of him among the toasts, jokes, and noise of the night.

Meanwhile, the general was approaching across the hall, pushing apart the passing guests, in a civilian, tight-fitting suit, with his feet and knees twisted slightly forward and his heavy hands at his sides in round clenched fists. The general's head, with short bangs, resembled a large boulder with chiseled, narrow lips, an impudent grin, and drilled in clever and cruel eyes.

Berner rose to meet the general. Feeling the gaze of the audience turn to them, they exchanged a handshake.

"I wish you, Yakov Vladimirovich, a bull's health, a snake's agility, and the army's courage. To feel like you are in a tank!" The general grinned, showing his short, yellowish teeth. His eyes glittered, not in friendliness, but cold cruelty.

"And I hope that the fortune comes true, as it was told by a witch, who was a disciple of the late Vanga. She was my guest and did a reading on prominent politicians. You were represented by the king of diamonds."

"And what did the old witch say?"

"She foretold of a glorious kingdom and a golden-domed Moscow. She said that Russia cannot wait for you. And you will take your crown. But evil people will try to take it away: sixes, eights, and all kinds of weeds. Presumably, she prophesized that you would become president, but warned against Communist conspiracies."

The general thought of himself as the next president of Russia. In his stone forehead, like a light bulb, burned this singular, inextinguishable thought. He entered alliances, offering himself to the most diverse and often incompatible political groups. He went to meet important people in America and Europe. He promised everything and everyone and especially valued his connection in the banking community, expecting money from these connections for his election. Berner, who was within the circle of these acquaintances, laughed at the general and at his appearance as a godfather. In fact, he seriously considered the general for the role of dictator, since he would be capable of suppressing chaos with an iron fist and pacifying popular revolts which would be fueled by the Communists. The bankers would give him power in return for the security and preservation of their capital.

"The old witch has a good nose!" the general said with gusto. "In your environment, Yakov Vladimirovich, people have a good sense of smell."

"And with good money!"

"You promised me a meeting with the bankers. I would like to speak to them—naturally, behind closed doors. There, I would like to outline my views on the future of Russia. I will give guarantees in exchange for their support. This meeting will be compared with the meeting between Hitler and the German bankers, where he promised to defeat the Communists.

"For my Jewish friends, this is a very sensitive comparison!" Berner laughed, touching the general's sleeve, where he could feel the muscles of the former paratrooper. "However, they are above prejudice and see you as a supporter of the new statehood.

They looked into each other's eyes, illuminated by spotlights, which someone's obliging hand directed at them from the mezzanine. Berner peered into the small, stone-headed, cruel eyes of the general and felt how he hated him. He answered him in the same way, knowing that he was deftly and accurately using the general, and then, at the right time, he would get rid of him. He could also feel from the general thin rays of hatred coming from his stone head and concluded that he thinks the same about him.

"See you soon in the new year!" Berner said, bowing.

"See you soon," answered the general, and he walked forward in a straight line past the tables and to the wall, as if he wanted to break it, like a wrecking ball. He then disappeared into the blue, frosty blizzard.

Berner was not alone. A famous TV anchor immediately approached him, ahead of the others. Young, charming, with fluffy eyebrows, impudent, and with a cutesy grin, he wore a splendid black frock coat with a crimson rosebud in the buttonhole. For show, he hugged Berner. His hugs, thought Yakov Vladimirovich, were a little longer and closer than usual.

"Well, Yakov, I must congratulate you!" the TV journalist deliberately said quite loudly, for the public to hear, as he called to Berner with the familiar "you." "Thank God, the war in Chechnya has begun! Russian tanks are marching across Grozny!"

"You know already?" Berner wondered. "Where did you get this information?"

"Space reconnaissance spotted columns of tanks in the center of Grozny! Here is my receiver with a live broadcast!" He touched his crimson bud, having time to look at a young woman walking past.

The TV journalist was unpredictable, talented, and, until recently, friends with the opposition. He led a bright, courageous, merciless TV program, where he glorified the Soviet Union and Russian patriotism and almost called for an uprising. Berner managed to charm the ardent and narcissistic journalist. He offered him a lot of money, gave him a prestigious TV program, and made him express Berner's views and interests.

"You know, Yakov, this is my war! I waited for it, begged to God, and finally the tanks started rolling! I will be in this war, without fail! Will you give me money? Give me money for this war!"

"You want to pocket expenses for a local conflict?" Berner laughed, admiring his temperamental interlocutor, his crimson bud, black lace shirt, and eyes shining with delight.

"You must agree that any war is wonderful! Normal people are waiting for it to burst, and they even strive for it! For there is the aesthetics of war, the aesthetics of destruction and blood! I will make a film about this war, and it will be the metaphor for our time! You must give me money for a movie!"

Berner felt the fierce, sick passion of this handsome, unbalanced man. The world they both lived in was a disintegrating world, like a huge, beached whale. This whale was rotting, with holes opened in it, from which poisons and the stench of decay poured out, where the swollen insides bulged and slippery white ribs were exposed. On the carcass of the dead giant sat smaller, strong predators: animals, insects, and birds. They stuck their beaks, teeth, and proboscises into the loose flesh. They ate the rotten juices. Berner and this handsome man with a black frill and a rose were among these predators. They found each other, needed each other. Together, each in his own way, they tore off the loose, decaying flesh of the whale.

"You see, this war is like a boulder thrown into our political swamp," Berner said. "Waves and surges will appear immediately; society will be divided 'for' and 'against.' There will be terrible confusion, failure, ridiculous alliances, and stratification. We must take advantage of these surges, ride public opinion, and lead it in the right direction. This is your task! I will give you money for *your war,* but you will do *my task* with this money!"

Both laughed, looking at each other with delight. They understood and appreciated each other, their similarities and shared likeness, the commonality of their goals and the coincidence of their paths, and even the inevitability that one of them would brilliantly and treacherously betray the other. They will eventually scatter and exchange curses, but deep down they will be grateful for this magnificent, temporary union.

"Believe me," the journalist put his arm around Berner's waist with his strong, elastic hand, "what you did for me, I will never forget. I recently bought another horse, a gorgeous Hanoverian filly! You should come and see!"

"Alright, I'll come to your arena and we can ride."

They parted, followed by the admiring gaze of the guests. Now it was Berner's turn to go to the tables where others were waiting. His first stop would be his long-time good friend, Lev Vershatsky, who he approached without taking his eyes off the golden candles. He was a banker, an extraordinarily rich man, a philanthropist, a lover of sophisticated entertainment, and a master of the largest financial adventures that created opportunity or spoiled it in the financial rivers. These rivers, at his will, changed channels, stopped, swelled, destroyed, and devastated vast economic spaces. He doomed the North, Siberia, and the Central Russian Plains to drought and extinction zones, while diverting his river to the previously dried up landscapes of the Urals, Tyumen, and port cities on the outskirts where he gave rise to flowering and rapid growth. Banks and corporations enriched it immensely, creating Vershatsky's banking empire on the ruins of his competitors.

Vershatsky was richer and luckier than Berner. Their friendship, which lasted for a long time, began when they were both humble Soviet engineers who mastered the systems of computer control in their industry; their current friendship was a complex interweaving of sympathy, mutual support, jealous envy, and rivalry. Berner caused excruciating, unbearable suffering, and had a desire to destroy his friend.

And he will be destroyed in a few days, for Akhmet, Berner's chief of security, is already secretly following Vershatsky. Outside, he was tracking his whereabouts, looking for cracks and holes in his defense, and looking for miscalculations and mistakes of his guards so he could seize a few short minutes and send a sniper's bullet into him.

Berner sat down at the table occupied by Vershatsky and his young wife, his third in a row, like Berner's. The beautiful Natalie was a top model, whose charming face, long legs, and high breasts rustled and flickered across the lacquered pages of fashion magazines and lit up in the amethyst rays of street advertisements.

He sat down at a table with a bouquet of white roses that Berner had sent; it was a sign that he sees them, loves them, and will come to visit them.

"Yasha, today you are just on fire! This mulatto, this Phoenix bird! You have surpassed yourself. Give her to me for two days!" Vershatsky laughed, joyfully meeting his friend. He held out a long, swarthy hand. On his matte, pale face, almond-shaped eyes shimmered with tenderness and joy. His black, glassy hair was parted to the side. Thick, bluish eyebrows grew together over the crooked, bent nose.

"Don't give your bird to him, Yasha. He will return it without feathers and fried," Natalie said lazily, giving a pale hand for a kiss.

"I can't refuse Lyovushka anything! Birds, fish, hippopotami—I will give him anything he wants!" Berner replied, kissing her warm, perfume-scented fingers.

Their interests clashed when it came to the Chechen oil complex. Vershatsky's empire wished to swallow up the Grozny oil refineries. He has succeeded in many ways, where he has invested huge sums of money in officials, ministers, and rebellious Chechens. He prepared a complex political and financial scheme, with the result being that a group of Chechen oil refinery fields and pipes should go to Vershatsky. This scheme included the possibility of war, but the preferred option seemed to be political, with the involvement of Georgia, Azerbaijan, and Turkey. The enormous power of money, intelligence, political support, and computers seemed overwhelming to Berner. He decided to direct the enlightened optics of a sniper rifle into their plexus.

Letting go of Natalie's warm, graceful hand, Berner looked at his friend's white, large forehead and envisioned a small bullet-like hole in that forehead. He painfully wanted the throne with his finger placed in that hole in Vershatsky's forehead.

"But you said you wanted the Phoenix bird!" Berner forbade himself from thinking about the assassination plot, which was a key element of his strategy and, like the invasion of Chechnya by troops, he was solving a task beyond the power of politicians and bankers. He forbade himself from thinking about it, because he knew Vershatsky's superhuman intuition, which he used like a psychic in the fight against competitors. "You said the Phoenix bird!" Berner said distractingly, sentimentally. "Oh how many times you and I, Lyovushka, have been burned down and reborn from the ashes!"

"Yes, there's been plenty of ashes! That first failure when we started that damn auto repair business and got caught by the cops. I will not forget the poor investigator; he took that money with trembling hands and with the USSR tattoo." Vershatsky burst out laughing, and his strong breath bent the flame of a candle.

"And when we were hauling that container of computers from Malaysia! I put diamonds in the chief of customs' pockets. I didn't know if he would allow the load or take me to the prosecutor." Berner deceived Vershatsky's intuition and distracted him, like a bird pretending to be wounded, falling on its wing, distracting the hunter from the nest. "These were, as the Komsomol[4] members say, years of fire!"

"And the explosion that blew our Volvo to shreds! Imagine, Natalie, we were supposed to go together and stay together for a couple of minutes, even while going to the bathroom." Vershatsky took his wife's hand and played with her long, ringed fingers, as if it was a rosary. "I still don't know whether it was the Solntsevo group that fought for my real

---

[4] Komsomol was a political youth organization in the Soviet Union for the communist party.

estate, or the Chechens who climbed into Moscow."

"Whoever it was, not a week later they buried two Solntsevskaya gangbangers, and Kazbek, a Chechen, was never seen again as if he had suddenly turned into a concrete block for the foundation in the Southwest," Berner chuckled.

"You know, Natalie," Vershatsky kissed his wife on her long, white long decorated with the finest string of pearls, "I will never, as long as I live, forget Yasha's actions. In August of 1991, when the red cretins brought armored vehicles into Moscow, Yasha came for me, for my children and took us to Belarus, to a friendly park ranger. He drove the car himself, while armored cars and tanks approached! Yashechka, I will never forget what you've done!"

"How many lessons have we learned, Lyovushka, how many lessons! God must be pleased with us. In '93, when Rutskoy was kicked out of the Kremlin and this Chechen speaker snapped his finger to his Adam's apple, showing how Yeltsin was drinking, remember, you told me: 'Let's go. To hell with this, with real estate. Life is more expensive!' We then, Natalie, flew to London together, sat in the hotel, watched the tanks firing at the red-brown buildings, and drank into a stupor! This, Lyovushka, will never be forgotten! This is forever! Stronger than any bullet!"

As Berner said this, he suddenly felt startled. Vershatsky's sensitive nostrils could catch the subtlest aroma of treachery emanating from these words. He closed his eyes, as if remembering that room in the London hotel, the huge TV screen on which the White House was burning oily soot. On the table was an unfinished bottle of whiskey, a broken glass glistening on the floor. He closed his eyes so that Vershatsky could not see in the depths of his pupils a dull blue point, the rifle barrel aimed right at him. But Vershatsky did not notice the rifle.

"I know, Yasha, that it was not easy for you to decide on the Grozny oil complex. You naturally conceded it to me with a heavy heart. Trust me, I appreciate it. I regard this as the highest manifestation of friendship! My security has reported that you are ending all your actions against me in the government. It would be wild for you and me to have this quarrel! We have accumulated such experience, such power, and we will not waste it on fighting each other. We need not compete, but to distribute influence. Your Siberian affairs, Krasnoyarsk aluminum, and Norilsk nickel are quite enough for you. And I'll take care of the Caucasus. I have excellent positions in Baku and Tbilisi, and friends in Turkey. I can master the Caucasian knot and pull it off with an oil pipe. These red idiots want to return to the Soviet Union, where they rally in the square day and night!" Vershatsky pointed somewhere to a Gothic stained-glass window, behind which, as it seemed to him, the Red Banner demonstrators were raging. "It is we, the bankers, who will restore the Soviet Union, but not with the help of the party and the Politburo, but with the help of financial wealth, oil, and the Internet!"

Vershatsky spoke with inspiration on his favorite topic. The meaning of his philosophy, which Berner shared, was that bankers, united in a close group, should divide zones of influence, smoothing out contradictions, and become the new and only power in Russia. They nominated their own president, a leader of a new type who was young and brilliant, containing a global mindset, and capable of formulating a new doctrine for Russia. He would replace the sick, old man in the presidency, who was unpredictable and dangerous in his crazy whims. This new leader, so it sometimes seemed to Berner, Vershatsky saw himself. He painted for himself an attractive portrait of the future president of Russia.

"Listen," Vershatsky commanded firmly and strongly with his dry, swarthy palm that squeezed Berner's hand, "we must meet in the coming days. I will fly to Geneva for two days, and we will meet and discuss in greater detail. No politicians, no fools, only financiers! We will discuss without ties the problem of the presidential campaign. We must concentrate our resources, choose a leader, propose political solutions, and act immediately. Moreover, you know that Russian troops are moving through the streets of Grozny. This war, whether blitzkrieg or protracted, with either little blood or at the cost of colossal sacrifices, becomes part of the presidential campaign."

"How did you know about that?" Berner was amazed, looking with fear into the pale, handsome face of his friend. "Why did you not tell me?"

"But you didn't say anything either!" Vershatsky smiled thinly, and with a slight movement of his fingers, straightened his black and blue shiny hair at his temples.

Berner was frightened. Did Vershatsky, with his insight, recognize his treachery? He did not believe in the imitation of peace and harmony, and he unraveled the false moves made by Berner's security service, who withdrew part of the money from the "Chechen project" and spread rumors about the loss of interest in the "Chechen issue." Is it possible that with his "third eye," closed on his forehead by fluffy, fused eyebrows, he could read Berner's thoughts? And a shooter with a rifle had already been hired, already following him on his heels, sparkling like rushing mirrors on outdoor limousines. His favorite casinos and restaurants, addresses of his mistresses, schedules of when he returns home have already been detailed. Already on the map of Moscow, the routes of his movements have been marked, and, perhaps, today, on New Year's Eve, a sniper is waiting for him in the blizzard, with the sniper warming up, drinking coffee from a thermos, wiping off his fogged sight.

He experienced a moment of panic, from which the air fluttered around, and the flame of the candles bent over.

"Are you OK?" Vershatsky looked at him attentively, as if reading his thoughts.

"Something came over me. I must be ill," Berner smiled.

"Waiter, champagne!" he snapped his fingers loudly, beckoning the waiter.

Three glasses of champagne, sizzling with sparkling bubbles, appeared in front of him. Berner took the glasses from the tray, feeling the fragile crystal legs, and held it out toward Vershatsky and Natalie.

"Happy New Year, friends!" he toasted, clinking their two transparent glasses over the table.

"Happy New Year!" Vershatsky echoed him.

They drank cold, sweet champagne, and burned their lips in microscopic explosions. Without blinking, they looked into each other's eyes.

Berner left the table. He moved across the hall, filled with anxiety and terrible premonitions. A woman in an evening dress, elbow-length gloves, tangled in a silk scarf, threw a handful of confetti in his face. Smiling, he disgustedly brushed off the multi-colored paper garbage from his shoulders.

A feminine young man, moving his hips in a circular manner like an actor of the risqué Roman Viktyuk Theater, hung a thin thread of golden string on his jacket. And Berner smiled at him, taking off the thread with two fingers, like removing an ugly caterpillar.

He experienced growing irritation, as if an invisible creature had entered through the pores of his skin, the openings of his mouth and ears, and his dilated pupils. It grew, filled his insides, and turned into a mobile, pulsating worm. This huge, annular worm moved in him, pressed from within, determined his gestures and feelings, and he experienced a poisonous, maddening suffering.

He hated a hall filled with merry, insignificant, mediocre people who depended on his wealth and will. He hated the vulgar Christmas tree decorated with pretzels and mermaids. He hated the head waiter, a thieving, deceitful man disguised as a noble English lord. He hated his feast, in which several helpless, mediocre guests were impatiently awaiting his return.

The slippery worm that settled inside him demanded manifestations and actions from him. He suddenly wanted to set fire to this mansion and this hall, sheathed with bog oak, so that the fire would be hot. He wanted the dry walls to crackle, curtains and tablecloths to flare up, ladies' makeup and hairstyles to smoke, and everything to turn into flames, into fire, into heart-rending cries and horror while he, pushing himself off the ground and flying through the fire, looked at the fire from the blue Moscow sky, through the shining night blizzard.

This obsession lasted a moment and ended. In front of him was a TV reporter who recently had a short New Year's interview with him.

"Today your words were the most sincere and heartfelt!" she said.

Her partner with the video camera disappeared, carrying away tapes with recordings, and she, slightly intoxicated and excited, walked across the hall. Berner again, looking at her plump, bare legs, tight thighs, and large breasts protruding from the neckline, felt a greedy attraction to her. Irritation and hatred turned into an irresistible lust, which made him breathless. The ringed, slippery worm swelled within him, filling his groin, stomach, and throat with a tight, outward force.

"Do you want to see the house?" Berner asked her hoarsely, looking around the room, seeing that his wife Marina was enthusiastically talking with the high-society princess. "There is an art gallery here with many excellent avant-garde paintings."

"Show me the house!" the journalist answered flirtatiously. "I love avant-garde!"

They climbed a creaky staircase with an antique handrail to the mezzanine. They stood looking down at the dancers, at men's bald patches, women's hairstyles, squares of tables with burning candles and plates, and the top of the Christmas tree with its golden, six-pointed star.

Berner grabbed a thick, wooden handrail and pressed his thigh against hers. He did not look at her, but stiflingly and blindly desired to.

"Follow me," he said, leading her through the dim passage, penetrating the other half of the house.

An elderly, helpful attendant rose from the chair to meet them.

"Give us the key to the art gallery, Stepanich!" Berner said dully and took from the minister a heavy, horned, Gothic key that matched the stained-glass windows and carved ceiling decorations.

He opened the hall, where he let her into the velvety darkness. He then locked the door, which rang like an old chest.

"So many pictures!" she said drunkenly, peering into the darkness, where canvases were dark on the walls and images of humanoid creatures, animal-like people, abstract forms, strange ornaments, and figures appeared on them vaguely, barely discernible. "How interesting!" she said, not requiring him to turn on the light.

He came up behind her and hugged her tightly. He pressed his face, lips, and eyes to her hot, damp neck, to her bare shoulder.

"What is the meaning of this!? Don't!" She faintly resisted.

He rudely and commandingly led her to the sofa, taking and ripping off her dress along the way. He made her sit, then pushed her down on the leather sofa, pulling off the translucent shells of her dress.

"What are you doing!? I can't!"

He could smell her scent, her warmth, her strength, her pounding heart, her quick, greedy tongue and biting, sharp teeth.

"Stop, I can't!"

Everything happened in a sweet moment. He freed himself from the huge, swollen weight that sat within him, from the hot, lead-like weight that was destroying and burning him. This force, this red-hot magma and weight, he pushed into her. He poured into it his fears, hatred, thoughts of fires and sniper rifles, his disgust for people, the envy and jealousy for his friend, the tank columns in Grozny, his call to the minister of defense, the princess' porcelain teeth, Segal's pink, bald head, and something else, something deep, vile, something hidden that had no name.

Relieved, empty-handed, he got up and walked away from her, losing all the interest he had in her. Absentmindedly, he looked at one of the pictures, where some shaggy giant was carrying a dead, bleeding horse on his shoulders.

"What have you done to me!?" she said weakly, straightening her torn clothes.

He was free and inwardly pure. The vile, ringed worm left him. Perhaps he moved into it, curled up into a pretzel in her bulging, sweaty belly with a black navel.

"Please!" she continued. Mockingly and gallantly, he let her out of the hall, and the key in the lock turned and sounded like an echoing, old chest.

8

The entourage with Dudayev's limousine left the square, and the bodyguards followed them. The militants, as if they were drunk, all celebrated with their victorious round dance, where they fired their machine guns and several grenade launchers, smashing into smithereens the already knocked-out and dead equipment. But the number of dancers became less and less, the shots sounded less and less, and soon the area, like a meadow at night, covered with burning heaps, became depopulated. Only the crows whirled and shrieked. They sat on the wreckage of the vehicles, where they burned themselves against the red-hot armor and took off again with a heart-rending cry. The birds looked like huge, black and red, shaggy shadows on the clouds of smoke.

"We'll get out of here," said Kudryavtsev, looking uncertain around in the darkness at the distant corners of the square, where the oblique glow did not reach. "We won't get far without weapons. So, we must get our weapons!"

He had not yet commanded these three randomly selected fugitives. He was not yet a commander to them. He was just older in age, and wiser.

These three did not see him as an officer, nor did they feel like a fighting squad, but only a pitiful remnant of a defeated, incinerated brigade, from which they were wrested away by an inexplicable attack and from where they did not want to return.

"We need to rummage around the cars and get weapons," he repeated more insistently, seeing how the soldiers in the darkness were afraid of the illuminated space. "Otherwise, they will slaughter you like chickens."

"They will kill us anyway," whined the thin soldier. "There is no way to escape."

"Sure, we'll die, but we'll bring a few of them to hell with us!" the anti-aircraft gunner said unexpectedly and angrily. "If I had a machine gun, I would have already started shooting them."

"Let's go one at a time in intervals of five minutes," Kudryavtsev firmly suggested, deciding to not yet order them around. "First I'll go! Then you follow me!" he pointed to the anti-aircraft gunner. "Then you! Over there to that truck! Then to the column! Do not wander far. Find a machine gun and come back!"

He gave himself the go-ahead, overcoming the lethargy in his knees. He felt the sniper's gaze on him, as if a large, tickling fly had perched on his forehead. He ran out of the entrance, trying to break away from his long shadow, and darted along the glowing asphalt to the black truck.

He poked into the side, listening for a shout, automatic fire, or squealing bullets. The cockpit door was ajar. He peered into it cautiously. The cockpit was empty, and the keys hung in the ignition. He suddenly had a crazy thought: jump into the cab, start the truck, and speed away, without turning on the lights, and rush to break through. But the wheels on the driver's side front and two in the rear were shot through and unusable as the truck leaned over and stood on the rims. It was unsuitable for escape.

He peered out from behind the chassis, choosing a gap among the twisted equipment, where he could dive out and hide. The two BMP's absurdly locked their tails, spreading the guns in different directions. They resembled paired insects.

Kudryavtsev rushed to them and bent down, feeling his weakness and insecurity. He ran, skirting the pointed bow of the BMP. On the run he saw a melted hole in the side—the trail of one of the grenades—and in the open hatch he could see the dead driver in a tank helmet. The vehicle, judging by the number, was from a neighboring company. He did not stop and plunged into the acrid smoke, hiding among the torn tracks and rickety turret.

Very quickly he found a machine gun. The AKS strap was caught on the towing hook of the vehicle. Clutching the machine gun and pulling on the belt, the previous owner had a dead man's grip on the gun. Kudryavtsev had previously quarreled with this rude, quickly drunken officer, who fell into caustic irritability after a glass of vodka when the commanders of neighboring companies came together for a friendly party. Since then, they did not greet each other, and instead turned away from each other during meetings. Now the dead officer, with a hole in his forehead, with eyes bulging from internal pressure, hung on the machine. His white mustache lifted in a wicked grin, as if he had shouted some caustic foul language before dying. A tank burning nearby lit up his bared, wet teeth.

Kudryavtsev grabbed the machine gun but did not release the latch. With both hands, he yanked at the belt, ripping it off the hook. The dead man refused to let go of his weapon and fell on his side, hitting his face into the tank track. Kudryavtsev tried to pull the machine gun out of his clenched fist, but the dead, white fingers did not unclench. Kudryavtsev unwrapped each finger, one by one, which gripped like nails. He finally tore off the broken, dirty nails from the machine. This fight with the dead seemed to be a continuation of their quarrel. With a fierce jerk, Kudryavtsev ripped out the machine gun, the dead officer fell, and his parted mouth continued to swear silently, his hand with twisted fingers outstretched and looking at Kudryavtsev.

Kudryavtsev looked at the weapon greedily. The gun was in burst mode. Moving the barrel and stroking the foregrip, feeling the trigger with his finger, he peered into the openings between the smoldering machines and was ready if danger arose to strike with hammering fire.

He felt effective once again and, along with the weapon, made his movements flexible as he rolled over in a solid wave. His eyes continued to look vigilantly for any danger lurking behind corners and protrusions of the wrecked vehicles, as his hands guided a blued slot and a front sight in the direction of the potential danger.

He stumbled upon a tank surrounded by lumps of formless substances smoldering on the ground. The turret was blown off by an explosion, with a round hole, like in an iron cauldron. It continued to smoke and swell with red smoke that illuminated from the inside as it poured out, and in the belly of the tank something gurgled weakly, squelched like a thick brew. It was a scary sight inside the black hole, into the torn-up belly of the tank, where digestion continued within its cut intestines.

The drafts of cold and hot air generated wind which blew between the wreckage. Kudryavtsev felt the wind brush up against his cheeks, as if invisible creatures devoid of flesh were striking him. These creatures rushed about, hovering over the open hatches, unable to leave the steering wheels nor their positions near the bores of the guns and their sights. Kudryavtsev moved among the disembodied, invisible creatures and made his way through their silent host.

The four-barreled, rapid-fire Shilka, untouched by the fire, lowered its tubular barrels horizontally and did not have time to shoot. Its hatch was open like a cracked suitcase, with rags smoldering, and among the wandering coals, with their backs to the armor, sat the gunners. They pressed their shoulders to each other and pressed their heads together, as if they were napping. A yellow guitar with stickers was lying around the tracks. Both were shot in the chest at close range. Kudryavtsev, not coming up, pressed himself against the warm side of the burned-out car and peered at their faces, at their tangled hair, and at their yellow guitar. They resembled tired pranksters, tourists who had been drinking glass after glass of vodka. Somewhere in the grass there were crusts of baked potatoes and an empty bottle gleaming. Kudryavtsev walked away from the fire and made his way through the forest edge, where it was light and misty from the blooming cherry tree, while a nightingale sang in a ravine above the black water.

This vision was combined with the look of the shot gunners, which mortified Kudryavtsev and made him feel like he was approaching madness.

A shot rang out from behind, inside the BMP. Kudryavtsev instantly dropped and pointed his machine gun at the sound, ready to fire. Slowly he straightened up and removed his tense finger from the trigger. It was the surviving cartridge of the detonated ammunition that slammed inside the car; the bullet sluggishly rebounded from the cartridge case and fell to the bottom among the burning ash.

In the open troop compartment, he found two more machine guns. In the darkness, where he directed the flashlight beam, there was a mattress lying on the bottom, alongside an ammo box, and on it were the remnants of dinner: crumbs of bread, opened cans, and bitten apples. The soldiers in a panic threw down their food and weapons and fled. They must have been killed and were lying somewhere nearby under wheels and fallen tracks.

Kudryavtsev threw the two guns over his shoulder and pulled up a third, listening to the incessant cry of the crows. He was covered and protected from the sides by the ribbed armor of machines, but it was opened by the crows, which were watching him. The armor was a hindrance to them and prevented them from descending to the ground and seizing their prey.

He peered up. Gloomy clouds with holes and gaps moved through the flashing net of birds. Invisible, a space reconnaissance satellite hung over the square, and a wet sheet of developed photographic paper lay on the table of the chief of the general staff. Through his glasses, the elderly general looked at the images of the city at night, the fiery cross of a burning column, and among the cubes of wrecked cars, elongated like maggots, and among the dead soldiers there was one small, obscure point. It was he, Kudryavtsev, alive, with a submachine gun, pressed against the stern of the BMP.

He saw a bird perched on the edge of the hatch. The crow clung to the steel edge with strong claws, turned its powerful open beak to Kudryavtsev, and angrily and fiercely looked with its blue eyes in red rims. It was illuminated, the compressed wings and glazed feathers gleaming with fiery brass. And the bird's whole strong, focused body expressed greed and fear.

Apparently, the dead were lying close on the other side of the wrecked tank, invisible to Kudryavtsev. The bird aimed at them, but was afraid of the uncooled iron, smoldering coals, and Kudryavtsev, preventing it from taking possession of the prey.

Kudryavtsev felt hate toward the bird and disgust for its bony beak, whose body fed on the fallen, while its tail feathers were stained from its white droppings. He shooed the bird, wanting to drive it away. The crow swung on the lid, but did not take off, and instead, opened its beak, showing a narrow red tongue while it hissed hoarsely. This crow was stronger than him, for it was the birds that ruled the square. He was the one that left his brigade, threw his people to extermination, and now they, shot and burned, were lying dead on the ground. Kudryavtsev did not belong here, but the birds did, for they were voracious and cruel and took possession of the slaughter. The birds owned the battlefield, which Kudryavtsev left, and they both knew it.

He wanted to throw up a machine gun and shoot the nearby muscular bird, tearing it to shreds, turning it into a heap of bloody feathers. Bending his head, he walked aside, and it seemed to him that the bird, opening its beak, smiled after him, its blue eyes in red rings laughing.

He saw a BMP, and on the charred turret, he could see the half-erased and shot number of his company. The car oozed smoke, poisonous chemical streams. Having retained its contours and structure, it seemed like a skeleton, on which skin and flesh burned. The smell it gave off was the smell of burning gasoline and meat. He approached the stern and touched the door handle, but it burned. He grabbed the handle with his peacoat, turned it and opened it. From there, like a hot oven, greasy hot air hit him. Among the seats, charred wires and oxidized machine-gun belts, he saw a peeling skeleton, with cinders and blotches of meat, stretching out a bony hand to the door. On the wrist was a thick, gold bracelet that had lost its rich color in the fire. It was the same bracelet that was on the contract soldier depicting Santa Claus. There was another skeleton lying on the bottom, who he identified as the contract soldier who sang obscene songs with a whistle during the day.

Kudryavtsev, horrified, stepped back, plugging his nostrils and suddenly experienced a strange feeling, like a guilty joy: it was not he who was lying baked in the car, not his ugly body, with bones showing, with his hand sticking out of the troop compartment.

Backing away, ashamed of his sinful thought, he stepped back from the hatch, and a gust of hot air flew out of the vehicle, hitting him in the face.

He moved among the destroyed vehicles of his company, those that had time to twitch, break out of the column, and turn their machine guns and cannons toward the enemy; and those that remained in place and kept intervals, forming a row of baked boxes, reminiscent of the burnt bodies he saw, like they were left on a baking sheet in an oven.

It was his company, shot and burned, torn apart by exploding ammunition and cut by the plasma beams of cumulative grenades. These were his soldiers and warrant officers, who he knew by name, taught to shoot, shouted at in anger, rewarded for their successes, ran with during drills, took to the bathhouse, entered the barracks with at night, heard breathing in a dream, wrote to their relatives for in the towns and villages, and spent time with on the parade ground, goose stepping and hitting the ground with the soles of their feet as they marched and aligned with the brigade's battle banner.

Now the company surrounded him with burnt iron and heaps of mutilated bodies. Empty gun barrels gazed blindly everywhere; open hatches shouted silently. In the sky, irritated by his appearance, the crows cried.

All his soldiers and commanders were dead. But he was alive and for some reason arrived here, to the place where his company was killed. Someone ruthless and cruel wanted him to return to this point, to show him the oxidized barrels of their machine guns, the smoldering blanket of debris on the asphalt, and the place where a driver fell from his hatch. Someone wanted to place him here, among the destroyed company, and silently ask, "What are you going to do now? How are you going to survive?"

He could immediately put the barrel of a machine gun to his throat, pull the trigger, and the last thing his eyes would see was a gracefully smoking blanket of rubble crumpled on the asphalt. Or he could find a surviving tank among the broken equipment, start the engine, and, taxiing among the wrecked cars, break through to the Presidential Palace and fire the cannon at its lighted windows. Or perhaps something else, something unclear, that had not arrived yet to his clouded mind.

He suddenly saw the chief of intelligence. He was laying dimly lit by a dying truck. His arm was torn off. His head was thrown back with his golden hussar mustache, and his open mouth and eyes open to the sky expressed incomprehension, as if something indescribable and terrible happened to him from the sky and he died not from a grenade burst, not from a painful shock, but from the spectacle of a truly terrible world event that not a single person could endure.

Kudryavtsev looked at the chief of intelligence from afar without approaching, recalling his good-natured jokes, the dashing gesture with which he twisted his mustache, and the wedding ring on his hand, which was now torn off. He remembered his greedy, glowing eyes when a woman appeared next to him, and the sentimental, dreamy look he had when, after drinking vodka, he sang to the music of a guitar with his soothing tenor.

Kudryavtsev heard voices. They were heard from several directions at once, and they were accompanied by the creak and clang of iron. Hatches opened and then slammed; heavy armored doors creaked. Two Chechens came out to the illuminated space where the dead chief of intelligence was lying. Kudryavtsev could distinguish their leather jackets, similar hats, and beardless, swarthy faces with large noses. They were armed with captured weapons. Like Kudryavtsev, they placed two or three machine guns behind their backs. They searched the wrecked vehicles with their eyes.

They saw the dead officer and approached. One of them unbuttoned the jacket on the dead man and examined the belt, apparently in search of a pistol. The other carefully, so as not to get stained with blood, rummaged through his chest pockets and pulled out a lighter and a fountain pen and put them in his pocket. He said something irritably in Chechen. His comrade grunted, unbuttoned his fly, and, coming close to the dead man, began to urinate on his face, on his open eyes and golden mustache.

Kudryavtsev saw how the splashes fell on the face of the chief of intelligence. He raised his hand gripping the machine gun. But other

Chechens appeared from behind the wreck of the truck. Kudryavtsev, extinguishing his impulse, ever so carefully so as not to clink metal, retreated into the shadows. He hid in the twilight gaps of the column.

He walked away from the illuminated places where marauders continued to roam. So, he kept to the darkness, making his way back to the edge of the square. He was worried that his fellow surviving soldiers he sent for weapons would run into the armed Chechens.

Though he could not see them, he felt that he was being watched, but couldn't determine from where. He shrank and pressed himself against the radiator of the fuel truck and expected a flash of bullets to strike it. There was no flash, but the feeling that he was in plain sight, that he was being watched, made him slowly scan with his eyes to look for the direction from which the alarm was emanating.

This alarm, like a barely perceptible vibration of the air, came from under the tank, from the dark opening between the tracks. Kudryavtsev did not see the one who was hiding under the tank bottom, but it could not be a Chechen. It could only be someone from his company, alive, someone that survived the massacre, who huddled, as if in a hole, under the tank.

"Hey!" called Kudryavtsev. "Come on out!" He did not receive an answer, but he knew he was heard. "Come on out! Friendly! Don't fucking sit there!"

From under the tank on all fours, looking like a big dog, a soldier climbed out, followed by another, laying on their bellies. The first was already on his feet, fearfully approaching, and the second continued to crawl, elbowing along the ground.

"Where are you from? Who are you?" Kudryavtsev tried to give a confident voice with an encouraging tone.

"Tank battalion. Tank gunner," said the one who got up to his feet. He looked around fearfully, like a big, frightened, beaten dog.

They were two soldiers, both unarmed. One was in torn overalls, with a large scratch across his circular, awkward face. The other, in a vest, was frozen with sunken cheeks and a small, pathetic nose, which trembled and twitched, as if he had been concussed.

"Are you frozen or what?" asked Kudryavtsev, but the soldier did not answer and continued to tremble.

"As the attack started, everyone ran away... The engine of the tank stalled... I got out, and everything was on fire... I crawled under the tank, and then he followed me... The Chechens came and brought prisoners here... Then executed all of them..." He nodded toward something on the asphalt where it was horribly dark, "And then this pussy nearly froze to death..."

The second soldier was hunched over, his skinny arms wrapped around his hips, and it seemed that he was about to vomit and twist. Kudryavtsev took the machine guns off his shoulders, took off his jacket, and threw it over the soldier, over his trembling shoulders covered with a vest.

"Follow me!" ordered Kudryavtsev, and they obediently trotted over. He could hear the coughing and gagging of the one who was freezing.

They reached the last of the vehicles that were driving away from the square but stopped by grenade launchers. Lonely, at a distance, the truck was dark.

"Run over there!" Kudryavtsev said while pointing at the truck. "If anything happens, I'll cover you!"

He saw the soldiers running out of tune, crossing the empty, illuminated space. He felt a nagging, pitying feeling toward them. He was ready to shield them, to take upon himself the danger that threatened them.

He met them by the truck and, gently urging them on, drove them to the house, where the three others were already waiting for him in the dark entrance. High-strung and impatient, they were delighted to see him. They had weapons: three submachine guns and one light machine gun with a heavy hanging belt.

They were no longer helpless fugitives; they were not unarmed loners. They were well-armed soldiers, and he was their commander.

All five lined up on the landing, facing the window, behind which the square was pink and foggy. Kudryavtsev saw their serious faces staring at him, the barrels of their machine guns and belts thrown over their shoulders. He did not know what he would say to them yet, but this burgeoning word and ripening decision took possession of him.

"Let's break the ice," he said, addressing the soldiers. By addressing them calmly, he let them know that the terrible massacre was behind them and they were once again an armed fighting squad. "I am the commander of the first company, Captain Kudryavtsev. Introduce yourselves. Title, surname, position... You! " He pointed to one of the soldiers, who he already talked to, standing to his right flank, greedily grabbing the belt of a machine gun with his fist.

"Private Chizhov! Truck driver of an anti-aircraft missile battery!"

"So, Chizh,"[5] Kudryavtsev clarified. With this clarification, their relationship was simplified. A sudden, subtle warmth and irony swept over and rallied them. "You!" he pointed to the next, short, well-behaved, robust man, the one who held a light machine gun.

Throwing the machine gun over his shoulder and placing it at his feet as a show of property, he answered, "Sergeant Tarakanov, motorized rifleman!"

"So, Tarakan!"[6] Kudryavtsev spoke and gave him his nickname. He also clarified so that the soldier would not be offended, "The smartest, fastest, and best hunter!"

Some of the soldiers chuckled, not in a mocking way, but in a friendly way, and Kudryavtsev realized that his game was accepted; their reconciliation and cohesion were already taking place.

"And who are you?" he asked to the thin, harsh man, who was the third to run toward the house. Now he almost lost his harshness as he stretched out, sharpened his look, and formed up and strengthened his body.

"Senior Sergeant Nozdratenkov, sniper of the platoon!"

"Nozdra,"[7] said Kudryavtsev. He saw that everyone liked the nickname. Those who were already named accepted him into their company. And those who remained nameless were patiently waiting their turn.

"And you?" Kudryavtsev peered at the one who recently crawled out like a dog from under the stalled tank. Now he was a strong, tall, country-looking guy. He calmed down after he received a machine gun and found himself in the ranks of armed people.

"Private Krutykh, tank gunner."

"Krutoi!" without thinking twice, Kudryavtsev determined his nickname. Everyone smiled as their lips moved, repeating, and trying on the strong word, "Cool."

"Last but not least, you!" Kudryavtsev turned to the one who was standing in his warm jacket, not yet warmed up, hunched over, keeping the first drops of heat that appeared in him.

"Filimonov, motorized rifleman, private..." the soldier responded and coughed. He began to shake again.

"So, Filya!" said Kudryavtsev with barely noticeable affection, as they say with sick children, defenseless in their ailment and loneliness.

---

[5] In Russian, this is a small, singing bird.
[6] Tarakan is the Russian word for cockroach.
[7] Nostril.

Now they were all familiar, named. Their new names were supposed to separate them from recent humiliations and fears, from wiped-out cars. They combined them in a new unity, made them a new fighting compartment.

"I'll tell you what!" The decision, which slowly matured in his mind, since his empty, unarmed hands gripped the foregrip of the machine gun, since his eyes burned by the sight of the exterminated brigade and his mind, having survived fear and shame, returned to him with a feeling of unbroken will, this decision was put into words, at which point he turned to the soldiers. "We've managed to escape from this hell," he nodded to the window, on which fluttering reddish spots were fluttering. "We got our weapons back. We are several healthy, young men. We can try to leave, sneak through the gardens, and get to the outskirts. If we are intercepted on the way, we will fight, but we will break through. Someone will break through! But we also have other options," he paused, checking to see if everything was deposited in his head on top of hot ash and recent fear.

"We can take up defensive positions. Use the house as a reference point. When we entered the city, we were assigned a combat mission: to occupy the station square, to control the station and access roads before the Marines approach. Nobody canceled that order. We are what is left of our brigade; therefore, we are the brigade. We reached the target line with heavy losses and took up defensive positions. Most of the brigade was killed, but the Russian army was not defeated; there are other troops, divisions, corps, front-lines, and bombers. There are fresh units that are already on the way and are preparing to attack. I'm sure it will start in the morning. Our task is to support them, to keep this house, our stronghold, while waiting for reinforcements to arrive... I don't want to order you. I want the decision we make to be your conscious, voluntary decision. Only then will I be your commander."

They were silent, looking over his shoulders and head out of the window, fogged by their breathing. Behind the glass, like a kerosene lamp, a red fire fluttered elegantly, but none of them were elegant. The towns and villages from which they came were inhabited by a tired people mired in needs and worries, and they themselves had just escaped death. They wanted, like they could in childhood, to close their eyes and miraculously fly from this cruel city to their native villages, where their brothers and sisters and relatives, exhausted by expectations, were waiting. This dirty window, in which the red wick sullenly smoldered, the heart-rending bird cries over the bodies of their dead comrades, this tall captain with a large forehead calling on them to fight—they wanted the nightmare to end.

They were silent, breathing loudly, until something hissing in Filya's cold lungs could be heard.

"Comrade Captain!" said Tarakan, slightly sticking out his leg, touching it with the butt of the machine gun standing on the floor. "That truck that we were moving to, it contains ammunition. It has ammo, grenades, and Bumblebee flamethrowers. We should go there now, while it's dark, to stock up on ammo."

"Oh, we will," Kudryavtsev said with relief, taking command. In a commanding voice that did not tolerate objections, he ordered, "All four, except Filya! Go to the truck, forward! I'll cover you!"

He went down to the first floor and set up a machine gun at the doorstep, surveying his firing cone along the axis of the darkened truck. He then briefly said, "Go!"

The four of them bent down, swinging their elbows strongly, and rushed to the truck. He watched the burning debris, the surrounding houses, and the openings of the streets, ready to fire.

It was quiet, deserted. All four soon returned, heavily laden with ammunition, a crate of grenades, and two grenade launchers with charges that looked like sharp turnips straight from a patch.

"Maybe one more time, Comrade Captain!" Tarakan said in a gamble, putting the cartridges on the steps.

"Enough! We will hold out until our approach!" answered Kudryavtsev, dragging a machine gun into the entrance.

"Now we should inspect the house and build a defense."

9

The three-story building made of bricks was their asylum. It had a sloping iron roof, an attic, and two porches.

Kudryavtsev thought that they could create defensive positions if they open the attic doors and barricade the entrances and the stairs that connected through the attic. The firing positions would be the windows overlooking the square, as well as the attic windows overlooking the station. One end, facing the neighboring gardens and small streets, was without windows, and this made repelling attacks easier. The enemy could not penetrate the blank wall and throw grenades at them.

There were six of them. According to Kudryavtsev's plan, two of them could hide at the staircase windows and repel attacks from the square. Two others could hide under the roof and hold the station at gunpoint. Kudryavtsev himself and the last soldier would be a part of the reserve group. They would move under the roof between the stair risers, providing support in a circular defense.

They went up to the attic. Kudryavtsev shined a lantern at the lock, which was dangling on hinges, while Krutoi, puffing and sticking out his tongue, tried to break the lock with a bayonet-knife. He was bending the hinges, rattling, and then, angrily, shoved the door with his strong shoulder, dropping wood chips and screws.

The attic was low, filled with garbage and junk, with scraps of pipes and coils of wire. Kudryavtsev saw the edge of a stucco station, a sticky platform, and a piece of steel track with purple lights that looked like the eyes of astonished animals through the cracks in the opening.

"Tarakan! Nozdra!" he called to the soldiers, searching for them with a flashlight among the beams and asbestos pipes. "Here is your position.

Your sector," he poked Tarakan in the shoulder, "is from the edge of the square to the corner of the station… You," he turned to Nozdra, "look to the right, along the track to these damn gardens. It's a dangerous zone. They can sneak up and throw grenades. So hit anything that moves if you want to live!"

The soldiers silently pressed their eyes to the wooden bulkheads of the openings, and in the white ray of a lantern, steam flew and curled from Tarakan's mouth.

Krutoi knocked down the second door with a slight groan. He rolled down the dark stairs, cursing and swearing. When he got up, he was illuminated by flashlights.

Tarakan quipped, "You're not a man; you're a battering ram. Not a damn thing will be left standing in this house!"

This was the first joke that Kudryavtsev heard after experiencing this nightmare. That means the nightmare was ending. The rest of the soldiers felt this as well and Krutoi, who was the target of the joke, did not get angry, but instead chuckled.

"Now let's figure out how to block the entrances," Kudryavtsev said as he listened to the sounds in the building, still hoping to catch signs of life, perhaps the striking of a wall clock or the meowing of a cat. But it was quiet. Only the screams of crows and rare bursts of gunfire were heard from the outside.

The solders firmly jammed the doors of one of the entrances with a huge piece of pipe. Tarakan, being agile and sharp-sighted in the darkness, made a booby trap at the entrance. He fastened two grenades with a wire to a strumming and ringing sound. He was saying, "Welcome home, stinky assholes!"

The doors of the second entrance had no handles, so there was nowhere to put a pipe. The solders decided to block the entrance by barricading it with furniture.

Kudryavtsev illuminated the space with a flashlight, placing a small circle of light on the floor, so that the beam would not slide over the window. They found an unlocked apartment with a half-open door. One by one, they entered cautiously feeling shy to the sight of someone else's abandoned housing.

It was a single-room apartment. Its tidy, dilapidated decorations suggested that its inhabitants were lonely old people, a humble, complimentary couple. The room was cooled down with cold radiators. It smelled like smoldering fabrics and medicines, and the smell of old age emanated from the clumsy furniture, greasy wallpaper, many rugs, and napkins, white with lace and embroidery.

Walking deeper into the room, dragging a gun through the curtains, Kudryavtsev examined furniture suitable for a barricade from the doorway: a heavy two-tiered sideboard with carved columns, filled with plates and vases; a dresser with a mirror with some boxes on top; a wide bed, covered by a thin blanket and pillows. It was suitable for living, and everything could be used in the narrow entrance to block the passage.

The soldiers were closely huddling in the room, looking around at someone else's housing, where they were brought by the commander without permission and without knocking.

Chizh came to the sideboard, stroked the carved patterns, and leaned against the glass, examining the dishes. "We have a similar sideboard at home," he said. "A grouse is carved in the top. Grandma calls him Hunter."

Nozdra leaned his machine gun against the wall, bowed somewhere in the corner, and Kudryavtsev saw that he was making the Sign of the Cross. In the darkness, where the gun was directed, barely distinguishable, hung an icon. The soldiers fell silent for a moment and stopped stomping around.

"Well, let's take the dresser?" Kudryavtsev opened the cabinet doors, and a mirror flashed dimly in the darkness. "All the clothes need to go! Tarakan! Krutoi! Pull them down carefully!" He then went to the bed and jabbed his finger at the pillows that adorned the old man's bed. "Take this too! Chizh! Nozdra! Let's go!"

He saw how the soldiers shook out the heaps of shabby clothes from the dresser and rolled the mattress and blankets off the bed. He walked into the corridor, illuminating it with a flashlight.

The apartment was cold, and the heat was not working. The electricity was cut off, and the tap water was not running. But the bathtub was filled almost to the brim with water. This made Kudryavtsev happy—there were plenty of cartridges for the machine guns and a reliable supply of water for the soldiers.

He opened the small refrigerator in the kitchen. A flashlight illuminated a bowl full of jellied meat. A bottle of vodka stood among the medicinal vials. It was a supper, carefully prepared for the New Year, and it remained untouched. Now this dinner will go to Kudryavtsev and his soldiers. If this food was not enough and the next day the Marines do not make their way to the train station, he was sure that in other apartments, in other refrigerators, in filled bathtubs, a supply of food and water was left for them.

The dresser, which had been moved from its place, was already creaking and hit the floor. Krutoi sighed and scolded Tarakan. The dresser could not easily pass through the doorway, where it clung to, making noise piteously.

"Be careful!" Krutoi was angry. "Don't break the mirror!"

"Who's planning on using it? There are no women here!" Tarakan snapped. "Push it harder!"

"It's the old lady's property," insisted Krutoi, pulling on the dresser. "All of her life is contained within."

"We'll write it off due to the war," Tarakan puffed, pushing the dresser.

"Hey you, be careful!" Nozdra intervened, picking up the corner.

"It's bad luck to break a mirror." Tarakan stopped pushing, and the three of them, carefully, groaning and taking a breath, lowered the clumsy dresser to the ground floor and blocked the entrance.

The bed was brought out next and placed on the floor. The bulky furniture was fastened to the doors with wire, and Tarakan set up a trap with grenades, saying, "Welcome home, bitches..."

"Tarakan! Krutoi!" Kudryavtsev, pleased with the barricade, pushed the soldiers away from the dangerous string, invisible in the dark and connecting the grenade rings. "Your positions are on the second floor, first and second entrances! We will divide the ammunition into two and store it on the upper platforms."

With the help of the old furniture, iron pipes, and wires, the house was turned into a stronghold with four defendable positions, in which the soldiers were located on different floors, in different sectors. Cases with cartridges and boxes with grenades were divided in two and placed in the dead corners of the platforms so that in case of shelling they would not be hit by a bullet.

"Now let's have a bite!" Kudryavtsev said cheerfully, feeling relieved. A barrier formed between them in the house and the square, which continued to smolder and ring with shots.

"Thank God for this house," he repeated silently, running his hand over the rough, plaster walls.

They returned to the apartment, put their submachine guns at the threshold, and sat tightly around the table. They then abruptly took out plates, forks, and knives from the kitchen. They brought bowls of salad with vinaigrette and the jellied meat from the refrigerator. Kudryavtsev looked around at their close, hungry faces, all in scratches, with streaks of soot from the attic. Each bore the traces of suffering and danger.

He said to Krutoi, "Bring the bottle..."

He brought it from the refrigerator and put the vodka on the table, along with cups from the cupboard. Kudryavtsev uncorked the bottle and slowly poured the smooth, chilled vodka into the glasses. The soldiers watched him silently and seriously. The vodka gleamed faintly, and in this gleam, there were red sparks flying in from behind the window.

"Well, guys," Kudryavtsev said as he raised his glass. "Firstly, let's drink to being alive, that no bullet has found us. Secondly, to our dead comrades who will not be going crazy with us. Thirdly, so that we continue to live as we await our comrades who will come to our rescue. But in general, Happy New Year!"

He held out his glass over the table. The soldiers took turns, clinking glasses with the commander. Nozdra made the Sign of the Cross before drinking. Then everyone drank, pressing their glasses to their weathered, bitten, and burnt lips, while the square outside the window smoldered like a crumpled blanket.

"Well, we ate everything the old man cooked for themselves," said Krutoi, eating up with guilt the remnants of the jellied meat from his plate. "Probably, they wanted to pamper themselves, but we ate everything."

"Yes, but they would have probably offered this to us," Nozdra reassured him. "These were Russian people. I can see the icon hanging on the wall. They would have invited us."

"My mother always prepared the same jellied meat at our house," Chizh said thoughtfully, "although she put horseradish on the table. It tastes better with horseradish."

"Better jellied meat without horseradish than horseradish without jellied meat," Tarakan reasoned.

"Will there be ice cream, Comrade Captain?"

"Look at Filya, he's basically like ice cream!" said Kudryavtsev.

Filya returned Kudryavtsev's jacket to him and then put on some of the old people's clothes, including a spacious, long-brimmed coat, designed for men or women. He sat ruffled after drinking a glass of vodka, looking like a lapwing bird. Everyone looked at Filya and chuckled, though they were not laughing at him, but simply responding to the joke of their commander.

Kudryavtsev caught this subtle delicacy. He felt an instant, dizzy tenderness toward them. A translucent creature flew over the nearby square, strewn with burning tanks, and entered the house through a fogged window. It rose above them in a motherly love and sorrow where it covered them with its weightless cover. It lasted a moment and ended.

"Get in position!" he said, getting up. "To your stations! Don't sleep, keep each other accountable! Filya and I are in the reserve group!"

They got up, taking their weapons. They took chairs with them in order to have some comfort at their firing points, then dispersed through the attic and stairwells and took their positions.

Filya, wrapped in an old lady's sweater, took a nap on the sofa, preserving his newfound warmth and the feeling of satiation. Kudryavtsev stared at a reflection of light flickering on the sideboard and thought to himself.

Inevitably, the news of the brigade's defeat would spread throughout the high command. The minister of defense, who is celebrating his birthday, has probably already left his feast and returned to his office, receiving reports from staff officers and commanders of districts and armies. Reserve units are likely already moving toward the city, the fuel tanks of the aircraft being refueled, and rockets and bombs attached to them like pendants. In the morning they will strike at the city, followed by more troops. They'll not enter how the previous brigade entered, which was in a solid defenseless column, substituting their flanks and turrets for grenade launchers. They'll instead arrive in small groups of infantry, supported by helicopters and tanks, breaking the enemy's defenses. Slowly, house after house, ruins after ruins, punching bricks like a chisel, the troops will get to the square and to the three-story building where Kudryavtsev has settled with his makeshift team. They will attack on two fronts: one consisting of regiments, artillery, and tanks; and the other will be Kudryavtsev's tiny fire team.

He was sure that this would be the case. They would not be found until the new troops arrive. They will enter the battle at the very last moment where they will strike into the rear of the retreating Chechen detachments. And with this confidence he got up and went to check on the positions, to cheer up and check on the soldiers.

Chizh settled in a chair by the window between the first and second floors. His submachine gun lay on the windowsill, barrel to the glass. In the corner, shielded by a wall, stood a grenade launcher with a sharp grenade. Another cupboard was empty, and Kudryavtsev mentally pushed Chizh into it in case a machine gun started to fire into him from outside or a hissing grenade flew in. Multi-layer brick will protect the soldier from shots if he properly braces himself.

Chizh was sitting by the windowsill over a piece of paper. In the dark, in the faint reflections of light that peered in from the square, he wrote with a pencil. Kudryavtsev bent down, trying to decipher what was on it.

"I can't understand without night vision goggles. You will ruin your eyes like this."

"My eyes are like a cat's; they widen in the dark."

"Are you writing?"

"No, I'm drawing."

Kudryavtsev made out faint outlines and strokes on the sheet, but the meaning of the drawing was unclear.

"What are you drawing?"

"I just draw what I see, the square and damaged tanks, all that remains of our previous life."

"What for?"

"I draw all the time. If I find a minute, I draw."

"What are you, an artist?"

"I went to school for it but dropped out. They said my drawing skills are rather weak, and that I should hone it. So, when I have the time, I practice."

"Can you do portraits?"

"I draw the soldiers who are about to be discharged with them in their uniform and with weapons. They always seem to like it."

He continued to draw on a piece of paper obtained from the old man's apartment. Kudryavtsev was amazed: an hour ago Chizh was spared death. He was looking for him, surrounded by the clatter of bullets, explosions of flying grenades, a fiery slurry, filled with the bodies of his comrades. But his soul survived the fire and did not die, but only got scared. And now, when the fear had passed and there was a moment of rest, he began drawing, surrendering to his passion.

"What else do you draw?"

"Everything! Trees, people, houses. The day before yesterday the warrant officer put out his boots to dry, and I drew them too. It is a pity that my portfolio is burning in the wreckage."

Kudryavtsev again doubted whether he was making the right decision in taking up defensive positions in the house. Five surviving soldiers recognized him as a commander; they believed that he would save them, lead them out of the terrible city, and help them get back to their families. He supplied them with weapons, put them into firing positions, and again threw them into battle. Is he right in remaining to guard the mountains of charred bones?

He watched Chizh draw, pressing a piece of paper to the windowsill, covering it with an invisible and perhaps nonexistent drawing.

Outside in the square, on the white snow, from the surrounding streets, dogs ran out into the fire to the smell of fried flesh. One by one, in small flocks, they galloped and disappeared in the cluster of vehicles. People slipped through to the wreckage, one or two at a time, with carts, sacks, and bags. They were not militants, not the armed victors, but timid and cowardly marauders who decided to pick the bones of the dead. As in big cities with homeless people rummaging through dumpsters at night, plunging their hands into warm and smoldering garbage, so too, these marauders reached for the warm, uncooled dump of war, hoping to feed on it.

Among the wrecked cars, fights and brawls arose. Dogs and birds quarreled; rumbling people fought over the possessions of corpses. They snatched jackets, boots, watches, and wallets from each other. The dead, with bare, bony legs, and blue wrists, undressed, lay in the snow. The marauders pushed their carts in a bustle, hunched over the stuffed bales, and hurried to leave the square, to drag the prey to their dens.

Kudryavtsev adjusted the grenade launcher standing in the corner and quietly moved away from Chizh. He was examining the square with his cat-like night vision, drawing padded tanks, dogs, crows, and marauders.

Kudryavtsev went into the attic, and in the cold darkness, among the rafters and iron risers, he did not see, but felt a barely discernible field; a soldier was hiding at the dormer. Tarakan nestled comfortably on a wooden beam. The faint light of the square illuminated his face. Another window was cut into the opposite roof slope, and in case of danger, Tarakan could change position and fire in two directions.

"What's the situation?" Kudryavtsev asked, settling on the rafter, slightly pressing the soldier. "How does everyone feel?" Tarakan moved to make room for the commander. It seemed to Kudryavtsev that Tarakan was pleased with his appearance. The light mockery contained in the question was conducive to conversation.

"I think the tenants in the house are Russians," replied Tarakan. "They were likely evicted so that they couldn't signal to us that we were falling into a trap. If the tenants had stayed, they would have given a sign, even with a light in the window, or with a cry."

"Seems so," Kudryavtsev listened to the silence, in which not a single rustle was caught, as if all the inhabitants, including mice, spiders, and cockroaches had left the house in anticipation of an earthquake. The first shockwave destroyed the brigade. The second was gaining in strength, accumulating in the earth under the square, preparing to erupt at the lonely house with darkened windows.

"I will never surrender to them." Tarakan guessed Kudryavtsev's thoughts. "When the attack began, some of the soldiers retreated, but I got up in the hatch and fired back at the bastards!"

Tarakan fidgeted angrily, reaching for his gun, touching the weapon, and the soldier's sharp shoulder pressed hard on Kudryavtsev.

There was a rumble in the square. They both ducked down and pressed themselves against the floor, their hands in the darkness ready to pull their triggers. Illuminated with flickering lights, black smoky trucks rolled out onto the square, one after another. There were people in the back, with cars dragged through the snow to the shapeless remnants of the brigade. They stopped, resting their lights on the piles of debris. People started jumping out of the cabins and bodies, shouting something, pulling something off the trucks. They gathered and, as a crowd, went into the dark heaps of armored cars and tanks, scaring away the screaming crows.

The trucks turned off their headlights, and in one of the cabins the red dot of a cigarette butt flickered and went out.

"Tractors?" asked Tarakan. "They're trying to pull out the surviving BMP's!"

Kudryavtsev did not answer. The square looked like a circular circus arena. Until recently, it looked snow-white and clean, with a delightful shimmering Christmas tree, filled with the beautiful sounds of a grand piano. Now it was black, drenched in blood and smoke, filled with ugly carcasses and red fires. They who had retreated from the stage for a while had to return to it, to participate in the performance.

"Not all Chechens are scum," said Tarakan when the alarm caused by the trucks subsided and the minutes of waiting dragged on. "There are normal people among them."

"What makes you think that?"

"I studied with a Chechen at school; his name was Shamil. Normal guy. He collected butterflies, like me. Then he left. Maybe he shot at me today; who knows?"

"You collect butterflies?"

"I have a large collection. Before joining the army, I gave it to a neighbor as a keepsake."

"To your girlfriend?"

"No, neighbor."

They watched as the bodies of the trucks turned black. Kudryavtsev recalled how in early spring butterflies appeared in his garden. In the first warmth over the wet ground, a black-red spark suddenly flashed in the bare apple trees. A butterfly sat on the gray fence like a colored cloth. Kudryavtsev got close to the butterfly and saw how its wings and antennae trembled and its dark body pulsated. In the summer, cabbage opened its waxy, green-white leaves, in which precious, transparent water accumulated after rain. He recalled a tender, yellowish-milky cabbage butterfly with a thin, powder-coated body.

Kudryavtsev was looking at Tarakan's face which was stained with soot. He had a frowning forehead with a dark wrinkle. He tried to guess what his room looked like, with his desk, notebooks, and glass collection boxes.

In the square, among the ruins and rubble, crows shrieked ever so loudly, frightened flocks of them flew into the air, and dogs wheezed angrily and furiously. From the destroyed cars from different directions, as if they had been frightened by hundreds of stones, the dogs ran, and the marauders trotted away. Apparently, those who got off the trucks dispersed the vultures merely by their appearance, and they meekly scurried away.

Soon everything was calm again. There was no more movement. Kudryavtsev's wary eyes rested, and his finger slipped off the trigger.

"So what? You don't have a girl back home?" Kudryavtsev held out the interrupted thread of conversation. "Why haven't you found one?" he asked, while grinning, lips firm in the cold. He was not married either. His brief cohabitations with women only brought him trouble, irritation, and excruciating disappointments, which brought long, persistent pain. The question he asked was simply a standard question which is required to establish a relationship of trust with a soldier.

"Why should I get married so young?" Tarakan answered judiciously. "First, we should try to understand ourselves and our life. We should travel, see lots of interesting things. And only after that, we should get married. And then after marriage come the children, and the rest of your life they become the center of your world!"

"Where do you want to travel?"

"Everywhere. My neighbor back home, Eugene, is a hitchhiker. He's been to China, Poland, and Turkey. He's been to Italy twice, too. He saved up some money and now he has a good life. I will return from the army and do the exact same thing."

"What will you do with your money?"

"I'm going to go to Brazil. I want to catch butterflies on the Amazon River. It's my dream to catch one on the Amazon."

Kudryavtsev was surprised to find the innocence of his dream, in which adult pragmatism could coexist with a naive, childish desire.

"When you go to Brazil, make sure to bring back a mulatto for me."

"Mmm... a mulatto!" Tarakan liked this idea. He twisted his foot in the dark, imagining how he would bring a mulatto to the disco and, to the envy of his friends, dance a carnival dance with her.

Kudryavtsev continued to marvel at this stubborn youth striving for the future, which seemed happy and joyful. The misfortune they just experienced, the massacre, the death of their comrades did not break his young aspirations. And he, Kudryavtsev, with a heavy machine gun that rested on his knee, must direct this aspiring child into battle, into blood, into death.

The trucks in the square suddenly buzzed and turned on their headlights. Bluish smoke billowed in the white light. The drivers jumped out of their seats and began hastily to open the side compartments. People began to appear because of the damaged armored cars and tanks. They walked in pairs and carried a heavy, laden stretcher. They put them on the ground by the trucks. They lifted dead bodies from them, and swinging them by the arms and legs, threw them into the back of the truck. They could see how the dead were swinging their parted limbs in the air, and with a thud, the bodies hit against the truck bed.

The people with stretchers went back into the cluster of burned-out cars. Others took their place. Black, disheveled bodies flew into the air again, with more thuds of lifeless husks. On the trucks, uneven and disheveled piles gradually accumulated. And then several people, leaving the stretcher, climbed into the back, to level the mountain of dead.

It took an hour or more. The crows shrieked into the sky. The headlights were blue and white. Sometimes a pale, lifeless face, naked, without shoes, fell into the light. Everyone who was in the house, huddled against the black glass, watched how the dead bodies were loaded onto the truck. Three trucks with open sides, with black loose heaps that looked like peat, rolled slowly and heavily out of the square. Behind them on foot, the funeral team left exhausted.

10

Winter night was slowly smoldering with fire and oozing with smoke. The mortal danger that chased Kudryavtsev along the snow-covered street, along the iron gates and fences, that tried to overtake him with automatic gunfire, was now behind him. The brigade in which he served was his family, for in it he had many close and important friends, as well as enemies, and even comrades who he was completely indifferent toward, and together they constituted a living environment. That brigade now resembled a huge, disheveled dump, where putrid fires smoldered and smelled of burnt iron and flesh. While he was tucked away in a safe place, Kudryavtsev tried to understand the fatal mistake that occurred and led them all to defeat and death.

Most likely, blame fell to the general's ignorance and folly. The general had stupidly and arrogantly played commander in front of the officers, when he tried to emulate General Yermol's ways, when he was in the tent and walked around the map in his soft leather slippers, as if he were at home, with his striped pants tucked into woolen socks, and when he insulted the chief of staff, who doubted the ridiculous order. As a cadet at the infantry school, Kudryavtsev studied combat tactics for densely populated cities, where every window opening, every gateway turned into a grenade launcher's position or a sniper's nest. The firepower of the tanks, the hollowing fire of self-propelled rockets grind enemy strongholds. The infantry then occupies the ruins, finishing off stunned enemies and providing corridors for further advancement of the company. Stupid ignorance and arrogant nonsense drove the unprotected columns into the city and exposed them to attack.

The general was surely to blame, but the minister of defense also had a part. With his long nose, small forehead, and closely set bird eyes, he looked like a stubborn woodpecker. He decided to give himself a birthday present by storming a city full of enemies on New Year's Eve, so that the next morning on an ornate table where various gifts will be brought to him—blades in a silver sheath, engraved personalized weapons, a Swiss watch with a diamond, a gold snuff box with a singing bird—he'll find among them a correspondence which reads, "Troops congratulate the minister of defense. Russian flag placed at the Presidential Palace in Grozny." And the minister, damp after taking a dunk in his pool, donned in a pink terry robe, will read the message.

There also could have been treason, a traitor lurking at the headquarters of the district, who informed their enemies of the routes the convoys would take. After all, it was not for nothing that at the moment of entry over the Chechen village, a rocket took off and sent a soundless message to a distant foggy city. And at this quiet sign, snipers sat down at the windows and grenadiers lurked. They waited like hunters for when a nimble armored vehicle would jump out onto the snowy streets, under the yellow lights.

But maybe he himself is to blame. He let his guard down with flattering speeches, cordial words and smiles, golden grape bunches, and multi-colored curtains in the doorway, where gentle, girlish faces flashed. And it was so sweet to drink black and red wine from glasses, to touch a snow-covered wooden table with a hot hand, until when suddenly the platoon commander, stabbed with a knife, wheezed, and his blue eyes bulged as the blade entered his larynx.

Kudryavtsev was going crazy and tormenting himself with these thoughts. He sat in the attic under an iron roof and could not stop thinking about the events of the night. He watched how foggy reflections slowly moved through the square, as if a huge lump of black coal was burning.

He made his way under the roof, stepping into the soft attic dust. At the other end of the attic, by the dormer window, Nozdra was huddled, as if taking a nap. And Kudryavtsev, not wanting to disturb him, asked in a low voice, "Are you praying to God?"

"I'm just thinking," Nozdra responded. He didn't feel the mockery in the commander's words.

"About what, if you don't mind me asking?"

"How am I the one that survived? All the guys from the platoon died, and here I am, alive.

"What exactly happened there?"

Nozdra paused, as if collecting what little he had managed to understand and think up in the brief moments of silence after the recent deafening and blinding horror.

"When it started, I was sitting on the BMP. And then came the rumbling, and then fire! The vehicles bounced as if they were being hit with a sledgehammer. One's turret was torn off, and how it smashed into the ground! Nearby, a fuel tank exploded, and all the fuel flew into the sky and from there just burst into flames. The guys who ran got caught in the rain of fire. I only managed to say, 'Lord, save me if you can!' I don't remember anything else, how I ran, how I was saved. You called out, then I woke up. The Lord must have sent a guardian angel. He carried me out!"

Kudryavtsev, if he had not experienced something similar, would not have resisted mocking what he just said and dismissed it, thinking, that here's another weirdo who came to the army from a twisted, civil life, which creates a lot of young freaks. These young freaks are not able to pull themselves up on a pull-up bar or throw a grenade. These drug addicts, hysterical punks, fickle pacifists, those sick with consumption and asthmatics, the flat-footed, rockers, and feeble-minded motley and dystrophic congregations are those from which he, an officer, in a short time had to create a combat unit capable of winning a battle.

Now, having survived the terrible extermination of the brigade, having lost a company and survived, he was ready to explain what had happened as an action of evil, inhuman forces that destroyed the irresistible power of the army. But by the presence of a mysterious and good will among these evil forces, which chose him among thousands of doomed people, he was saved from death. In the snow-covered Chechen courtyard, flooded with wine, lamb fat, and the blood of murdered comrades, a sudden passionate and mighty force lifted him with wings, carried him over the hedge, and rushed him forward along the street, diverting the striking lines. He was led through explosions and fountains of fire into this deserted house, as if he had prepared this shelter in advance in anticipation of such a disaster.

Listening to the soldier, Kudryavtsev felt that he possessed some mysterious knowledge which was inaccessible to and surpassed him. Yielding in strength, intelligence, and experience, he can understand and explain the unexplainable for Kudryavtsev. He wanted to ask him about this knowledge and find out and, perhaps in the moment of impending danger, rely on this knowledge to find support and strength.

"Where did you learn to pray?" asked Kudryavtsev, fearing that

Nozdra would close up and no longer talk about his innermost thoughts. "It seems you pray any chance you get."

"My father is a priest, and my mother and I sang in church. I planned to serve in the army, then enter the seminary and become a priest, too.

"Ah, it's the family business. Is your church big?"

"It's beautiful. It has served us for two hundred years and has never closed down."

In the black, icy attic, in a gloomy, hostile city, near the smoking remnants of the brigade, Kudryavtsev imagined a church: golden, foggy, with the soft glow of lamps, stem-shaped candles, many humble and meek faces, relatives and friends, among which, if you look closely at them, you will see aunts, mothers, and grandmothers.

The vision was precious and redeeming, and when it disappeared in the icy attic, among the beams, pipes, and iron, it became warmer, as if the house had suddenly been flooded.

"When you pray to God, what do you ask Him? How to live? What to do? And can you ask, what will be our fate in this?" Kudryavtsev was surprised by his own questions. He tread carefully, trying not to frighten off the soldier, treasuring this inexplicable dependence on him. "Can you ask God what lies ahead?"

"Old Marfusha comes to our church. She is like a praying mantis. She travels to various monasteries and holy places. She is usually gone for six months and then reappears. She says, throughout all the churches, the icons cry. Tears flow from them. This only means trouble. To be in Russia is a big problem."

"It will get worse?"

"There will be more problems. We have an icon of the Archangel Gabriel in our church. A tear crept onto his cheek, as if the tar from the icon glistened. We saw the angel weeping."

"What for?"

"I don't know…"

Kudryavtsev tried to imagine a long, tall icon with a red lamp, heavy, weary wings lowered to the ground, a darkened, aged face among the dark folds, crumbling embellishments, and a tiny, bright spark of a drop of resin.

"How could this happen to us?" asked Kudryavtsev, looking at the square, where the burning machines started to calm down, the layered smoke was floating, and the night crows who had gone mad continued to rush about. "Who is so angry with us?"

"God. There must have been a grave sin," Nozdra replied matter-of-factly. Kudryavtsev had never said such things before and never heard it. He was surprised at how serious the words sounded coming from the soldier. The young man who survived the battle, who was scratched and smeared with soot, planted by Kudryavtsev's battle plans at the dormer window in anticipation, understood and knew something hidden from Kudryavtsev. Behind these closed doors, something so different from what he had experienced before, there was a different space, a different life that was inaccessible to Kudryavtsev. It seemed that the soldier came out to him from behind these doors and sat down for a short while at the dormer window, just to say a few strange, indistinct words and disappear again. To close the doors in front of Kudryavtsev, leaving in his mind a disappearing golden gap with a darkened angel with a sad lamp.

"If you pray, then you believe God will help. Pray well, so that we may be helped." Kudryavtsev asked the soldier to plead in front of someone powerful and inaccessible, to whom the way was closed for Kudryavtsev, to vouch for him and convey his requests. He suddenly experienced an acute aspiration, a passionate attraction associated with his own defenselessness, there, through the iron roof, up to the sky, inhabited by a mighty, good, nameless force. He turned to this force with a request to save them all from death, to take them out of this house, from this burnt square. So passionately and naively he asked for it, his soul strained and hurried so hard that for a moment it seemed that someone's huge, warm palms stretched out to him through the roof, scooped him out, and carried him away, carried him to his hometown, to his small-town home, to the plank fence draped with his mother's shawl.

He woke up. A crowd of people was moving across the square, across the white snow indirectly from the smoldering debris. This crowd was disorganized, swirling, and elongated, as if they were carrying some kind of heavy log or rail. When they approached the area full of light, they moved along the houses toward the buildings near the station.

Kudryavtsev could make out a long column of people surrounding the station with guards. The guards were wearing leather jackets with Chechen hats and caps. Those who marched in a column wore tank helmets, soldier caps, and unbuttoned jackets. They were escorting prisoners. Kudryavtsev was struck by a black, sticky trail left in the white snow. He had only seen something similar from wounded elk running through the forest.

From that range, it was possible to attack with their machine guns. By sending frightening bursts over their heads, the guards would fall on the snow, defending themselves from the sudden attack, and then the prisoners would run and scatter, fleeing into the surrounding streets. Or, by gathering the soldiers in the attic, they could rush the square and blitz the guards before they knew what was happening, take the rescued prisoners to their safe house, arm them, and create a force to be reckoned with.

But in the next minute, both ideas seemed insane. There could easily be a retaliatory attack from many invisible enemies lurking in the neighborhood. Kudryavtsev, without raising his machine gun, looked longingly from the attic.

The prisoners were suddenly mixed up and staggered on the spot. The escorts shouted, aimed their assault rifles, and pushed the convoy forward. The prisoners, in obedience, moved on, stretching out in a sluggish line, as if they were tied with a long rope.

A man remained sitting, hunched over, leaning on the snow with his hands, and a guard jumped up and started kicking and hitting him with the butt of his rifle. He walked away and aimed his machine gun. Kudryavtsev expected to see a short flash, but two men ran out from the prisoner convoy, grabbed their fallen comrade by the arms, and the three of them hobbled and wandered off to catch up with the others. The escort shouted and threatened with his machine gun, showing he was not afraid to shoot them.

All of Kudryavtsev's soldiers were alive, armed, fed and placed at firing positions. They remained invisible to the enemy, hidden in the depths of the darkened house. They should retain the element of surprise for as long as possible, not giving away their position by light, nor sound, nor the smoke of a cigarette, at least not before the beginning of the expected morning attack, before the arrival of fresh soldiers. Once they find themselves flanking the Chechens, they will strike, mix up their defenses, and facilitate their own advance.

Kudryavtsev went through the attic to the other half of the house. He went down past the quiet, closed apartments to the second floor, where Krutoi was sitting by his window, almost invisible and seemingly breathless.

"Are you sleeping?" Kudryavtsev asked quietly, feeling the stiff sleeve of his peacoat.

"No, I'm not," he said in a barely audible voice, as he slightly fogged up the flickering window with his breath.

"What are you thinking about?"

"The battery, damn it, it's not charged! I told the ensign to change the battery, because ours was dead! 'No, no! The rear will come up, then I'll change it!' So then the rear came! The tank stalled and they couldn't move it. If they had a battery, they would break us out! Fuck, they won't capture us!"

"Did you burn the tank?"

"It's fine! Load a shell in the cannon! The engine won't start. I wish I could look at that bastard ensign right now!"

Kudryavtsev thought that he shouldn't look at the ensign just then. The ensign is probably lying somewhere shot next to a tank with his feet bare and crooked. Or he was turned into a grimy skeleton with a bare, scabbed mouth. Or he was walking now, wheezing, in a column of prisoners, as a Chechen escort poked him in the side with his machine gun. It would have been better not to look at him.

"Where are you from?" asked Kudryavtsev, resorting to the simple tried-and-true question that brought unfamiliar people together, not only a soldier and an officer.

"From the Omsk region, the village of Gorbovka," he said calmly, as if his own words had warmed and revived him.

"A peasant's son?" Kudryavtsev chuckled.

"You could say that!" he agreed. Suddenly, Kudryavtsev had a strange thought: sometime in old age, having lived a long life, he would go to the village of Gorbovka. There he will be met by an elderly, silent peasant, dirty from hard labor. They'll recognize each other. They will sit together in a country house. A bottle of vodka and a bowl of sauerkraut will shine on an oilcloth under a lamp. Drunk, they will remember their hiding place in the stone house in Grozny and how they sat side by side at the window, holding their machine guns.

"What kind of family do you have and what kind of farm is it?" this question seemed appropriate, being able to distract them from the dire situation they were in with the thoughts of loved ones, and displace them in time, to where they survived and thrived.

"What family?" Krutoi willingly shared. "I have a mother, father, and sister. My father left the farm that was owned by the state and bought his own land. We keep a cow, a heifer. He then bought a horse so that we can plow."

"A horse? Why not a tractor?" asked Kudryavtsev, not wanting to lose this calming dream that distracted them from their misfortunes.

"A tractor burns diesel fuel and needs oil. No way we could get enough. We will always be able to feed the horse. In the summer it can graze, and in the winter we can plow in a ravine," Krutoi explained. Again, it seemed to Kudryavtsev that the soldier was in some way more experienced and wiser than he was. In addition to the temporary army life, with tanks, cannons, batteries, and slovenly warrant officers, where this ill-fated trip to the city and the terrible defeat had occurred, this man had another, separate life, where a remote, wet ravine awaited him with dark grass and angelica flowers, a house with blue windowsills, and a grassy mound where a red horse grazed in the light rain.

"I have a photo in the tank," said Krutoi. "It's of my sister on the horse. I would show it to you. It's a pity that I left it there."

Krutoi looked with regret at the square, at the burnt column, where among the twisted equipment stood a surviving tank with a stalled engine. And in the turret near the gunner's seat was a photograph of a red horse, with a guy and girl squinting in the bright sun.

"What's your sister's name?" asked Kudryavtsev. But the soldier did not have time to answer.

They heard voices outside. The voices were approaching and sounded unintelligible behind the glass. They both jumped away from the window, grasping their weapons.

Shadows flickered in the snow. They were vigorous, armed Chechens, being led by a commander. As they walked past the house, they spoke very loudly. Kudryavtsev watched the Chechen in front and, despite the twilight, could recognize Ismail, who was not wearing any head covering and had his hair pulled back. Even in the darkness, his handsome, tanned face was visible.

Other Chechens followed, and among them, Kudryavtsev also recognized one, the same gray-haired old-timer who sat next to him on the bench. They were accompanied by several young, armed men, and behind them was a boy in a funny, red hat that repeatedly lagged and then caught up again.

Passing the house, the boy fell behind, bending down and picking up some of the sticky snow off the street to make a snowball. He then threw it through the dark windows of the house. The snow hit the wall and splashed wet snow everywhere, while the sound of the heavy, damp snow echoed throughout the building, like in a resonant, empty bucket.

The Chechens left, and Kudryavtsev got up with relief, relaxing his hand that was holding the machine gun.

He returned to the unlocked apartment, from which they had taken the furniture. In the kitchen, on a sagging sofa, he saw Filya. He was hunched over, wrapped in an old woman's rags, and crying. In the darkness, he could see his skinny shoulders shudder. He could hear sobs, which, as soon as Kudryavtsev appeared, turned into wails.

"What's the matter with you?" Kudryavtsev asked, leaning toward him.

"I'm scared!" Filya choked, covering his face with his hands. Kudryavtsev tried to take his thin, cold fingers away from his face, feeling plentiful, warm tears on them. "They're going to kill us!"

"Come on, pull yourself together!" Kudryavtsev tried to shout, with a tough, commanding voice to interrupt the sobbing of the soldier. "Set aside your tears—that's an order!"

"We can't stay here..." Filya exclaimed with a groan. "They will find us and kill us in this place!"

"You're not a helpless child!" Kudryavtsev started to feel a dislike for him, with growing disgust at his sobs and pitiful, bouncing shoulders. "You are a soldier! You have comrades in here with you!"

"I'm afraid," Filya repeated, squeezing himself into the sofa with his thin shoulder blades, as if he wanted to hide from Kudryavtsev, from his unfriendly voice and heavy machine gun.

The helplessness of the soldier and the fear that Kudryavtsev aroused in him suddenly struck painfully. He was ashamed of his rough voice, his hardy, well-trained body, and his aggressive superiority over the soldier, whom he tore out of the frying pan and immediately sent him back into the fire, into horror and death.

"I'm sorry to hear," Kudryavtsev said quietly, sitting down next to him, hugging him lightly by the shoulders. "Calm down, brother, it's going to be alright!"

The soldier suddenly pressed himself against Kudryavtsev, and he, hugging him, felt how thin and weak he was, how his narrow, trembling chest trembled from his tears.

"I have to go home! My mother is alone! She has asthma! She could have an attack! When she suffocates, there will be no one to call a doctor!"

Kudryavtsev felt a bitter compassion for him, a previously unknown, fatherly tenderness. He stroked his bobbed hair and admonished and persuaded him like an offended, upset child, "Well, okay... Don't... Everything will be fine... Everything will be okay..."

Filya gradually calmed down. Sobbing, he continued to cling to

Kudryavtsev until he laid him neatly on the sofa.

"Just relax," he said as he got up, leaving Filya to lie on the couch. "Prepare breakfast for everyone in the morning. You will rotate with Chizh... Here, let me cover you up."

He went into the bedroom and found a blanket piled in the corner. He brought it and covered Filya, tucking the blanket under his feet. Filya huddled on the short sofa, where he silently and gratefully sighed, placing his palms under his cheek.

Kudryavtsev stood at the window and looked at the decaying square. His soldiers lurked around the house, in the attic, and in the stairwells. Filya sobbed in his sleep. Thrown snow stuck to the wall of the house. Kudryavtsev, who reflected on the horrible day and the exorbitant night swollen by the catastrophe, asked whoever was in charge of life and death to save them from death. If this Mighty Being heard him, he promised he would return Chizh to his albums and drawings, Tarakan to his boxes of butterflies, Nozdra to the angel with a sad lamp, and Krutoi to his red horse. And if Filya meets his mother and Kudryavtsev sees his father's house, then in gratitude for that miracle, he will change his whole life. He will work hard and overcome any challenge before him and donate his money to the poor. Or he will hide on an island among the cold sea and alone, among waves and ice and night auroras, begin to reflect on how the world works and who controls and reigns in the universe.

He made a vow, not knowing if the one to whom he made it exists. He picked up a pillow from the floor, went up to the third floor, threw the pillow on the steps, sat down, and pressed himself against the wall. He closed his eyes, and under his swollen eyelids, the gasoline tanker began to explode silently, splashing out fountains of fire. The black turret of the tank blew off and flew into the sky. Two fiery tankmen ran, embracing, falling, and engulfed in sticky flames. The wine sparkled black and red in his glass. Ismail's bulging eyes gleamed. A knife with a bone handle plunged into the lieutenant's throat. A crow was sitting on the hatch cover, opening its scarlet mouth. Everything spun and flew like a soundless merry-go-round, while he, a boy, chased a pearly butterfly and galloped on a gilded horse. Then everything disappeared in a blizzard.

11

The guests left the business club in the morning after a bright and tiring night. Ladies in sparkling fur coats and men in half-open long coats and came out onto the illuminated porch, onto the red carpet covered with snow. From the stuffiness and hot wax aromas, they fell into a blizzard, into the flying, blue snow. The gatekeepers carefully took them off the porch and helped them get in their limousines. Cars flashing with diamond lights, dusting up the fluffy snow, were carried away into the snowdrifts, whirlwinds, and foggy glow of the streets.

Berner put his wife in a heavy, wide-ranging Jeep, into its velvety warm depth, from which a muscular, alert chauffeur peered out. The Jeep was a gift to his wife. Marina loved to ride in this high-speed carriage on wide wheels and a mighty engine. "Get some rest, dear. I'll be back later. I'm off to visit the hero of the day!"

He watched the ruby taillights disappear into the blizzard. He enjoyed the cold wind and streams of snow that deftly flew under his scarf, where they easily dove into the interior of his Mercedes, into the spicy twilight smelling of delicious varnishes. Akhmet sat in the front seat next to the driver. The guards filled the escort car, and both, scattering purple signal flashes, rushed into the blizzard.

"Let's go to the banya to meet the minister!" Berner ordered, pressing himself into the suede seat. He was not tired; instead, he was cheerful and fresh. Freed from apprehensions, in anticipation of imminent success, he was looking through the glass at the long, silvery whirlwinds flying along the facades and windows.

Moscow was empty. The streets were covered with lots of snow. The traffic lights, the blurry flames of shop windows, the streetlights, the stars, and the glow of advertisements flew past them.

The journey through the bright and illuminated Moscow intoxicated Berner. The city belonged to him. Amber facades were highlighted in his vision, and huge crystal showcases shimmered, displaying gold jewelry, furs, cars, grand pianos, bottles of imported wines, pink hams, and fish living in emerald aquariums.

Everyone else was carried away by the blizzard, and they freed the streets, squares, and crossroads for him, so that he, Berner, could fly through the beautiful night city.

The neon lights of the casinos created a sort of iridescence, like the tail of a peacock. The bank building resembled a blue crystal filled with thickened air, dry because of the cold. The illuminated nightclub entrance flashed with continuous waves of light, like a shell.

It was a new Moscow, which was not like the dull, dark, dilapidated one where his youth passed, where sad images of his anxious childhood lurked in the courtyards and doorways. This Moscow was taken away from its old decrepit rulers and given to them, the people of the new era, to rebuild it. Mansions and palaces were renovated and the Empire facades were dressed in precious pink, green, and golden colors. The domes of the erected cathedral were gilded. Moscow was washed with young energies and showered with New Year's silver, where it seemed to him like a charming woman with a pearly smile, ruddy lips, and dark hair parted in the middle.

He felt Moscow so passionately and tenderly. He rushed along the embankment along the river filled with sugary looking ice spotted with black holes, behind which, like a pink glow interspersed with red stars, the Kremlin soared.

He suddenly and irresistibly wanted to visit Red Square during these first hours of the New Year.

"Turn to the bridge! Let's go to the cathedral on the square!"

"Sir? You want to go straight to the Kremlin?" asked Akhmet with a straight face.

"Not now! In a couple of years!" Berner replied, not knowing if he was joking or believed in such a possibility.

They raced across the bridge toward the cathedral rising out of the blue air. It looked like a huge, multi-colored thistle that had risen from the snow-covered square.

The car stopped at the cathedral. Berner stepped out and was immediately swept away by the huge snow drifts. They dragged him along the stone parapet and threw scalding handfuls of snow in his face, as his eyes were dazzled by the tiles, scales, and white, ornamental carved stone. The cathedral shook its domes in the blizzard like a huge dinosaur. It was breathing with ice fire, puffing with white mercury, sticking out its red tongues.

Okay, Berner thought as he walked around the cathedral, leaving behind the blurry shadows of his bodyguards. *Now this is Mother Russia!*

He went out to the square. It curved in front of him, and the curvature seemed to be the curvature of the earth itself. The Kremlin, pink, powdered, jagged, and serrated, was so huge that it was barely obscured behind the bulge of the earth. It was bristled with burrs and golden, bushy crosses and with blackened openings and gaps.

The square was white, with black paved stones. It seemed like a huge glacier or a polar cap, into which it was frozen, stuck in hills, squeezed by the terrible pressure of ice, this red icebreaker. The ruby stars, surrounded by a frosty glow, stood over the square like wild stars ignited in the black and blue polar abyss.

So exhilarating! thought Berner, experiencing a sweet, mystical horror at the square on which for all ages, fleeting life tried to gain a foothold on this earth, settle down, cling to the cobbles, but it, like a leaf in the tundra, was blown away by a terrible whirlwind and carried away into the abyss. *No, it won't blow me away!*

He came to this square as a winner. Princes, kings, patriarchs, opera boyars in high hats, cuirassiers, guardsmen, commissars in leather jackets, and leaders in caps and hats, with their processions, parades, columns, honor guards, and hearses—everyone was blown away, carried away into the black and blue chimney of the universe where, foggy, frozen stars were blazing into the sky. But now he has come.

Berner was freezing. Through the thin soles of his shoes, his feet froze to the square as if he was standing on a red-hot magnet. But he felt good. The area belonged to him. The Kremlin with the Terem Palace and Georgievsky Hall with the gold inscriptions of the guards' regiments were his. The Tsar Bell and the Tsar Cannon, Ivan the Great and the Archangel Cathedral, and the tombs of the Russian tsars belonged to him, Berner. And a crazy thought arose here that in Red Square, in the center of Moscow and Russia, he, Berner, will celebrate his fiftieth birthday. On this square, where Stalin spoke from a microphone, from where the regiments went into the hazy military distance, where standards with crosses and swastikas fell on the granite of the Mausoleum, here, on this square, he, Berner, will celebrate his imminent anniversary on this earth.

He will stand on the Mausoleum, wave his hand affably, and smile. A wave of festive, inspired people will pass by like a Carnival of Rio de Janeiro with dancers, drums, and tambourines, rock singers from all over the world, thundering drums and pearlescent guitars, models of the world's best designers, the winners of beauty contests in captivating poses, top models with dazzling lacquered covers, and Oscar-winning Hollywood stars. And he, Berner, tanned, in a white suit, loving them all and loved by them, will wave his hand and blow kisses from atop the Mausoleum.

This thought did not seem impossible to him. His wealth, will, and power, before which the country will bow, will be enough to carry out this plan. And so that the square would know about this, so that it would feel his dominance now, he wanted to touch the paving stones with his commanding hand to leave his mark on the square.

He bent down and began to shovel the snow with his numb hand, revealing a dark, blue stone.

Slowly he brought his hand closer to them, placing his white fingers in a black square. He pressed it to the stone, and he felt a terrible shock, as if he had touched an electric wire, as if a bare, high-voltage conductor had been brought to the stone. The square shocked him, throwing him away. He fell on the parapet of the cathedral, looking up in fright at the visible domes. They began to move, rotate, crunch with their stone teeth, and squeal with gears and shafts. It was not a cathedral, but a huge meat grinder that took Berner, crushed his bones, broke his skull, and squeezed out a bloody mess.

He was thrown through the eerie rock crusher of Red Square, as it spat out into the snow the sticky debris of his ground bones and the red slurry of his worn flesh.

He woke up from his delirium with the foggy pink Kremlin and the motionless cathedral covered with snow in view, and his bodyguards bent over him.

"What happened, Yakov Vladimirovich?"

"We must go!" Berner said, not understanding what had happened to him. "To the banya... To the minister..."

The minister's banya was located almost in the center of the city, among stone gorges, surrounded and hidden from sight by a high fence and vigilant guards.

The armed guards let Berner and one of his bodyguards in, who followed with gifts: a Persian carpet brought from Khorasan and a crooked saber in a gold sheath with sayings from the Koran.

"Please come in!" the colonel's assistant, in a light tracksuit and beaming with affection, greeted them.

They passed a small dressing room where a communications center was located containing an array of telephones connecting the banya with the Kremlin, the ministry, military headquarters, government districts, and the space and missile forces. The signalman on duty bowed silently to Berner.

They then passed the second dressing room, reminiscent of a museum room, with a portrait of Peter the Great, busts of Suvorov and Kutuzov, and commemorative pennants, souvenirs, and models of submarines, missiles, and aircrafts.

They entered the third dressing room and dining hall, where the bath aromas soared, smelling of shampoos, delicious food, and drinks. There was a wide table with benches topped with bottles and food. At this table, naked, throwing off the sheets, sat the minister and his closest associate, the general in charge of the army's psychological and moral issues. Both were tired, pink, and damp, having just been in the banya from behind the door, where a blazing heat and a ringing brazier, white as a spine, lay. This was the famous ministerial steam room, created by the best specialists of the military-industrial complex using the blueprints of the Finnish saunas and utilizing the recipes of Buryat sorcerers who knew the secrets of Tibetan medicine.

"Greetings, Comrade Minister!" Berner, in the doorway, comically put his hand to his temple in a Polish salute, with palm turned out. "I have arrived at your disposal to pay you my respects and wish you a happy birthday! Please, open my gift!"

Berner turned to the guard, who put a woolen roll on the floor and rolled out a black, crimson, and smoky gray carpet covered in rhombuses, monograms, and mysterious oriental signs. He laid a curved blade over the carpet, pulling it halfway out of its sheath. The minister gazed at the gifts with his sharp blue eyes set in the pink rims of his sore eyelids.

"A magic carpet!" the entertained minister laughed cheerfully, shaking his big, bony head and large, flabby body that was unaccustomed to exercise. "And the sword—'Off with his head!'"

"Everything is mine, said the gold. It's all mine, said the steel," Berner picked up his laughter. "Long live the alliance of steel and gold!"[8]

"Come and greet me!" called the minister. Berner, who was still in his expensive evening attire, approached and hugged the minister, feeling his slippery, beaded sweat, steamed body, and moist, flabby lips.

"Well, little by little! Happy New Year, as they say!" As if by habit, the general grabbed a bottle.

"Wait, let him enjoy some steam first! He looks cold; not only does he have a hooked nose, it's worse that it's blue!" The minister rudely though lovingly patted Berner with the heavy paw of a paratrooper on his thin bones, which hurt Berner. "Come on, Yasha, take off your suit. Otherwise, you'll look like a condom without its tip!"

The comparison hurt Berner, as did the mention of his hooked nose. But he did not show it, nor allow himself to be offended. The minister spent most of his life in barracks, shooting ranges, and battlefields, which completely excused the nature of his humor.

Berner undressed in the dressing room in front of a large mirror. He stripped off his wide-shouldered suit, silk tie, thin socks, and underwear. In the mirror in front of him appeared a thin man with stooped shoulders, a sunken chest, thin legs, and overgrown, yet sparse hairs in some places. His body was pale and faded, like a stunted stem, on which hung a large, downcast head. He experienced a disgust for himself, for his precariously placed feet, the pimple on his chest, an ugly scar from appendicitis, and his sluggish genitals. He tried to flex his biceps, pecs, and abs, but the picture came out comical, and he, torturing himself, wanting to prolong the suffering by standing in the pose of a bodybuilder like a grasshopper or a praying mantis. He returned to the dining hall, where two strong men clinked their glasses of whiskey. They looked at him mockingly with drunken, blue eyes.

"Come on, Yasha, let's get some steam," said the minister, stepping out from the table, heavily. "Bartender! Sit here and mix us whiskey and soda!" he ordered to the general, not letting him into the steam room.

The minister and Berner went from the cool, fragrant dining hall and penetrated through the dense door into the dry, hot heat, where the air was like a foggy, transparent flame, where the beach chairs glowed like

---

[8] "'Everything is mine,' said the gold. 'It's all mine,' said the steel" is a passage from one of Alexander Pushkin's poems as a metaphor for a dispute between two delusions (gold being money, and steel being weapons) that what you can't buy you can take by force, and what you can't take by force can be bought with money. It presents a philosophical question of which is stronger: gold or steel?

polished bone. Berner felt scorched and was horrified by this red-hot hell. He felt his nose burn, as if there was fire in the room. It seemed to him that the sparse hair on his chest and groin began to smoke and smell like it was on fire.

"We'll not add any more steam; we'll have a dry heat!" said the minister. Like a monkey, he deftly climbed to the very top, moving his pink buttocks. He sat with his heavy chin sticking out, and he bared his teeth, breathing in what felt like a mixture of fire and air, from which his eyes bulged and turned blue. The slightest glassy layer of sweat formed on the minister's white and pink, blotchy body.

"I'm already down here in the lowlands," Berner groaned, tucking a cool seat under himself and making sure to stay close to the door.

"Little by little; little by little…"

Berner hated banyas, especially their fierce variety, accompanied by food, drink, and a frantic, meat-packing-plant-like rumble, where pink, ragged carcasses swayed amid boiling water, steam, roars, and groans. Once as a child, with a respectable neighbor, he ended up in the Sandunov Baths. The spectacle of the semi-dark steam room looked like a huge cave, where, huddled closely, a herd of naked people stood: bony, old men; sullen, frowning men; gentle youths and babies. All of them were covered with steam and emitting noise as they burned with fire, and their groans and cries were heard under the arches of the cave. The screams—this was a spectacle that he staunchly connected with the image of hell or Nazi gas chambers, and when he heard about the Last Judgment or the brutal extermination of Jews, he recalled the Sandunov Baths.

Now he sat huddled, waiting longingly for the sweat to break out on his skinny loins and drooping shoulders. From below he looked at the minister, at his calloused feet with yellow nails, at his bumpy, beaded shoulders, at the red scars and welts showing traces of battle wounds. Unblinking blue eyes peered over at Berner from under his sticky bangs, intense like electric torches.

"I was curious as to how the operation is going. How is Grozny?" Berner asked casually as he was sure that the minister invited him into this foggy underworld to have a conversation without the risk of being heard and recorded.

The minister was silent. He pushed out a copious amount of sticky sweat from all his pores. He sucked in streams of heat into his lungs. Then he raised his hand and, making a parting gesture, said, "Troops are coming and going…"

"Pray tell, did they start the offensive today? After all, they wanted to start the operation in mid-January!"

The minister was silently squinting and squeezing sweat from his eyes. He wiped it with his spread fingers from his shoulder to his chest, leaving a red line on his body.

"There was a conversation between the president and the American president Clinton," he said. "The pipeline from Absheron will go through Chechnya. It should be calm there by February. Then the Americans will invest. The president ordered the advance."

Berner knew about the call to the president. Through friendly relations with the president's family, to whom he had provided many continuous delicate services, he had heard about this call.

American oil companies were developing Caucasian oil. So these companies invested billions in oil fields, pipelines, and a tanker fleet. They unceremoniously broke the borders, reconciled fierce enemies, and quarreled with recent friends. They reeled on the black axis of the oil pipe of the Caucasus. Berner was involved in this project that promised enormous profits. He flew tirelessly to Tbilisi, Baku, and Yerevan. He had within his network a web of presidents, prime ministers, and other politicians invisible to the eye. He himself was caught in the invisible world net like a tiny, shiny fly.

Sitting in the steam room with his eyes closed, he recalled a recent trip to Istanbul: the blue expanse of the Bosporus, a white ship, and the glass facade of a skyscraper reflecting the rising sun.

"Sorry to remind you again," Berner, burning his tongue, pushed the words through the boiling air, where droplets of sweat instantly evaporated, and the steam broke up into stinging dry molecules, "but you promised to keep all the production facilities that I marked on the map intact. Not a single shell, not a single bomb should fall on them! The money has already been transferred to the account of the specified company; you can verify it. And they will continue to do so. However, each shell that falls on an oil storage facility will reduce the amount that will be transferred. Sorry, but that's how it is…"

The minister glistened in the mist, with a drop of sweat on his nose. He looked like a huge, yellow, thawing ham, and Berner looked at him with disgust as he inhaled the poisonous air flowing from the minister's body. He was breathless and could feel his heartbeat, and he dreamed of getting out of this gas chamber-crematorium, as soon as possible. But stoically he stayed to extend the conversation.

"You gave me this contract with Azerbaijan," said the minister, beating sweat from his eyebrows, where a few drops, greasy and hot as wax, flew into Berner's face. "Two Azeris came from Aliyev, and weapons will arrive there per the contract: all the tanks, armored vehicles, and self-propelled guns straight from the factories, brand new. Could it come out that these arms will go from Azerbaijan to Chechnya? Will it cause the Azerbaijanis to work against my group?"

"You have an intelligence service," Berner replied. "Track their routes to Chechnya. Let your falcons bomb them if anything happens. There is no objection here. The money has been paid."

The minister was like a melting snowman. All in luster, moisture, and fumes. A red carrot protruded from the middle of his face, and it was not clear how he took Berner's words. Did he hear them at all through the billows of dull, hot air?

"And one more thing," Berner added, rearranging his skinny feet and looking at the dark, fast-drying print. "As promised, I will give you supplies of food, fuel, and ammunition for the entire group during the Chechen campaign. We will agree on prices later. Payment will be to the account of the same company."

Berner, sitting on the lower step, felt the heat roll down on him from above, like hot cobblestones. He wanted to jump out into the cool dressing room. He cursed the primitive amusements to which the sullen, heat-resistant statists from the "Russian" circle of the president—the Security Council, the Federal Grid Company, the Ministry of Defense—indulged in. They preferred to solve state problems in an informal setting. He was forced to meet with them in steam and drink with them, to hunt moose and scrape animal blood from a hot frying pan, to choke on poisonous vodka. He took a break from them by being in the company of intelligent people on an elegant yacht gliding along the Bay of Biscay or Lake Geneva, where he could drink only weak drinks and wines, either warmed up or with ice crystals, bathe in a large marble bath full of bluish fragrant water, and retire to a spacious, pearly tiled bathroom, with a small, carefully selected library. He endured baths and hunts as a temporary and inevitable evil, which will end with the removal of these narrow-minded, poorly educated statists from the president's cabinet.

The general's face appeared in the doorway in the glass window. He did not dare to enter without an invitation. He pressed his nose to the glass, flattened it, made terrible crayfish eyes, and opened his mouth, depicting a monster. He wanted to attract attention to himself.

The minister watched for a long time how his entertainer made faces until he finally waved, inviting him to come in.

The general rushed in noisily with a stomp, dragging with him an enamel basin, in which lay soaked, dark-green brooms.

"And here we are!" he stamped with his foot. "I came here for you! To count your bones!"

"Beat him!" the minister ordered. "And then he sits so awkwardly, like a dog on a fence! He has imported branches as a gift! Made from eucalyptus! From the Sukhumi battalion!"

Berner tried to resist, raising his thin arms pleadingly, angry that he was compared to a dog. But it was useless to fight. The entertainer had already spread the dry sheets on the hot wood. He was already squelching in the basin with the soft broom that squeezed green juice. With a forceful and tenderly voice, he held Berner down and exclaimed, "Now it's time for stretching! But for now, we will knock out all this nonsense!"

Berner lay down on his stomach, eyes closed and terrified. He heard a eucalyptus bunch rustling above him, catching up with hot whirlwinds that made anyone want to howl in discomfort. The general from above slammed down a sticky, scorching heap on his upper back. He pressed down so that Berner's breath was caught in his throat. He tried to wriggle out, but huge, dexterous paws restrained him, and more biting blows fell on his back, on his buttocks, and on his calves, which caused him to shudder, moan, and squeal.

"And now we beat along the spine... And now across the spine..."

Berner was on the verge of fainting, surrounded by a hum, whistling, falling bumps, and the smell of tar and ether. The butcher general tormented him, crumpled his body, and drove his huge finger like a chisel along his spine.

Terrible images of torture and agony arose in Berner's semi-conscious mind. He hated these two men, afraid that they would strangle him and fry him here. But he endured "for the cause," tenaciously holding this "business" in the depths of his darkened reason.

"That's enough!" said the minister. "Otherwise, you will leave his wife a widow! Take him with us into the snow!"

They pushed him out of the steam room, but did not allow him to go to the table where the coveted beer was, and with friendly and rather painful cuffs they drove him to the barely noticeable door in the wall.

"Let the banker do a somersault!"

Both men, huge, red, and enveloped in steam, pulled him by the arms and whipped him like a biblical martyr. They kicked the door, and the three of them rolled out of the warm, illuminated dining hall into the snow, into the frost, under the blue sky, to a loose snowdrift, from which, when they appeared, a soldier in a sheepskin coat and felt boots with a wooden shovel ran away.

"Yasha, go ahead!" The minister kicked Berner, and the red-hot man tumbled into the depths of the snow, clogging his eyes, nostrils, and mouth with soft snow, like cranberries, sprinkled with powdered sugar.

Nearby, both military men were floundering, roaring like a bear with delight. Berner, almost crying and feeling that he was about to die, burst out of the snowdrift and returned headlong back to the dining hall, and from there to the steam room. He then fell on the couch, breathing heavily like a dog, watching the snow melt and disappear on his trembling stomach.

Soon the minister and his companion rushed in happy and heroic, as if they had accomplished a feat. They perched themselves upstairs, red, cast, blue-eyed, as if molded from colored porcelain.

"Here, brother Yasha, taste a Russian bath!" Then they rested at the table. These brutes poured themselves whiskey, and Berner greedily sipped on cool, German beer. He could not quench his thirst, as if every cell of his dehydrated body was absorbing every last drop of golden beer.

"Let's drink to our leader, to our minister!" the general, entertained, raised a toast as he spoke menacingly, but at the same time politely. "Our president respects him! He loves the army and the officer corps! He is accepted by the people! Because he is not only a military man, not only a strategist, but also a politician with a capital letter! Your career, Comrade Minister, is far from over! You still have big things ahead of you and very big assignments! But, as they say, not a word of this will be spoken!"

The general made a stone face and put a fat finger to his lips. He poured a glass of whiskey for himself, and then stood there, rolling his eyes, sticking out his wet lip, and released a long stream of air.

The minister sat swaying, stooping his bare shoulders. He fixed an unblinking, evil, blue gaze at one point.

"Don't drink in my honor, but in honor of the Russian soldiers who are now, at this moment, fulfilling the order of the supreme commander in Grozny! There is no other soldier in the world like a Russian soldier! He defends Russia, her people, and it is greedy not to give him any awards! Yes, I would send a whole dump truck with orders and medals ahead of the advancing units! I would shovel them onto the streets, so that the units that entered the city would pick them up from the asphalt and affix them onto their chests!"

His head with wet, short bangs bent to the table. He rested his heavy fists on the wood and looked at Berner with hostility.

"The Russian soldier lays down his head for you, banker! I suppose, not a single son of yours, not a single foster child of yours will get up on the command 'Forward!' Your sons are not there, only the workers and peasants' children! And you pay them with what? If only you gave them good boots! Fuck, all you do is think of yourself! You even try to save money on the Russian soldier!"

He was filled with a dull, feral anger, which, like sap, rose through his bones and joints, as if along wood fibers. His head swelled, and, like a crown with heavy, damp foliage, it hummed and swayed.

"I tell you, if you ever harm even one soldier, I will rip you to shreds!" He hit the table with his fists, the anger showing on his face as he clenched his jaw, with his teeth gritting. "You sons of bitches, your end will be terrible! Where have you pushed the Russians? A Russian person cannot die! The oil is yours; the steel is yours; the aluminum is yours! What belongs to the Russian—a horseradish? Wait, your turn will come! Soon, you motherfuckers will understand who the boss in Russia is!"

This drunken hatred from his blue, cruel gaze was directed at Berner. The minister hated him. He took advantage of his bounties, received benefits for his services, and was part of invisible projects related to the supplies of the army, with the sale of military property, including military vehicles and aircraft. He hated Berner with a deep, hidden hatred that suddenly, after fire and snow, after vodka and whiskey, bore itself like a fossilized mammoth in a mountain after a landslide.

And Berner was intimidated by this naked force that was ready to destroy him. So, he responded to hatred with hatred.

In the minister, in his friends, in the directors of military factories, in the heads of power ministries, in governors, in these tongue-tied village peasants, Berner saw a threat to his well-being: his banks, overseas accounts, mansions, influence on the president's family, and the lifestyle and flair with which he furnished houses, ran TV channels and the press. He built a complex, constantly changing pattern of behavior in which these men, unknowingly, served his interests. They replenished his wealth, increased his power, and moved him forward to victory. This power was so great, so disguised that in a moment, when he pushes it forward, this power, like an earthquake, will sweep away all these clumsy, arrogant peasants at once. They will be cut down with a dazzling razor, leaving only their ribbons and empty beer cans.

But this he only thought, and he did not allow his offended feelings to show. He chuckled lightly, dipping his lips into the yellow beer.

Cautiously, tiptoeing into the dining hall, the entrusted colonel entered and said, "Comrade Minister, we are in contact with South!"

"They are impatient!" the minister turned his head like a bull with its horns bound in hay. He shook it off, got up heavily and, covering himself with a towel, staggered out to the communications center, where, among the array of colored telephones, his call was waiting.

Through the open door, the minister's indistinct roar was heard, a moment of silence, and again a roar.

He appeared at the door, sober, confused, and pale. The towel trailed behind him in his fist. His body, naked, on strong, crooked legs, seemed to be flattened, as if it had received a blow from above.

"Assholes!" he hissed. "Set up a brigade!"

"Something happen in Grozny?" Berner asked, sensing that something was wrong.

"The brigade has suffered heavy losses! Send those faggots to the tribunal!"

"They will break through!" the general tried to calm him. "Let's drink a little!"

"Shut up! To the Ministry! Scramble all aircraft! Bomb their asses to kingdom come!"

"Don't forget about the factories!" Berner protested.

"To hell with them! I will leave a large crater in their place!"

They were dressing quickly and nervously. They pulled on trousers with stripes, and without buttoning their shirts, they climbed into their tunics. The assistant helped the minister to get dressed in his peacoat.

The military personnel left, and Berner, naked, was still sitting at the table. He drank beer slowly, wondering if Vershatsky, his friend and partner awaiting a sniper's bullet, knew about what had happened.

12

Kudryavtsev woke up from the cold, which drove sharp gimbals under his shoulder blades, as well as from something inexplicable, like the approach of sound. He opened his eyes; the dim light from the staircase window illuminated the untidy wall, some inscriptions scratched in the plaster, and the dirty ceiling with a smudge of soot and a stuck matchstick. His gaze moved lower, to the first floor, where there was a landing with three closed, padded doors.

One of the doors opened, and a woman appeared on the threshold in the pale light, like a vision.

Kudryavtsev remained seated, and it seemed to him that this was a continuation of his dream. The woman barely touched the threshold and seemed to sway, agitated, like a cloud created from fog in unsteady light and air currents. She seemed like a mirage where you could stretch out your hand and touch her, but you will only meet emptiness and the mirage will disappear.

But she didn't disappear. She was filled with flesh, volume, and color. The door sounded faintly, and footsteps could be heard. The woman went out onto the landing and looked up at Kudryavtsev. She was tall, with a large, white face and parted, blonde hair. A light, loosely buttoned coat was thrown over her shoulders. Kudryavtsev, finally coming to his senses, examined her dense legs, her belly protruding under her coat, and her large breasts. He raised his weapon, without pointing the barrel, and asked, "Who are you?"

"I live here," the woman replied. Her voice was low and dull as if she had just woken up. It sounded soft in the frozen stairwell.

"Where did you come from?" he repeated the question roughly. The anxiety did not go away, but more and more it turned into amazement. The appearance of a woman in the walled-up house, with banners on the porches and vigilant soldiers overlooking the house, seemed improbable. Only a disembodied creature could pass through brick walls.

"I was here in my apartment."

"What about the others?"

"Everyone was driven away. The Chechens went to the apartments. They told us you were twenty-four hours away and we had thirty minutes to get ready to leave. They fired into the air from their machine guns. So, I hid in the closet."

"Did you see us arrive?"

"I saw how you retreated. I thought you'd come to help us out. But you were defeated."

"Did you see us enter this building?"

"I heard you, but I was afraid to leave. And now I'm out."

Kudryavtsev suddenly had a strange feeling, as if the house, which seemed empty and coincidentally appeared on the way of their escape, was in fact prepared for them by this woman. She guarded them, opened the doors for them, and let them in at the moment of mortal danger.

"The entrances are mined," said Kudryavtsev. "Don't try to go there."

"I'm not leaving," she replied.

Filya leaned out of the apartment below, gray from the cold, with bags under his eyes from the suffering he had endured. He was not surprised to see a woman.

"Comrade Captain," he said plaintively. "You ordered breakfast, but everything is eaten. There is no bread or jellied meat!"

"I have some food," the woman said. "Come with me!" she called to Filya.

Tarakan appeared from the attic at the sound of voices, staring at the woman in surprise.

"You told us, Comrade Captain, that the Marines will arrive in the morning. This must be them."

Kudryavtsev was happy to see him smile, even if they were blue from the cold.

"We were able to get into that apartment over there and stayed without asking. May the owners forgive us," he apologized to the woman, the keeper of the house, whose property they had invaded.

"Good people live there," she said. "The Kurbatovs, Andrei Nikitich and Maria Lukinichna, they are pensioners. They will forgive you."

"Quiet," Tarakan pointed and placed his ear to the staircase window. The nostrils of his small nose sucked in air and quivered as if he wanted to smell the approaching danger.

Kudryavtsev, on his tiptoes, so as to not make any noise, went down to the window and looked out. The area was foggy. Smoke rolled through the streets, and the gnawed skeletons of armored cars had turned into black, shapeless fragments of iron scraps. Dirty, greasy splashes of debris were scattered and smeared into the snow. Where the snow had not melted, the tracks of people, dogs, and automobile wheels scattered across the white ground in different directions. A barely noticeable path led to the house, connecting the entrance with a distant truck on flat wheels. Kudryavtsev looked at the gloomy scene of the carnage with a yearning glance; it was a huge graveyard left over from the brigade. At the same time, he scanned the square vigilantly in all directions to look for potential danger.

He went to Chizh and heard Tarakan almost silently slide down the steps after him. The three of them, stretching their necks in different ways, bowing their heads, listened to the approaching voices.

"Away from the glass! Away from the glass!" Kudryavtsev, with a wave of his hand, ushered the soldiers into the depths of the stairwell. He retreated into the gloom. He could see the illuminated, snow-covered area while remaining invisible.

Chechens were approaching the house. Ismail walked ahead, spreading out his legs for stability as he was slipping on the melted snow. There was a machine gun on his shoulder. Around his neck was a lush, bow-like scarf. His tar hair flung back in heavy braids. Now, in the morning light, he looked even more like an actor who played noble, romantic heroes in historical films. Kudryavtsev noted this similarity and immediately felt an acute hatred for him. He remembered how he shot picturesquely across the table, shooting right into the soldier's wrinkled forehead.

Others followed quickly behind him in fashionable leather jackets and also had guns thrown over their shoulders. One of them had a grenade launcher primed with a pointed grenade sticking out from behind. They laughed, gestured, and pointed at the wreckage of the tanks. One of them slipped, driving them through the snow, but with his other strong hand caught himself before falling.

Following them, lagging behind and gasping for breath, was a mustachioed face enveloped in the steam of his own breath; the familiar old-timer was in a long coat and a low astrakhan fur hat, and he was in a hurry. For some reason, he was without a large weapon, so his pistol must have still been tucked into his belt. He said something, trying to attract the attention of the younger soldiers, but they did not turn around as they were busy explaining something to each other with their fingers.

The group was closed by the same nimble boy in a funny, red hat sticking out like a sore thumb, the one who threw the snowball at the house last night. He tried to catch up with the adults. On his side over his coat dangled a heavy bayonet-knife, a trophy presented after a night of slaughter.

The main group had already passed the house, but the boy lingered absentmindedly, without interest, looking at the windows. He must have seen the imprint of his snowball on the brick wall. He bent down and began to collect more sticky snow, making another snowball. He continued slowly, wondering where to aim.

Suddenly, Filya appeared, holding a plate with slices of bread and some kind of sliced food. Shuffling loudly, plopping down the steps, he coughed and whined plaintively, "No gas, no electricity. Neither tea nor boiling water..."

Tarakan turned around and tried to shush him. He pressed a dirty finger to his purple lips and shook his fist at Filya, who did not understand why they were threatening him and so approached the window to put the plate on the windowsill.

"What happened?"

The boy then saw him through the glass and was stunned. The snowball remained un-thrown. With a weak cry, the boy rushed to catch up with the retreating group with all his might. You could see how his hat was shaking, his bayonet-knife dangling on his side.

"Damn it! You idiot!" Tarakan swung and punched Filya in the face with a crunch. He staggered back, opened his mouth, and a trickle of blood ran from his nose. "I'll kill you, you faggot!"

"Stop!" Kudryavtsev pushed Tarakan away with his shoulder. "We can figure this out later!"

Filya was choking on his tears, silently crying, smearing the blood on his face. There was a plate of sandwiches on the windowsill. The gray square was fogged through the dirty glass of the window. It was quiet; only the rare call of a crow could be heard. With the onset of morning, the crows took off and flew back to the suburban landfill.

"Positions!" ordered Kudryavtsev in a strangled voice.

With an angry narrowed gaze, he drove Tarakan up into the attic, and the crying Filya away from the window. He pressed himself against the wall, looking out into the square, holding the machine gun vertically, so that at any moment he could dip the barrel down and direct it to the square.

Time dragged on slowly, like fibers of raw smoke. Kudryavtsev looked around the neighborhood, in which the fuzzy outlines of city buildings were drowning. Where are the troops? Where is the offensive? Where is the roar of cannons, the barrage of fire moving from square to square, rubbing into the dust fortifications and clearing the passageways for the infantry? Nimble combat vehicles should be rushing into the hacked corridors through the brick dust, hammering the enemy with machine guns. The vehicles would stop, hiding behind the ruins, and as their heavy doors open from the stern, the troops would pour out of them. They would then run, firing their weapons, taking cover in the piles of broken stone. Where are the helicopters, their long, newt-like bodies and carpets of explosions? Where are the Marines with their discordant cheers and white and blue flag with a red star?

These thoughts rushed to Kudryavtsev's mind as he was clinging to the wall, feeling that their silent, tranquil hideout in the house was coming to an end and that through the yellow fog many attentive eyes were trained on them, listening closely with sensitive ears.

There was no offensive by the troops. There was no artillery attack and no Marine attack. Only from a distance were rare shots and stray automatic fire heard.

Without voices, without laughing, without speaking, the Chechens returned. Now they walked carefully, keeping in a tight group. The boy in the red hat was not with them. They were holding their submachine guns in their hands, and they could hear the snow chomping under their feet. They stopped at a distance from the house, peering into the windows, floor by floor.

Kudryavtsev was afraid that a cloud of steam would burst out of the unglazed attic window, from which Nozdra was hiding.

The young Chechens stayed at a distance, hunched down, raising their submachine guns. Ismail, slowly springing up, began to approach like a big, strong cat, ready to jump back and attack. Kudryavtsev saw his broad, bronze forehead with large eyes under his black eyebrows. It was possible from the upper steps through the glass, to strike the enemy at close range, plunge the group into a dense, well-formed formation, and make them into a lush bow aiming for the throat.

Ismail went to the door and became invisible. Below, one could hear the rustling of his feet and the jingle of the barricaded door strapped to the old man's closet.

"Hey!" he called softly. "Anyone here? Come out!" He paused and listened. Rustled yet invisible, he went along the wall. He came to another entrance and tugged at the locked door, which was blocked by a pipe. "Come on out! We can make a deal! Let's talk!"

Kudryavtsev was afraid to move, even crack his joints or fidget. He squinted his eyes at the pile of grenades in the corner and thought about throwing one through the window to cause a short, blunt blow.

Ismail moved away from the house and again became visible. He looked around the windows, stroking his black, hard, stallion-like hair.

"You'd better open this door, I tell you! We'll throw a grenade in the door! If we find you, you'll get a bullet!"

He stood, turned around, and quickly withdrew to the rest of the Chechens, almost in a run, shivering, as if feeling a fly along his back following him. He began explaining something to them as the old-timer in an astrakhan hat stretched out his hand and moved it from one entrance to another.

The grenadier, twisting his elbow, removed the pipe from behind his back. He put it on his shoulder, directing the protruding grenade rutabaga toward the house. He stepped aside so that the jet stream would not hurt his comrades.

Kudryavtsev ran down the steps and sat down on all fours against the wall, sitting with the slow-moving Chizh and Tarakan next to him.

"Grenade!"

They heard an incoming grenade slam and immediately hit, breaking through the entrance and exploding, filling the stairs with the roar of an explosion, as wood chips, smoke, and heavy water bounced many times from the walls, rolling down the steps. While the building was still being destroyed from the explosion, Kudryavtsev squeezed out of the floor, threw the barrel of the machine gun to the window and, blindly, at random, shot a burst. Then he immediately slumped to the floor, lying there listening to the screams outside.

Slowly he raised himself, raising his head above the windowsill, ready to instantly fall and hide.

A man lay in the snow. The rest of the Chechens fled. They looked around as they continued to run, hiding in the foggy nearby gardens.

The old-timer was lying in the snow, head pointing toward the house. His astrakhan hat fell off and was laying in front of him. The head, merging with the cap, seemed unnaturally large and elongated. Kudryavtsev thought he was dead, but he stirred, scraped the snow, and raised his head. A mustached face lifted and fell back into the snow.

"Finish him off, Comrade Captain!" Tarakan stomped impatiently by the window, ready to push the barrel through the window.

"Wait!" interrupted Kudryavtsev, peering at the wounded body.

The man lying on the ground was the first to be shot and hit by Kudryavtsev. His will, passion, hatred, keen eye, and a lucky shot cut off a living person, and the pain that he experienced from the wound, which may have been fatal and tormented him, was the result of his action.

Yesterday, before his eyes, his soldiers were treacherously stabbed and shot to death. Hundreds of his comrades, life-loving and healthy people, were burned alive and torn to shreds. And this wounded, elderly Chechen, the first response to this brutal beating, was not a full-fledged retribution. Still, the sight of a wounded animal still struck Kudryavtsev.

He was understanding that these were the first shots, which would soon be followed by others. The danger threatening their lives was rapidly approaching. This was not the time to worry and reflect, but the time when all mental strength should be preserved, directing them into the inevitable battle. Yet, amazement remained, since the man who was lying face down in the snow was shot by him, Kudryavtsev. A bullet from his machine gun was stuck in his body, among the bones and torn tendons.

The old-timer took his face away from the snow, extended his elbow forward, and slowly began pulling himself up. He pulled out another elbow, pulled himself up more, and fell again. He could be heard shouting something plaintively.

"If I were you, I'd finish that bitch!" Tarakan said enraged.

Kudryavtsev understood that the charred brigade, crumbled into shapeless pieces, filled with killed and burnt comrades, was calling for revenge. The stabbed, cherub-like lieutenant, killed by a headshot, the skinny contract soldier, shot down by a burst, called for this revenge. But all the same, he could not raise his gun, target the person lying in the snow, and open the crown of his head with a single aimed shot.

The old-timer crawled, stopped, and began to crawl again. A pinkish trail followed him in the snow. Apparently, the bullet hit him in the groin or stomach, and he, cooling off the pain, pressed himself against the icy ground. It was not clear why he was crawling to the house, where the bullet had come from. Perhaps in a darkened state he moved to where the people were, hoping for help. Or his clouded mind, like a homing head, chose the line along which the bullet had struck, and he could not deviate from it.

Kudryavtsev was looking at the old man with gray, disheveled hair, at his snow-stained coat, and at his dragging legs in wet pants. The old-timer did not appear to be an enemy. He lived in the same country as him, gave lectures at the institute to people the same age as him. What hatred made him crawl on his stomach with the desire to pull out a pistol and shoot Kudryavtsev? The same one that, like a meteor, struck the brigade, incinerated it, and left a stinking fire pit.

The old-timer crawled remarkably close. He raised his unseeing eyes to the windows and began to sing something, melancholy, like the howl of a wolf. He sang for the Russians who shot him to hear his death song.

"Where are the troops?" Kudryavtsev thought with anguish, listening to the high, gurgling, and wheezing howl of the Chechen.

Kudryavtsev went down to the first floor to examine the damaged doors. The explosion broke the doors, as well as split and moved the shelves that blockaded it. There was a narrow light clearing that led out into the street, through which burned boards emitted smoke.

"You can drag the wood away," suggested Tarakan. "Let's close the gap."

"You can't hold them alone," Kudryavtsev responded.

He pushed Chizh away from the window and, hiding behind the ledge, fearing a stray bullet, began to watch again.

A man ran out of the gardens, out of the alley. Ducking and wagging, he rushed through the empty space, fearing a shot. He ran to the truck and disappeared behind the tarp body.

A minute later, the second, to match the first, ran, bending over, wagging like a snake. In his hands was a large, yellow object resembling a jug. Kudryavtsev did not shoot, wanting to understand the meaning of these risky dashes. What was the object that looked like an enamel jug that the Chechens dragged along with them?

The third Chechen from among those accompanying Ismail, holding his gun, ran to the truck, where he ducked into the cab.

"I wish I had a grenade launcher in my hands," Tarakan said, "so I could blow them to smithereens!"

"There in the back is a box of flamethrowers," said Chizh. "They will explode, and scraps will fly from the sky!"

The truck was parked far from the house. The simultaneous detonation of a set of flamethrowers filled with aerosol could knock out glass and scorch the walls with a fiery heat, but no more. And yet it was not worth the risk. It was not worth spending one of the two available grenades on this distant, difficult target.

The truck jerked and made a buzzing sound, but the tires were flat and caused the truck to stoop. The Chechens hiding behind the body caught up with the rest and hid again. Their leather jackets, machine guns, and something else, yellow, varnished, like a jug or a bowl, flashed through.

The engine buzzed again as the truck drove off, jerking and wobbling on the rims. The Chechens covered themselves with the tarp body, and the one in the cockpit bent down and was almost invisible.

"These bitches are running the engine!" Tarakan was irritated. "We could have done it too! At night we'd have been out of here!"

"If they keep it up," said Chizh, "the battery will be dead, and then they're fucked!"

The Chechens drove the truck under the protection of its chassis. Kudryavtsev realized that they wanted to get close to the wounded man and pull him out, while shielding themselves from bullets. The truck was close to the home; it could have easily been hit with a grenade launcher, but now a simultaneous explosion of a set of flamethrowers threatened to destroy the house. And he watched the truck jerk and waddle on its rims as the Chechens deftly took cover along its sides.

The truck jerked a couple of times and froze. The battery had died, and the starter couldn't get enough power. The truck was parked close to the house, and behind it a freshly made trail stretched through the snow.

The wounded man stopped crawling. He turned on his side to face the truck. They could see how hard his chest and stomach were breathing as his trousers turned black from the melted snow and blood.

"Russian soldiers! Let me take our dead!" came a metallic voice with a whistle and rustle from behind the truck. Kudryavtsev realized that the polished, yellow object was a megaphone. The Chechens, risking death, approached the house to save the old-timer.

"Let them, or what?" Chizh said in confusion, peering out from behind the ledge.

"Do you want a bullet between your eyes?" Tarakan pulled him back. "Let them come out and we will shoot them like dogs!"

"Let's be reasonable!" continued the metallic voice, which

pronounced the Russian words with an irregularity that could be detected through the megaphone. "We will take our man and you can leave. We will not touch you! By Allah, we will not touch you!"

Kudryavtsev listened to the cold wheeze from the megaphone. He didn't hear it at first, but then he noticed shuffling and rustling behind his back. He looked around and saw Filya who was full of energy, with his mouth open, gasping for breath as he ran down the stairs, down to the entrance. Kudryavtsev didn't have time to grab him as Filya unexpectedly flew over the wreckage of the barriers they used to try to block the door, pushed his way through the narrow gap, and ran out of the door.

"Filya!" yearning, Kudryavtsev shouted piteously after him. "Where are you going, Filya!"

But he didn't turn around. Waving his arms that poked out of short sleeves and bouncing on long legs, he was still dressed in the ridiculous, old man's rags. He ran not at the man with the megaphone, but to the side, through the snow, to the nearby foggy gardens, which seemed like a refuge or salvation to him. He chose the direction not with his mind, not with his eyes, but with a frightened, yearning heart. He was heading to his distant home, to his mother, feeling her through the vast expanse of the snow-covered wild land, tied to her by an invisible umbilical cord. His mother silently called him through the snow, carnage, and smoky battle columns.

Kudryavtsev could only watch him, and he felt pain and powerlessness, as he was not able to catch up, stop him, give him a hug, and shield him from the machine guns of these merciless people yelling from a wheezing megaphone.

Filya had already fled far away when a burst of bullets rumbled from behind the truck. These bullets found their target and overtook him. Filya trembled his legs for some time, carrying the fire that shot through him. Kudryavtsev felt this fire in his side, as if his rib had been broken. Filya fell and curled up into a ball, like an embryo. He took the position he had taken in his mother's womb, where he joined her in death.

Tarakan, pale, took a grenade from the floor. With his left hand holding his machine gun, he hit the window with the butt, knocking out the remainder of the glass, and with his right hand, he threw the grenade. He threw it under the canopy to where the old-timer was laying in the snow. The metal pomegranate fell, jumped, and rolled up to the old-timer. It then hit him with an oblique explosion, ripping out a part of the flesh from the lying man. The old-timer turned over in the snow, mangled, with a sticky, red lotion covering what used to be his face.

The smoke from the explosion flew away in a small cloud as the old-timer lay in the snow. In the distance, like a dark pod, lay Filya. All around them there were many confused, intersecting footprints in the snow.

13

Kudryavtsev looked through the shattered window blowing in the wind. Below was a truck with a set of Bumblebees, and in the area there were Chechens lurking. Also nearby was the dead old-timer, lying with a shredded face from the grenade. Filya was curled up into a ball. A dreary thought overcame Kudryavtsev, *When will the troops arrive?*

The woman silently walked to each soldier, carrying sandwiches and water. She brought a glass to Kudryavtsev, and he drank the precious water, but he could not understand the expression in her eyes. She was either afraid, or she pitied him, or she was asking God knows what.

"What's your name?" asked Kudryavtsev.

"Anna."

"Anna..." he repeated. The name sounded hollow and cold, like this deserted home. But he was grateful for the home, and he was grateful for the name.

"If you want to leave, try from the first floor, from the window. They won't notice."

"I'll stay."

"There will be shelling."

"Doesn't matter."

She carried her pitcher full of that precious water further, to where Chizh had perched on the stairs. Kudryavtsev got a strange feeling from her cold name, booming, like a fading sound.

He began to think that he had made a terrible mistake. At night, when they got their weapons, they should have left immediately. They should have thrown themselves into the black and red shadows of the fire to the buildings near the train station. From there they should have retreated along the train tracks, leaving behind the death and horror. If they were pursued, they would have engaged in a fleeting battle and went for a breakthrough. Six submachine guns, a light machine gun, and grenades would have cut the path to retreat and pierced the corridor through the loathsome, city night. By morning they would have been out into the foggy steppe and in the empty fields, bypassing the village, moving to the north to their native borders.

Now in this stone house, as fugitives, he condemned four soldiers and this silent woman to death. He exposed them, like Filya, to the bullets of their enemies.

His decision to take up defenses, to defend the station square before the arrival of the Marines, to carry out the general's order was absurd and insane. The brigade was defeated, and there was no one to carry out the order. It was defeated through the fault of the general, and no one had the right to demand from the handful of surviving soldiers that the order be fulfilled. No troops will come to the rescue. The generals are cowards and thieves. The minister is a liar and a hedonist. He was probably steaming in his morning bath, soaking from the night drinking. In Moscow, there are swindlers who have lots of money, corrupt deputies who are drunk, high, and repugnant, and the president who is clumsy like a twisted stump. They squandered the Motherland, as well as ruined and defaced the army. The remains of the untrained peasant sons, on worn-out equipment, with a meager supply of food, were thrown like sheep to the slaughter to a war unclear in terms of tasks and goals. They were sent to a city inhabited not by enemies, not by Germans, but by Russian aunts and old Chechen men. These compatriots, pouring wine into glasses, bringing skewers with lamb, stuck a knife into the pink throat of the platoon commander, baked the brigade into coals, and just shot Filya, who lies in the snow like a small, dark animal. And maybe it's not too late to blast the grenade launcher into the truck, blow up the Bumblebees, throw a red ball of fire over the square, and rush to the station, to the train track leading out of the city to the steppe.

He sat and grieved, but something prevented him from giving the order to retreat; it was some kind of sad thought. It charged him, the captain, forgotten by the generals, to defend the station, guard the cooling brigade cemetery and the dull steel track, along which in an hour or two, if the troops remained in Russia, if the Russian people remained, the Marines should approach.

He saw a man emerge from the neighboring gardens, whitewashed by the snow that had not yet melted, over which the tiled and iron roofs were reddening. The hunchbacked and ruffled man was alone in a coat and winter hat. Awkwardly, like an old man, he moved his unstable legs. He carried a blue, white, and red flag in his hands. Not a white surrender flag, not a green flag of Chechnya with the image of some kind of beast, but a tricolor Russian flag, which looked unusual and ridiculous among the defeated Russian brigade.

"Some kind of madman!" said Chizh, peering out cautiously and incredulously. "He's hunched over!"

The man did not walk toward the house, but obliquely, toward the truck. His intentions, his route, the place from which he came out, and his destination were not clear. He gave the impression of being a blind man walking with the flag for many miles, for many days in a row. Now he was crossing this square, which came across his path, unaware of yesterday's carnage. He will pass with his flag through the wreckage of tanks, groups of Chechens, neighborhoods of houses and dumps, and then dissolve in the winter fog.

The man went to the truck where he lowered the flag. The hiding Chechens accepted him, and for some time they were not visible. A minute later, the man showed up. In his hands was the megaphone, yellow as a huge lemon. He coughed several times, and the device directed the old man's metallic cough into the windows of the house.

"Russian soldiers, umm... I'm talking to you, a deputy of the State Duma! A deputy..." the man spoke in a relaxed old man's voice, interrupting himself with strange bleating interjections. This relaxation, reinforced by the megaphone, filled the square with the old man's weakness, and this weakness was of an oppressed type.

"I am a deputy..." the megaphone howled, as if a huge fly flew into it along with the wind, drowning out the words. Kudryavtsev could not make out the name of the deputy—either Korablev or Kobylev. "I am here on behalf of the Duma, umm...and the Russian public, umm...which is outraged by the war unleashed in Chechnya, umm...and demands an end to hostilities..."

It was inexplicable that an elderly deputy appeared among the bleeding square of Grozny with the smoky remnants of the brigade, among the Chechens, who joyfully and ferociously celebrated their victory. They tried to finish off the last fragile stronghold of defense, the soldiers who had settled in this house. Kudryavtsev clenched his melting remnants of strength into a fist to withstand the blow of the victors, and

this old man with an unfurled Russian flag came under the protection of
Chechen guns, blowing and bleating into the Chechen megaphone. It was
like a mirage arising in his overworked mind.

Separated by the foggy space, the yellow spot of the megaphone
continued to vibrate, as if the snipe's voice was broadcasting, "The
invasion of Russian troops into the small country of Chechnya, umm...is
regarded by the world community as an act of aggression, umm...and is
contrary to the Constitution. The long-suffering Chechen people suffered
a century-old genocide, umm...as in the days of the Tsar, so as the days
of Stalin... Needs protection and self-determination, umm..."

The old man seemed to be holding a huge, yellow bird. It was his
voice, his metallic squealing, heard by the soldiers. This bird squealed and
vomited a speech about the long-suffering Chechen people to him,
Kudryavtsev, who had just lost his brigade in black and red, like delirium,
after seeing how the burnt corpses of his comrades were loaded onto the
platform and a column of prisoners was driven to march with guns to their
heads. In the winter garden, his platoon commander choked on blood, by
a planted Chechen knife in his throat. The Chechens who handed over a
megaphone to the old man had shot Filya. And now this stunted deputy,
having turned into a yellow bird, is broadcasting to them about the
Constitution.

"Stop shedding blood, umm... Russian soldiers, I tell you as a
representative of the Russian government, umm... Lay down your
weapons, umm... This will not be considered captivity, but an act of
conscience!"

A blind, mad force arose from within Kudryavtsev's soul. He was
fuming as his heart pumped hot blood into his bloodshot eyes and he
started to lose himself in blind rage. The mumbled voice of the old man,
superimposed on the iron vibrations of the megaphone, was heard not
only by those who were entrenched in the house, but also by the soldiers
that were burned, turned into charred bones, who lay among the tanks,
hung in the cooling hatches, who looked through sunken, boiled eyes
pecked at by crows. They listened and waited for Kudryavtsev to answer.

"What is this asshole saying?" Chizh turned uneasily to Kudryavtsev.
"What does he want?"

"Go into the apartment unit," ordered Kudryavtsev. "Find some
cardboard. Roll it up into a makeshift megaphone. I will answer him."

Chizh fled, and Kudryavtsev took his place on the chair by the broken
window. He continued to listen to the megaphone whistles and shrills.

He tried to uncloud his mind and took the gun away that was standing in the windowsill.

He was trying to understand why this deputy was not here in the house with them alongside the doomed Russian soldiers, but instead alongside the Chechens, whose guns were dirty with the soot of the burning brigade. Why are the authorities in Moscow, all these journalists, artists, and talkative men and women who flooded the TV screen, not with these Russian soldiers choking on their blood? Why do they hate Kudryavtsev, his face, his weapon, his uniform, his speech, his way of living, which is nothing more than loyalty to the oath he gave to his unhappy, beaten, and pecked homeland, reminiscent of the crushed, disfigured brigade? Why do they hate him, Kudryavtsev?

Chizh ran up from the apartment, rolling a dirty sheet of cardboard on the move, on which traces of an old lady's teapots and pans were visible. He handed the newly-fashioned megaphone to Kudryavtsev.

"Russian soldiers!" the old man continued to squawk metallically, blowing his bile out of the yellow, poisonous vessel. "I guarantee you humane treatment by the Chechen authorities, umm… I will personally take you to the plane, and you will fly to Russia, preserving the honor and dignity of the soldiers. Lay down your weapons! Come out! Do not spill blood!"

Kudryavtsev felt a hot, stifling hatred explode in him, as if he had bumped his face against a red-hot steel plate.

He pressed the cardboard horn to his lips and directed it through the split window. He shouted, blowing all his hatred into the square, "You are a stinking goat! Faggot! Chechen trash! Go away, bitch! Take away your tri-colored doormat and hang it in your bitch Duma! Or I'll smash your rotten head with a Kalashnikov! You sheep, you'll be hanging from a lamppost! If you don't shut your mouth in the next ten seconds, I'll shoot! One… Two… Three…"

He saw how the Chechens grabbed the deputy by the collar and pulled him to shelter. From there, because of the damp tarp, the megaphone wheezed and whistled for some time.

"Bitch! That corrupt bitch!" Kudryavtsev repeated, feeling the sweat pour over his face and his hair stick to his forehead. "Pederast!" He was sitting on the chair, feeling terrible emptiness and fatigue. The machine gun was trembling on his knees, and he kept repeating, "Where are those troops, dammit?!"

For a short time, the white square, covered with footprints, remained deserted, but people slowly emerged from the foggy alleys. They were in a tight formation, seeming from afar as a band of drunken revelers who were hugging, slowly, getting tangled up in their legs as they approached. Kudryavtsev peered, expecting a new trial. The square was still an arena for the next group of artists. And they were spectators at the dirty windowsills. The performers from the stage were ready to shoot into the auditorium, at the boxes, and from there, from behind the unwashed glass, in response, automatic rounds and grenades would fly at them.

People were approaching. A white flag fluttered above their heads. A tricolor banner had just been carried past the window, followed by his hatred and longing. Now a dirty, white rag was fluttering, and a threat emanated from it, promising the same longing and hatred.

People were advancing. Kudryavtsev could now distinguish them and understand why they were moving in a slow, close crowd. Some of them were in army uniforms, in gray-green trousers, overalls, peacoats, tank helmets, or with bare heads. One had a bandaged forehead; another had a rewound neck. Their hands were clasped behind their backs, and as they walked, they interfered with each other, as if they were being tied by a rope.

Among them were armed Chechens in jackets and hats, covering themselves with prisoners and controlling their disordered movement. Kudryavtsev recognized Ismail from a distance, his big, shaggy head. He was the one holding the white flag, waving it in the damp air. Among the prisoners as they approached, among their gray, blurred faces, one seemed familiar to Kudryavtsev. He looked tensely, sharply, resting the foregrip of the machine gun against the windowsill.

The crowd of tired, heavy, wandering people with bent bodies and elongated necks resembled barge haulers who pulled themselves into belts and pulled an exorbitant load along the shoals. Among the barge haulers, who were resting their feet on the ground, Kudryavtsev recognized the brigade commander. He was no longer that clean-shaven and ruddy commander, with a daring little mustache over his pink lip, who he remembered in the morning coming out of his tent and, stretching tiredly, wiggling his plump shoulders. Now the brigade commander was in torn overalls, without a hat, his dark mustache seeming like dirty smears of soot, his puffy face swollen with untidy stubble. Even from a distance, it was clear that this face was asymmetrical. One half was swollen, and there was a bruise under his narrow, bloated eye. The brigade commander walked in a swaying motion, and his body, which was recently sleek, pampered, fed with tasty food, able to bed any woman, and exuding the smell of expensive cologne, now suffered at every step, and his effort showed.

The whole group approached the truck, and those who were hiding behind it already got out and hid behind the prisoners. They built a wall facing the house and stood with their hands behind their backs, looking at the windows.

"Are they being used as a meat shield?" asked Chizh, not understanding. "Shout at them through your megaphone, Comrade Captain; tell them to lay down, and we will hit the Chechens!"

"Wait," said Kudryavtsev, continuing to peer at the prisoners, hoping to recognize among them the soldiers and officers of his company. But those who surrounded the brigade commander were unfamiliar, warrant officers and soldiers from other battalions and companies.

Armed Chechens hid behind the prisoners' backs, and the deputy with his tricolor flag was also hiding there. Ismail's hands held the yellow, bright, glowing megaphone.

"Hey, guys!" Ismail's cheerful voice was heard, saturated with a metal crunch and rustle, as if it was wrapped in foil. "Let's get out of this together! Come out one by one, and put your weapon in the snow! I guarantee your lives, I swear by Allah! We'll send you home with the Red Cross! The deputy will take your letters and tell your family that you are alive!"

He spoke slightly distorting the words in his accent and changing the stress, but these irregularities could be the result of the megaphone's distortion. The yellow megaphone was placed between the heads of two prisoners, and they, deafened by the harsh sounds, moved their heads in different directions. Kudryavtsev could see Ismail's bronze forehead and resinous hair.

"We, the soldiers of the Chechen army, fight only armed enemies! You saw what we did with your tanks, which came to crush our women and children! But we preserve the lives of the unarmed! The commander of your brigade is here! He wants to tell you to give up!"

Ismail lowered his megaphone, stood behind the brigade commander, and put the yellow bubble in front of his face. The brigade commander's hands remained tied. The lower half of his face was obscured by the megaphone, and Kudryavtsev saw his disheveled hair and swollen eyes surrounded by bruises.

Kudryavtsev tried to understand what cruel irony connected the brigade commander of yesterday, who in the heated general's tent just stood there as the chief of staff was berated when he predicted the defeat of the brigade, with this one today, tied up and beaten. Yesterday, he had allowed the angry general to offend an officer and did not dare to incur the anger of his boss by defending him; knowing the risk he carried out the order, which was delivered by this general, who was tempted by becoming a colonel and leaving to travel to Moscow and enter the academy, away from dead country roads, putrid outhouses, and mud-stained armor. But today's commander, severely beaten, who shamefully lost the brigade, stood among his enemies, listening to their victory cries.

The brigade commander was silent until Ismail pushed him from behind, and the heavy body of the brigade commander swayed forward. He coughed hoarsely and spoke into the microphone, "What is your name, and who else is with you?"

He fell silent, and the crows could be heard croaking. Kudryavtsev was in a tight spot. What was he going to do? Where was the battle he prepared for? He previously explained the tactics of defense and offense, types of weapons, and methods of struggle. Where is the long-awaited, promised battle in which he will test his will and reason, his bravery as an officer, use the power of the weapon entrusted to him, where he will crush the organization and the will of the enemy? Instead of this battle, there was an unexplained massacre, the massacre in the garden, with him sitting in the cold house, Filya being shot down, the old-timer torn apart by a grenade and the humiliated and broken brigade commander trying to persuade Kudryavtsev to surrender.

Experiencing despair and a melancholy similar to madness, Kudryavtsev grabbed the cardboard megaphone, pressed it to his lips, and shouted in a howling voice, "Comrade Brigade Commander, it's me! The commander of the first company, Captain Kudryavtsev! Fulfilling your order, by taking up a defensive position to block the railway tracks! If you, Comrade Brigade Commander, standing on the bones of the brigade you destroyed, order us to surrender, we will blow ourselves up with grenades, but we will never stand next to you; we will not let you bind our hands! Go on then, Comrade Brigade Commander, give us orders!"

He threw away the megaphone and looked at the prisoners, at the brigade commander, at the visible machine guns and Chechen hats, at Ismail's black, stallion-like hair. The brigade commander swayed again from being hit. Hoarsely, with a whistle, he shouted, "Kill them, Kudryavtsev! Shoot these sons of bitches with everything you got! I order you, Captain, fuck them all up!"

They took away the megaphone, and his face was twitching. His small moustache was hopping over his screaming mouth, but it was impossible to make out any words, only incoherent sounds.

The guards beat the prisoners, drove them from the square, and hid behind them. Scraps of the red-blue flag and the yellow of the megaphone appeared in the tangle of hurried, stumbling bodies. Kudryavtsev, seeing off his commander, shouted after him, "Comrade Brigade Commander! Can you hear me, Brigade Commander?!"

They were no longer visible. The fog and snow were evaporating. The old-timer was lying close by, excised by the explosion, and nearby was Filya's cold body.

Why is this happening to me!? Kudryavtsev thought in anguish.

His pupils, unblinking, looked at the white square covered with the black blots of footprints and the windowsill with the tin can containing cigarette butts and a sharp shard of glass hanging in the frame. Through it was a hazy, empty space accompanied by the occasional cries of crows.

Time trickled on without any signs of human life in the fog. Something invisible and inaudible was happening. His pupils scanned the fog and felt a pulse of light and trembling of air molecules reacting to this invisible and inaudible action.

He saw the boy in the red hat run out of the front gardens. With a slight bounce, he briskly ran to the square, dodging, playing, carrying some kind of cloth bag under his arm. He was not afraid of the submachine gunners who had settled in the house, as if he did not know about them. He looked like a frisky goat.

He approached the house and looked cheerfully at the windows, where he threw the bag as if he was throwing a ball.

And while the bag flew and the rag slipped from it, the boy ran away. Kudryavtsev no longer followed him with his eyes, but watched as something round, like a rye crumb, hit the ground and bounced. This crumb in the distance stopped, and Kudryavtsev saw and realized that it was the brigade commander's head which was turned toward the house, where it stood on the stump of his neck. Tendrils bulged over his parted mouth. His eyes were glassy, and under one of the eyes was a dark bruise. The hair on his head was stuck together, sticking out in sharp braids. It seemed that the brigade commander was buried up to his neck, with his body in the ground, and his head peeping out.

"Comrade Brigade Commander..." uttered Kudryavtsev soundlessly.

"How could this happen, Comrade Brigade Commander..."

Tarakan came from above and went down to the window. The three of them silently looked at the severed head of the brigade commander.

14

The space in Kudryavtsev's gaze consisted of a triangle, which was trampled on by chains of footprints. Dark paths connected at the top of the triangle, where the corpse of the old-timer lay, twisted like a stalk. Filya and the brigade commander's head, sitting on a red stump with squinted, wet eyes under his eyebrows, rested at the other two points. In this triangle, bisections, sides, and half arcs were drawn as scattering dotted lines by the footprints of the people who ran through. Sitting on the cold steps in the back of the staircase, Kudryavtsev tried to unravel the situation tactically: his sectors of fire, how he was mismatched on troops, and if he would ask to risk his men's lives.

Chizh drew in his crumpled notebook. He drew the triangle that was made up of the two corpses and the severed head. He meticulously drew the traces connecting them, as if he was restless, still running around, and measuring the distance in steps.

From the fog, from the iron fences, from the wet winter gardens, the megaphone spoke again persistently and deeply, as if they were letting out tin, hollow birds toward the house that whistled as they flew by. They hit the house with a grinding noise and fell like empty cans.

"We propose a ceasefire! We wish to take the dead! We are releasing the women! Do not shoot!"

Kudryavtsev prepared for a new test, not a battle, but a painful temptation, which he was again asked to withstand, which he must overcome and reject.

The women appeared in a small herd, all dressed in black. They moved and at the same time smoothly rotated, like tea leaves in a cup. Their small, round dance surrounded the armed men, and they were still using the yellow megaphone, which looked like a piece of cheese, but it was obscured by their dark clothes.

There were young women in fashionable fur coats, leather boots, and black, Islamic, facial coverings. Underneath the facial coverings, their beautiful, swarthy faces with thin noses and black, parted eyebrows could be seen. There was a short, obese woman in a badly buttoned, untidy coat and a mourning shawl that covered half her face, which looked as yellow as a baked apple. There was also an elderly woman, who walked with a cane, barely moved her legs, and was clothed in felt boots and galoshes. On both sides she was supported by two girls in bright coats, who looked playful and flexible, like goats, but they were also covered with black facial coverings. Among them were armed Chechens and Ismail, with his shaggy forehead and his megaphone.

Kudryavtsev assumed that Ismail was the leader of a small detachment that controlled the surrounding streets. It was in his territory that the house was in which Kudryavtsev had settled. Chechens from other detachments were distracted in other directions, taken away from the square, but Ismail with his small detachment would be able to destroy the house.

"Don't shoot!" he said from the megaphone in the center of the round dance. "Don't shoot at the women!"

The women, holding hands, approached slowly. They stopped, waiting for an old woman who was lagging behind. When she caught up, they walked again.

From the depths of the house, through the window, Kudryavtsev saw the group surrounding the yellow melon of the megaphone. Suddenly he felt an instant, fierce rage, a desire to shoot and kill them all.

The Chechen women saw the torn body of the old-timer, and they began to mourn. These beautiful, black-browed, young women, the fat, obese woman, and the old, bow-legged hag in black clothes, had just been present at the execution of the brigade commander. From behind their facial coverings, they watched earlier as the brigade commander fell to the snow with a knife under his shoulder blade. They saw as a nimble Chechen pressed his knee on his lively, wheezing chest, and deftly cut off his head, cut through the vertebrae, and grab the head by the hair as it gushed forth sticky blood. The women looked from behind their curtains, as if a ram was being slaughtered in the garden, just as they watched the murders at the feast half a day ago. They set the table and placed plates alongside jugs of wine, knowing that in the darkness near the braziers there were weapons hidden. These mournful, plaintive women would look with admiring, unblinking, uncaring black eyes, if Kudryavtsev was captured and his trembling body was cut to pieces.

He felt such hatred for them, for their husbands, brothers, grooms, for their dark-haired children, for their entire Chechen family such that his finger fell on the trigger with the front sight aligned with the group. He was ready to cut them all down with lead, shredding their mourning clothes, their earrings, and their fashionable coats and leather boots.

"Shouldn't we kill them, Commander?" Chizh guessed his condition. He pressed his gun to the doorframe and turned pale with impatience and anger.

But suddenly, the women began to wail. It was like a song, like sketchy, wind-washed sounds. Their voices were like the sound of wind in a palisade made up of thin, trembling poles, each one making a dreary, rattling note. These rising and falling sounds combined with the cries of crows in the gray sky, who had returned to the ground where the dead lay and the commander's severed head stood. It seemed that it wasn't the women who were singing, but someone invisible, soaring in the clouds, mourning all of them, mourning those who died last night among the torn apart tanks and armored cars, those who were shot in the morning on the melted snow, and those who were yet to be killed during the cloudy, cold day.

His rage passed, and it was replaced by powerlessness and incomprehension. He remembered how his father was buried. Behind the coffin where his long-nosed, purple-eyed father lay, stood his neighbor Pelageya, who was nicknamed Pigalitsa. She lamented, throwing back her sharp-billed, bird-like face, choking with a scream and a cry, and then with force she fell down, almost onto the coffin, emitting a long, unabated groan. Everyone around began to sob and moan quietly.

When he heard the Chechen women's cries, he experienced something similar, not the need to cry, but a longing and a moment of understanding this cruel world. As if all power and blood had been cut off at once, his hand sluggishly slipped from the foregrip of the machine gun.

"Kudryavtsev, come out unarmed!" the megaphone rasped and whistled. "I'll meet with you unarmed as well! We'll just take our dead and disperse! I will not shoot, I swear by Allah!"

"Don't go, Comrade Captain; they will kill you!" Chizh tried to dissuade him, seeing how Kudryavtsev put his gun against the wall and headed for the exit. "It's a trick, Comrade Captain!"

"If anything happens to me, drop them all," said Kudryavtsev. "If they kill me, kill their little folk choir along with them."

He made his way through the wreckage of the wardrobe and through the hole where the door used to be before it was punctured by the grenade launcher. He came out into the light and felt insecurity in the open air. It was as if a stone shell had dissolved off of his shoulders, or an impenetrable body armor had been taken off, and he was vulnerable, completely in plain sight on the gray-silver square. He took a few steps forward, moving away from the brick wall and stepping into the triangle, where the souls of the dead fluttered and soared silently and disembodied, each above their own corpse. He saw Ismail split the herd of lamenting women unarmed and also enter the triangle, carefully feeling the ground as if under his feet there was not asphalt but thin ice covering rapids.

Kudryavtsev slowly approached the lying old-timer, avoiding the pellets and cranberries of blood-soaked snow. It seemed that in the head of the old-timer a black-and-red bird hit the snow with its wing, where it left a trail of claws and feathers. Half of the old-timer's face was ripped apart. His mustache seemed peeled off at the part of his lip that was torn off, and his wet trousers were pulled down almost to his knees. Under them, the old man's blue underpants showed in an undignified way.

Kudryavtsev, entering the triangle, did not move to the farthest corner from the house, which was where Filya stood like a mound, but headed to the side of the brigade commander's head. As he approached, he did not take his eyes off the dead man's head. The head looked at him tearfully from under raised eyebrows. The hair was sticking out in sharp, frozen tufts, and the half-open mouth was trying to express and explain something to Kudryavtsev.

Kudryavtsev went up to the head. He pulled off his jacket and covered it. It was now hidden by the impenetrable hard cloth of his jacket.

As he moved on, Ismail walked toward him in a long coat and silk scarf, with his hands in his pockets.

They were close to each other when they stopped. Kudryavtsev felt the noiseless blow of his hatred, which was so strong that it caused the air to vibrate and pulsate, pressing on his forehead and eyes. The answer was hatred, as if a black-and-red lantern powered by a ruby generator of hatred had been lit in Kudryavtsev's chest, and a laser beam burned down from Ismail's bronze forehead.

"I'll get you anyway, bitch!" Ismail said quietly. "I'll take off your skin piece by piece, listen to how you squeal!"

"You're a foul goat!" said Kudryavtsev. "I'll cut off your goat balls and throw them to the dogs! But they won't be able to stomach such rancid flesh!"

They stood facing each other, furious, trembling, ready to rush each other and fight hand to hand, ready to beat, tear, bite, and thrust in with their claws and teeth, a fight to the death, like a traditional dual, just two men finding out who has the stronger will. Whoever steps on the breathless chest of his opponent, he will be the owner of the ring and subsequently end the night battle.

"We will destroy you pigs with the tanks!" said Ismail. "We'll start up your fucking tanks! And we'll put your tank operators in them, and they will fuck you up! You have an hour of your life left!" He pulled up the wide sleeve of his coat and looked at his gold watch. "The tank will come in an hour! We'll demolish your whole house!"

They passed each other, almost touching shoulders, and then began to retreat, each to his own stronghold.

Filya was lying on his side, his slender back arched, his hands between his knees, as if he wanted to warm them. Kudryavtsev bent over him and touched his forehead with his palm, just like when feeling the forehead of a child, trying to see if they have a fever. His forehead was barely warm. Filya was cooling down, but remnants of heat were still stored in his thin, slender body.

Kudryavtsev lifted him, marveling at how easy it was. Filya's head was thrown back, and his thin, dark veined neck was exposed. Kudryavtsev turned and carried Filya to the house, experiencing not pain, not compassion, but a strange amazement, for it was he, Kudryavtsev, in the light of a winter day, in the first hours of the new year, carrying a dead man in his arms.

He had caught up with Ismail, who was carrying the old-timer in his arms. Without stopping, they parted. Kudryavtsev had no hatred, but still held his amazement.

Kudryavtsev brought Filya into the house. He walked up the steps past the quiet Chizh. He put Filya on the floor of the landing. Tarakan approached, dove into the apartment, brought out a sheet, and covered Filya. His thin, long body was completely covered with his sharp nose sticking out from under the sheet.

Kudryavtsev looked out the window. The Chechens were slowly leaving the square in a soft fog. They carried the dead body of the old-timer and surrounded him in a close crowd. When they disappeared, the barely audible screams of women could still be heard.

They were all sitting together in the destroyed old man's apartment, where Anna fed them bread, cold potatoes, honey, and some berry juice. Leaning against the wall, she silently watched the soldiers chewing, as Kudryavtsev poured pinkish water into a glass. Her large, white face with light shadows seemed sad, as if she were watching her hungry children eat.

"This long-haired Chechen said that a tank will be coming for us," Kudryavtsev said as he listened to the sounds in the square. He tried to discern the rumble of a tank engine and the tinkling crunch of tracks among the crows. "He said the tank will come in an hour. They will put captured tankers in it, and they will shoot the house."

"Are they willing to shoot their own people?" asked Krutoi, who was a tank shooter, turning his freckled, peasant face to Kudryavtsev. "Are they really that barbaric?"

"They won't even know who they are shooting at. It's just a home!" explained Chizh, as he looked at the walls covered with wallpaper, through which a high-explosive shell would fly in. "They'll put a gun to your head and make you do as they order!"

"The Brigade Commander didn't," said Tarakan. It was quiet. The crows screamed. The jacket Kudryavtsev put on the severed head was hunched over in the snow. Filya was lying on the landing under a sheet. The woman still looked sad.

"I have a thought," said Krutoi, wrinkling his forehead, sticking a dirty finger to the bridge of his nose, where his fluffy, gray eyebrows converged. "I have a thought, Comrade Captain..."

Outside there was a growing whistle and then a short push against the wall along with a booming rumble. The smoke of the explosion drifted languidly past the window.

"Get to the shelter! To the stairs!" Kudryavtsev barked, pushing the soldiers from the table, pushing them into the corridor. "Get on the stairs, I said!" he aggressively shouted at the woman who hesitated in the doorway.

Another whistle echoed, and another explosion shook the wall. Kudryavtsev ran down the steps to the window and looked out from behind the ledge. A grenade was approaching from the fog, leaving a smoky trail. It fell in front of the house, where it turned into a dirty, red explosion. It left a ragged pothole in the snow, and soot remained in the air, looking like smoke in the shape of a man who stood up.

Invisible grenade launchers sat in the misty bushes. From there, the house was under fire at random. Kudryavtsev looked out with half of his face from behind the protrusion, with his eyes tense, trembling in their eye sockets. He waited for the shot to calculate the position of the shooters along the trajectory of the grenade.

A black dot surrounded by soot flew out of the fog at the same time as the pop. It approached, enlarged, and flew into the window of the old man's apartment, where it struck inside with a tight explosion, filling the staircase with a crunch and a crack, an explosive wave bursting from behind the open door. The apartment continued to crunch and crumble. Kudryavtsev examined the misty intertwining of branches from where the grenade had flown and released a long, half-magazine burst, shooting through trees, nearby houses, and gardens, filling them with bullets.

Then he hid, waiting for a new grenade. But they didn't shoot anymore, and smoke was pouring out of the old man's apartment, crunching and flaring up in it.

He rushed upstairs and ran in. The grenade planted by the window thumped into the sideboard, where it exploded inside and was stopped only by the wall. It scattered the dilapidated shelves of the sideboard, chopped the dishes, baskets with spoons, bags of flour, and cereals. All these, scattered, were in pieces and smoking. The sideboard was on fire, the wallpaper on the wall was burning, and the curtain was slowly smoldering. The apartment, which was home for the old couple that lived there, was destroyed and enveloped in fire, acrid smoke, and decay.

Kudryavtsev grabbed a pillow that was lying on the floor and began to beat the fire on the wall. He pounded into the flames that engulfed the remains of the sideboard. He ripped off and trampled the curtain, coughing and gasping.

Anna came to his aid. She moved around the room with strong steps, carrying water from the bathroom with pots and then splashing them on the fire. The fire soon died, but the charred scraps of wallpaper and the charred boards of the sideboard were still smoking.

Kudryavtsev sat down wearily on a chair, drawing in the smoke of the burnt old woman's supplies. All around were multi-colored shards of debris, bent spoons, and forks. All their wine glasses and porcelain dishes, which were exhibited to guests on holidays and other gatherings, had shattered and turned to rubble.

"Come on, I'll pour some water on you," the woman said quietly.

"Your face is full of soot."

She helped cleaned off his face in the bathroom, and while he splashed icy water on his face and saw her close, white hands, he suddenly wanted to press his lips to her close wrist.

"Where did you come from?" he asked, lifting his wet face.

"I live here," she responded.

Where are the troops? thought Kudryavtsev, already knowing that the troops would not come today. In the coming early twilight, the attack aircraft will not show up. The artillery shaft, the harbinger of an assault, will not rumble in the vicinity.

They sat on the stairs, on the cold steps, with their submachine guns at their feet. Filya's body was laying long and white behind them. Kudryavtsev, who had left his warm jacket on the ground outside, put on a tight sweater from the old man and a jacket that did not fully cover his chest. He then waited for the approach of the tank. It had to turn into the square because of the accumulation of broken equipment and then run to the window, push the grenade launcher against the window frame, aim the turret, and fire into the house with a black shell.

"I have an idea," repeated Krutoi, as if their recent conversation had been interrupted not by the explosion of grenades, but by a striking match, from which they lit a cigarette. "I'll go to my tank." He abruptly nodded to the window, where in the twilight the iron ribs and shin bones of the burned cars were blackened in the snow. "An armor-piercing shell is loaded into the barrel! If the bitches drive the tank, I will manually deploy the turret, where I can hit them at close range!

"Don't do it," Kudryavtsev responded listlessly. "One of us is already under a sheet. You'll be shot, like Filya, after the first ten steps."

"They fucking won't!" Krutoi disagreed. "It's starting to get dark. If anything, you can cover me. I'll dress up like a woman, in a skirt and scarf, and I'll even grab a purse! They will think that I'm a beggar or a marauder and won't shoot!"

"Nonsense!" Kudryavtsev dismissed the idea, irritated by his naive insistence, reminiscent of a child's game of hide and seek and dressing up, a prank stuck in Krutoi's village mentality, inappropriate in a moment of danger.

"Why is it nonsense?!" Tarakan supported Krutoi's idea. "There are so many rags in this grandmother's wardrobe! We'll dress him up as an old lady, open a window on the first floor where the bushes can hide him, then let him loose, and he can drag his little purse!

162

Kudryavtsev looked at the faces of the soldiers, on which, through fatigue and soot and dark shadows of insomnia, a cheerful, boyish expression played. He suddenly felt old, shriveled up, and incapable of a gamble. Young soldiers viewed danger differently and weren't so averse to risk. Their young blood encouraged risky strategies, even if they could be deadly.

"Let's try, Comrade Captain!" Krutoi insisted. "At the same time, I'll grab the photo of my sister on the horse. It'll be a pity if the picture gets destroyed!"

"Let him try," Nozdra also brought in his support. "God will be with him."

These three, Chizh, Tarakan, and Nozdra, encouraged the fourth in this deadly mission. But they did not realize the size of the danger. They envied him, who had the opportunity to interrupt the dull sitting in the house, to go and frolic, to do a valiant act, as if there was no terrible night, no massacre of their brigade, no murder of Filya. They were so young, so frivolous and forgetful. Kudryavtsev was a cautious, wary old man by comparison.

"I don't know…" he hesitated. "Fine, try it, dress up as an old woman, we'll see…"

The soldiers cheered up, and the jovial haste with which they rumbled up the stairs, skirting around the body of Filya, hurt Kudryavtsev. He followed them into the apartment. Anna, who appeared silently and unexpectedly every time, as if a phantom passing through walls, followed Kudryavtsev into the room.

The soldiers rummaged through the old couple's junk. They were shaking up old dresses, coats, and skirts. They took out and threw away the faded red tablecloth and some worn, moth-eaten furs.

"Krutoi, try it on!" Chizh threw him a woolen skirt, and throwing off his jacket, Krutoi began to pull the skirt over his head, thrusting his shoulders and chest through it. The skirt cracked, sagged, and stuck on his hips. "Come on, Krutoi, almost there!"

Krutoi struggled with the skirt. He pulled on a blouse and a sweater. He then put on a coat. He covered his head with a scarf. Not being shy in front of Anna, he pulled off his pants from under the skirt, and put on the old lady's leggings.

Tarakan laughed, thrusting a wooden club into Krutoi's hand. He rolled out a filthy shopping bag on two wheels from the kitchen. "Come on, granny, go to the store! We need some bread!

"Oh, you are so naughty!" Krutoi said as he portrayed an angry, old woman. "I'll beat you with my cane!"

He looked like a tall, bony aunt in his skirt with wrinkled, tattered leggings and a scarf tied low, under which cheerful eyes peeped out.

"Now I will beat them with this stick to the forehead!"

Chizh, Tarakan, and Nozdra gathered to make him into a presentable elderly woman, and they pinched him, shook him, and tugged at his skirt. As Krutoi spun, he stepped on broken shards, and he hit Tarakan twice with the cane.

Anna stood silently in the doorway and looked on with sadness. Kudryavtsev let them have their fun. He decided to wait until they were tired, and then he would strictly order them to stop this stupid masquerade and send the soldiers to their positions.

He heard a distant, barely perceptible rumble with a faint screeching. He realized the sound was a tank engine shaking the air with heavy exhaust. The tracks rolling over the front rollers made a weak, squealing noise. The sound disappeared and then repeated, carried in by the wind through the broken window. Kudryavtsev listened intently as the sound wandered behind houses, behind the wreckage and carcasses of cars. It then completely disappeared. Again, the sound of the tank, which was not yet visible, was brought by the wind into the room.

"Chizh, get the grenade launcher!" shouted Kudryavtsev. "Everyone on the first floor! Lie down by the walls!"

"Comrade Captain, I'm going to fuck him up!" Krutoi looked at Kudryavtsev from under the woman's scarf with a stubborn and demanding look. "I will stab him with armor-piercing rounds!"

Kudryavtsev imagined a tank appearing on the square in the gray gloom. First, the turret will flash among the humps and debris of the brigade. Then it will roll out into the open and slide on its tracks, turning in place. It will then aim the heavy cannon at the house. Then, there will be a minute of silence followed by a red plasma explosion. That explosion will be a terrible blow to the wall as it breaks through the facade, flying into the house, smashing the floors, as it destroys beams, stairways, and steps. The anticipation of the explosion was aching in their bones, as if they could already feel the fragments of the grenade and debris piercing their bodies.

"Go fuck them with the armor-piercing round," Kudryavtsev said dully. "You!" he turned to the other soldiers. "Break open the window on the first floor, and let him out!"

Krutoi, leaning on his cane, went out of the room. Behind him was Tarakan, grabbing the bag with wheels on his elbow. Anna was next, silent, with a white, sad face. Nozdra cleaned up the unnecessary clothing from the floor. Kudryavtsev remained, listening to the sounds of the square, looking at the red tablecloth thrown on the floor.

The tank, roaring, rolled in the distance, as if it was a stray animal. He was looking for an exit to the square from the maze of streets, front gardens, narrow passages, and iron obstructions.

Chizh brought the tube of the grenade launcher along with a grenade. Stepping back from the window, Kudryavtsev put the pipe on his shoulder, took aim, and shifted the sight from the twilight, foggy trees to the burnt cars and the shapeless mounds of wrecked trucks.

"Come on, Krutoi," Chizh quietly said to himself, looking out onto the square. An old woman's figure appeared in the gray, fading square, wearing a scarf and walking with a cane and a humped back. This figure dragged a fragile stroller which limped, stopped, and rested. Kudryavtsev waited fearfully for machine guns to strike obliquely across the square and surround the old woman with flying dotted lines, where he would be noticed and run back, abandoning the stick and the carriage.

But there were no shots. The old woman rounded the truck and trotted toward the dark rubble, poking her stick, leaning toward the ground with her heavy, coiled head.

"Pray that he gets there," Kudryavtsev said to Nozdra, while he fumbled with the grenade launcher over the misty trees, ready to strike with a long arrow at the first flash of the enemy tank.

"I'm praying," Nozdra replied, moving his lips. He must have called for help from an angel with red wings that had dropped to the ground in the village church.

Kudryavtsev reproached himself. He was amazed at the ease with which he agreed to this foolish venture in which he sent a soldier to almost certain death. At the same time, he believed in success, which gave him a rush of superstitious thoughts. He knew that Krutoi would deceive the Chechens and get to his surviving tank which was lost among the exploded graveyard of vehicles.

"He made it!" Nozdra sighed with relief, looking at how the figure of the old woman stomped around the massive machines, nimbly diving into the crowd, and disappeared among the inclined turrets with drooping cannons and ribbed sides.

The sound of tank exhaust approached the home. The crunching and tinkling of the tank tracks became distinct. Kudryavtsev readied the grenade launcher on his shoulder, looking out for the invisible tank.

He did not pray for the soldier, because he did not know a single prayer. But having lost sight of Krutoi, he felt him and flashed in search of him with invisible radar. Silent flashes and impulses emanated from his chest and heart as they looked for the soldier among the wreckage, which created an uninterrupted living connection between them.

With a special clairvoyance that he felt within himself, Kudryavtsev watched the soldier. Here he clung to the oxidized stern of the BMP, looking at the shot machine-gun belt. With a short dash and unwinding of the scarf from his head, he rounded the truck with a puddle of spilled fuel. He then dove under the drooping cannon, jumping over the smoldering roller torn off by the explosion. Among the mutilated, burned-out vehicles, he suddenly saw his tank, which had survived, but stalled, with its turret turned to the side.

This clairvoyance was as an unexpected gift, as if another creature had possessed him and looked through his eyes with special vision in which it sent long rays penetrating through the obstacles between them.

He saw Krutoi grabbing the braces and climbing onto the armor. He then deftly plunged into the hatch. He made his way through the narrow belly of the tank among greasy blankets and abandoned pots and cans. Sitting on the gunner's chair and manually overcoming the inertia and the weight of the gearbox, he rotated the multi-ton tower. Above the optics of the sight, near the breech, where the armor-piercing projectile was laid, a photograph was glued to the armor. In the picture was a horse on a grassy plain, and on the horse sat a thin-legged girl.

In the twilight above the contours of the immovable debris, something shifted and changed. Howling and slamming the engine he rolled the tank, spinning the wheels on the dimly illuminated tracks. It threw flying soot into the air and disappeared behind the black piles of debris.

Kudryavtsev's clairvoyant gaze dimmed, as if soot covered his eyes. The last thing he managed to make out was the inside of the resurrected tank containing two wounded tankers bandaged up with Chechens pointing guns to their heads.

Kudryavtsev directed the grenade launcher pipe to the window, waiting for the tank to return. Insurgents poured into the open space, agile, fast, and with pointed grenade launchers. They were in black, like devils, in a scattered formation. They were on the prowl, making sure their tank was safe.

Kudryavtsev imagined the howling of music to which these black, humanoid creatures were jumping. But it was the howl of a tank engine. The vehicle came out from behind the wreckage, turned sideways, and carefully moved its rollers to aim at the side of the armor and the turret for a well-placed shot.

But Kudryavtsev hesitated and did not fire. The tank, sliding along its track, turned about its axis, with its front armor facing toward the house, aiming its thick cannon. The grenade launchers fled, not wanting to get hit by the shock wave of the shot.

Kudryavtsev took aim, feeling the cannon aiming directly at his chest, feeling a dull pressure within his breathing ribs, but hesitated again, and still did not shoot. In these last possible moments, he thought to himself, *Did Krutoi not find his tank? Or, in the frozen bulk, did he fail to turn the gearbox manually, to move the turret of the gun? Or was the target obscured by the hulk of an iron body, which made a direct shot impossible?*

His finger began to press on the trigger, feeling the elastic resistance of the spring. A second ahead of him, a flash emerged from the black dump of debris, and a shot crashed, as if the cannon had been killed for a moment. An armor-piercing shell hit the side armor point-blank and drove a sparkling chisel under the turret. It tore out a block of armor inside, turning it into thousands of stabbing needles, which exterminated the crew and undermined its ammunition load. The tank jumped from the impact and threw out a fountain of fire in a poisonous, blinding salute. Thick, prickly, greenish sparks flew. The tank looked like a smelting furnace, in which the shutter was open and the melted metal was released.

"Krutoi, fucking A, well done!" shouted Tarakan, throwing up his fists, like a football player who had scored a goal. "Right under the bastards' noses!"

The tank was burning and surrounded by a glow. The grenade launchers, scattered by the explosion, fell to their knees and fired their glowing grenade fires into the black fragments all in one direction. They found a living tank among the rubbish. In the twilight, an explosion burst in a second fountain of white-green light with molten mercury plasma pouring out.

Two burning husks were illuminated in the square. Two wrecked vehicles emitted a metallic spirit.

"Krutoi is dead! Dear God, he's dead!" Nozdra stretched out his neck and listened, as if he wanted to distinguish among the explosions and shots to hear the light rolling away of Krutoi fleeing.

It became dark, and they were still waiting for Krutoi's return. Hours passed, and Kudryavtsev kept peering into the gloomy square for a glimpse of a fast shadow running toward the house. But it was empty, gloomy. It was snowing lightly, and in the square in two places among the black ruins, there was a barely noticeable glow, as if two dull winter moons were rising and clouded by wind and snow.

Tarakan found a stick in the kitchen. He attached the red tablecloth to it and then placed it in the broken window. The wind picked up the heavy fabric and swayed it along the facade. The flag looked black and silent as it fluttered in the night.

15

All day Berner slept on the cozy sofa in his home office under a fluffy Australian blanket. He woke up in the evening, when the tall, icy windows were dark blue and the patterned leaves of frost shimmered faintly, as if the thistles were frozen into pieces of blue ice. From the sofa, under his dark blanket, he gazed with delight at these motionless, fragile thickets.

Icons hung on the wall, a collection that he collected from antique dealers. He ordered them in distant cities of Siberia and the Russian North. Saints, apostles, and prophets were hung on the walls, and right above him, on a thick, eaten away, and blackened board, St. Nicholas, with a white-beard and forehead, pressed a holy book to his chest, where he baptized Berner with long fingers like flower petals.

It was quiet. Only downstairs through the suite of rooms could the voice of his wife, Marina, be heard on the phone laughing. Her warm, homely laughter, the ancient gilding of the icons, the softness of his fluffy blanket, and the thorny ice patterns on the windows evoked a sweet feeling of peace, well-being, and reliable security in Berner, which he relished in during these first hours of the new year, a short, one-off day of respite, after which he will again rush into dangerous and exciting adventures.

He took a bath. With delight he plunged into its marble tub, feeling soft ovals on his hips and back and watching water fall from the shiny tap with a velvet rumble. Pink, berry-scented shampoo foam floated around his shoulders and chest like whipped cream.

He dried himself with a terrycloth towel and a rustling hairdryer.

Standing in front of a huge mirror, wielding a comb, he parted his hair to the side and then combed it either in profile or head on. He gave his face a formidable, unapproachable expression, and then sweet and seductive.

Feeling cheerful and refreshed, he bypassed the living room where Marina was talking, not wanting to distract her. He threw on a light sheepskin coat, put on a shaggy wolf cap and went out onto the porch.

It was frosty and wonderful. All around him was snow, an untouched, virgin snow with soft piles, under which rose bushes and flowerpots took refuge. In the blue air, the windows of the service rooms glowed elegantly and festively, and the greenhouse was green like a damp lantern. In the distance by the high fence, frosty and heavy, stood fir trees. Their forest silence and stillness along with the precious glitter of the windows gave Berner pleasure. These were his spruces, his winter greenhouse, his garage with magnificent cars, his snowdrifts and bluish trodden paths, and his huge palace with semicircular windows, visible far from the highway, like an alien ship descended upon the forests near Moscow.

The snow on the path squeaked appetizingly as Berner stepped on with soft, comfortable boots into the depths of the plot to the fence, where huge, shaggy dogs were running along a tight vein, sliding in a ring. Wire was stretched along the top of the fence, barely noticeable, and neat porcelain insulators gleamed white. From the neighboring forest, only chickadees and woodpeckers could fly to the site. The hidden electronic system and high-voltage current reliably separated the territory from the rest of the gloomy and unfriendly world.

The Caucasian Shepherd Dog was shaggy with pellets of snow and ice, as he threw himself heavily and happily on Berner's chest. She doused him with steam from her hoarse, wheezing breath like a psychotic spirit. He fought with her, dragged her by the fat scruff of her neck, grabbed her wet, hot tongue, and thrust his fist into the white fangs sticking out from the gums. They floundered in the snow, moving along the fence. The ring, sliding along the metal vein, rustled and jingled, and it seemed that bluish sparks were streaming from the wire, from the dog's neck.

In the middle of the site, where a huge, multi-colored flower bed had been laid out in the summer, a few guards were now crowded. They helped the pyrotechnician prepare the fireworks with which Berner wanted to please the guests he expected for dinner.

"How are the fireworks?" he asked cheerfully as he passed.

"They'll be just like the ones in Red Square! Probably even better!" the pyrotechnician joyfully responded, setting up long firecrackers, rockets, and firecrackers on a tripod.

Berner dove into the cramped, warm bunker, where he threw off his sheepskin coat and hat. Through the insulated door he entered the winter garden. It was humid there, stuffy, like in the tropics. It smelled of sweet decay and barely audible aromas of flowers. Teardrop-shaped mercury lamps hung from the ceiling, and under them were transparent tropical plants, tenderly green-feathery palms, curly hairy araucaria, glossy rhododendrons, and pink-purple orchids. Over the branches flew tiny, squealing birds flashing with emerald breasts and white and turquoise heads.

In the middle of the greenhouse was a stone-lined pool. In it were floating, huge, green basins of Victoria leaves. Among these green islands a flower rose on a succulent stem, where it unfolded snow-white, as if carved from butter, like petals with a golden core. In the dark depths, among the roots and underwater stalks, colorful fish flashed like lights.

It was paradise, as Berner called it, the place where he loved to come in rare moments of peace to restore a tired spirit, an exhausted mind, to bring together a torn, scattered world.

He sat down on a small bench under a palm tree, so that the white rosette of the flower was reflected in the dark mirror of the reservoir. He tried to concentrate on the pure contemplation of delicate petals, breathing stamens, and juicy pistils, like a tiny, gilded statue of Buddha.

In this contemplation, he rejected all concrete disturbing thoughts and experiences. He forbade himself to think about the situation with the stock market and the upcoming issue at one of his large factories, to think about the morning meeting with the minister and about the possible destruction of Grozny as a result of an air raid, and to think about his friend Vershatsky, whose fate was a foregone conclusion and whose life was running out with every minute.

He brushed aside thoughts about a new political project concerning a multitude of deputies, journalists, analysts, and pop stars, the purpose of which was to cut off and neutralize unwanted groups of influence that surrounded the president.

He chased away the accidental memory of how, in their youth, he and Vershatsky picked up a young, frivolous woman on the embankment and spent the night with her in the artist's studio. And likewise the second unpleasant memory: in childhood, in their dirty Moscow courtyard, he was surrounded by a group of neighboring hooligans who teased, mocked, and then painfully beat him.

He swept aside all this, just as the fallen leaves are swept aside, just as the wet, fallen snow is removed, and just as thick hair is removed from a woman's face. Gradually, the disturbing thoughts flew away, and in the center of his tranquil consciousness was only one white flower with a golden core. He himself became a flower and was surrounded by snow-white petals. He was a tiny, golden Buddha placed in the center of the universe.

This contemplation did not last long, and he returned to the real world refreshed, ennobled, and solemn.

In the hallway, he shook the clean, rapidly melting snow from his boots. Marina sat with her feet on a comfortable ottoman, dangling a small slipper embroidered with gold. She was still on the phone, exchanging New Year's greetings. Her homely, loose dress concealed her fullness. Her neck was open, only wearing a thin, coral colored necklace, and Berner hugged her and kissed her warm hair as he walked by. He experienced not attraction, but tenderness to her big, beautiful body, in which the fruit, their child, grew and ripened. *Little Berner?* he thought touchingly and chuckled to himself as he hugged his wife.

"Tell them to set the table," Marina said as she covered the receiver with her hand, slightly dodging the kiss.

The servers had already brought dishes into the spacious, white, dazzling, two-story dining room with a huge crystal chandelier. Plates, silverware, bottles, and porcelain dishes with cold snacks were placed on the tablecloth.

Car signals were heard outside. The heavy gate opened, and three limousines drove in one after the other, sparkling with diamond headlights, illuminating the snow with long beams. Guards holding back the barking dogs helped drivers to arrange their cars more conveniently, to fit them alongside snow-covered flower beds, flowerpots, and statues.

The guests entered under the white arches, squinting at the glitter of the chandelier. They looked sideways at the set table, hugged the hosts, and rewarded each other with compliments and congratulations.

These were people close to Berner, his friends at home, and his relationships with them remained unchanged for many years. They were held together by common interests, a common worldview, and common enemies.

Kosharov was one of the president's advisers, a tall, awkward, bony-headed, good-natured, big-lipped mule, overgrown with an unkempt rusty beard. "His face is the hybrid between a broom and a shovel!"

Marina angrily joked, irritated by Komarov's manner of eating quickly and voraciously.

Together with him came Goloshenko, the manager of a television company controlled by Berner. He was small, graceful, with chiseled hands and a white, porcelain face set with violet-blue, maiden eyes. He stifled himself with ladies' perfume, had manicures, and sometimes sang under the piano in a nightingale voice close to a coloratura soprano. Marina could not restrain herself and, wanting to offend him, said, "You should wear something that shows off your cleavage!" But Goloshenko was not offended, but only burst into a pearly laugh.

The third guest was the renowned film director Tambovkin, who was swollen with sickly fat as dark as paraffin. He was round, busty, and constantly smelling of something pungent, reminiscent of alcohol or vinegar. When he got up from his chair and left, it seemed that after him there was always a damp, quick drying sweat spot.

"In my opinion, if you leave him to sleep on the couch, then by morning he will be overgrown with mushrooms," Marina snapped, cautiously sniffing at the place where Tambovkin had just sat.

Their wives came with them, in casual attire, with a limited set of jewelry and not very well-groomed hairstyles.

They trampled and laughed, sitting down at the table amicably. They ate quickly, with a big appetite, and even got a little drunk. They exchanged kind jokes and harmless New Year's gossip.

After dinner, the women retired to the living room, where they started lively conversations about the hostess' pregnancy, about the new design of the living room, about a wonderful new chemical that prevents cloudy water in pools, about an art gallery where the most fashionable artists are exhibited, about resorts in the United Arab Emirates, and about what kind of dress was worn by the eldest daughter of the president, who for some reason has grown very ugly in recent months.

The men went up to the office and sat in deep, comfortable chairs. They rested after a hearty supper.

"Let me repeat myself, friends, but honestly, our Russian intelligentsia is the best in the world!" Goloshenko plunged into the depths of the armchair, looking like a cozy, domestic cat, shining with his violet eyes.

"You know, we love to celebrate the New Year in bohemian company. Well, there are all sorts of pop stars, comedians, fashion writers, and artists. And this time the divine Rostropovich was with us with his goddess of a wife. Well, of course, as usual in this company, there were all sorts of jokes, skits, slight outrages, and ambiguous anecdotes. And Rostropovich fooled around with us, amusing himself like a student! Suddenly, they were carrying a cello! It was carried solemnly, like an icon, in the light of searchlights, and it shined, as if strewn with gems! Rostropovich took the instrument, fell on one knee in front of his wife, and sang Mozart's 'Little Serenade' in one breath. There was something medieval, chivalrous, and Shakespearean in this! We all understood that there was a genius among us! We were all witnessing the magic!"

Goloshenko made a gesture with his small, fragile hand, repeating the movement of the bow, trying to convey to his friends the inspiration he experienced.

"Well, we, as officials, celebrated in such a simple way!" Kosharov laughed, running his thumbs into his tattered, mossy beard. "We drank and ate. We watched a film, and then staged a carnival! I dressed up as Leo Tolstoy, barefoot and in trousers. He walked between tables and preached non-resistance to evil. They say it worked! But the finance minister was the best. Dressed up as a bum in some rags, he walked around with a hat and collected tips! He collected maybe about three million!"

Kosharov burst out laughing, exposing his large horse teeth, with which it seemed he could gnaw through a thick wire.

"Well, if you told a story, I will too!" Director Tambovkin pulled his head into his shoulders, and a double collar of fat formed around his head. "You of course know our administrator of the film club is a rather arrogant and funny gentleman. For some reason, he imagines himself the leader of the democratic intelligentsia. In this regard, he does a lot of stupidity and vulgarity. One of our actors, a mockingbird, brilliantly copies the voice of the president. Immediately after twelve, the administrator is called to the phone. He picks up the receiver and hears the president personally wish him a Happy New Year and thank him for his contribution to the cause of reforms, where he informs him that he is submitting him to the Order of Merit for the Fatherland and is sending him to the Vatican as part of a delegation of clergy led by Patriarch Kirill. The poor administrator went crazy! He returned to the hall and announced the president's call to everyone! Then the prankster that tricked him came back after about a minute and, in the same voice of the president, added, 'Besides, Solomon Yakovlevich, you must convey to the pope my personal message!' Unhappy, Solomon realized that he had been played. He then began to cry like a deceived child! But by the end of the holiday, he got as drunk as a lord!"

Tambovkin laughed hoarsely and coughed. His head swayed softly on the pillow of fat on his neck.

"Now, I'll tell you what, friends!" Berner said solemnly, with a domineering and agitated intonation, as he changed the course of the conversation, turning the frivolous conversation into a different, previously prepared topic. "You know about the conflict that erupted in Grozny, or whatever you might consider it, but this is war. It is unknown how long it will last or how much it will cost. But like any war, it seeks to achieve many goals at once, some of which may directly contradict each other. We will not discuss all the goals that can be achieved, but let's discuss the most important one."

He knew himself for the ability to clothe vague, unclear ideas into convincing forms and images. During their very expression and formulation, he conjured up vague thoughts, almost premonitions, against his will, lined up in a logical chain, and he acquired the refinement of the project that he proposed to others, involving them in his game.

"Last time, we stated that the threats to our well-being have shifted, or rather, they changed places. Thank God we were past the red-brown threat. After they were attacked by tanks, they sent some of them to Lefortovo Prison and simply bought others, for in the Duma they no longer pose a threat to us. They are but only a ragged red scarecrow. We will use this communist-fascist doll in any, including presidential, elections."

The men were agreeing with him and nodding. He was grateful to them, this narrow circle of friends, tested in the bloody autumn of '93, when they were all threatened with violence and mayhem. But they courageously, without flinching, opposed the communist revolt with the might of their finances, television channels, and organizational efforts, which made it possible to nullify the red revenge and the destructive outburst of the rabble. They were pushed back into their holes, smelly doorways, shabby, communal apartments, coffins, and prison cells.

"The threat of a new brown danger now comes from the military, the generals and governors, the Russian Party surrounded by the president, which has violated the agreement, broke parity, and is hatching plans for a fascist putsch directed against you and me. Our business is our worldview, our culture. If this war that they unleashed ends in a quick victory, then the Russian Party, or 'the party of war,' as it should be called, will rise on the wave of chauvinism and cut us down. The dictatorship they are contemplating will be purely fascist. If we are responsible politicians, we must not let them win. Their quick victory in the war is our complete ruin and downfall! Their defeat is our rapid win! We will cut them off and kick them out of politics!"

While he talked he had time to wonder how these scattered thoughts took on an elegant form. They lay down in images, like a gifted saber in a precious sheath, a violin in a Moroccan case, or a pearl Parker pen in a mahogany pencil case. He recalled his morning meeting with the minister and his small, sweaty forehead with drunken, sly eyes. He hated him and his "peasant party," their culture, arrogance, and cruelty.

"We should work out the foundations of the plan today, now, and start implementing it tomorrow. The high command, the people around the president who are responsible for military policy, must be demonized. They must be presented to society as immoral idiots. The troops themselves must be deprived of public support and presented at best as unfortunate youths thrown to the slaughter, and at worst as executioners and punishers. Every wounded and crippled soldier, every coffin should be shown to the people close-up. We will give money to mothers whose children went to war; we will take them to the troops, to the front lines, to hospitals and morgues, and we will film their tears. We must mobilize the deputies close to us for constant anti-war protests in the Duma. We should especially rely on the noble representative of the president for human rights, who is in Grozny at this very moment. His voice must be heard around the world, and the world community must put pressure on our president. We must support the Chechens, showing them as heroic fighters for independence. All this, taken together, will smear the Russian Party with blood, along with the president, and he, having lost the war, in horror will distance himself from those people who started it. He will cast them off and turn to us. We will then cleanse him of this blood, clean his bloody, hawkish face, and return him to the people as white as a dove."

Berner marveled at his own eloquence. He felt that his voice, gestures, breathing, and facial expressions were controlled by some other being than himself. This being was cheerful, energetic, and omniscient. It moved into him and pulled his flesh over itself, where it hid behind his name and appearance. From there, it acted confidently, quickly, and accurately.

The guests, infected with his energy, had gotten accustomed to seeing him as a leader, as a master of original, victorious projects, which he echoed and improvised. Each person offered his own contribution, whether it be TV programs, the invitation of prominent cultural figures, telethons, or subtle intrigues covering the presidential administration, journalists, and the diplomatic corps.

So, they made their plan. Satisfied with themselves, they praised the host and got up from their chairs and returned to the dining room, where coffee and ice cream were waiting for them.

"Well, friends," Berner got up, holding a small glass of cognac, "the New Year has come, and let this year make everyone's wishes come true! Marina and I, God willing, will have an addition to our family." He hugged his wife, and she, like a cat, gently clung to him. "So that we remember our meeting, so that we have a dazzling year, I want to give you a gift, some New Year's fireworks in a heavenly bouquet of flowers!"

The guests put on their fur coats and hats and poured out onto the porch powdered with snow.

Berner gave his signal, and rockets flew into the sky. They fell from the explosion like lightning snakes and carried away a fiery, hissing flash into the dark blue heights of the sky. They exploded with a crackling clap, opened shining tents in the sky, hung precious chandeliers, and scattered colorful bouquets. Fiery merry-go-rounds whirled in the sky, liquid plasma waterfalls poured out, and constellations appeared, brilliant, flickering nebulae alongside spirals, snakes, celestial lamps, and sparkling chandeliers.

The tops of the trees lit up like daylight. The snow was unbearably blinding. Dogs barked and ran. The guests were amazed. The fireworks over the palace were seen far away on the highway, and the drivers took out the limousines to enjoy the magnificent spectacle.

Berner was childishly happy about this festival, the flaming turntables, and fiery water cannons. He admired the flowers that the magic gardener planted in the frosty skies. He prayed wordlessly that his plans and hopes would come true, so that he and Marina have a son, so that the Grozny oil plant would become his property. He also suddenly wished passionately and earnestly that Vershatsky was killed.

The firework exuded its fiery element and went out. Only in the sky, where recently the huge night sun was shining, was a tiny golden spark still swinging, not wanting to fade.

The guests said goodbye, babbled, and exchanged good-bye kisses. They got into their limousines, turned around in the snow, which shined in the long diamond beams of the headlights, and all left the estate.

Marina left him on the porch. She went into the house, tired and content, and must have gone up to the bedroom, decorated with soft blue silks, where she would sit down in front of the pier glass, look at herself, take off her bracelets and rings, and slowly undress. Berner, seized with sudden sadness, looked at the black forest, at the hazy sky, in which fires were boiling and blazing not a minute ago. They burned a huge bonfire in the sky, which was now cooling down, all covered with fog and mist.

In an animal-like manner, sensing the master's anxiety, his chief of security Akhmet quietly approached. He stood nearby in the crumbly snow. Berner watched the golden semicircular imprint of the bright window lying on the snowdrifts.

"When?" he asked, and Vershatsky's beautiful head with a proud nose and forehead rolled and sank among the golden snow with blue shadows.

"Tomorrow," Akhmet answered. Berner heard the snow crunching under his sole, shattered by that brief word.

"Where?" A ring rang out and rustled far off the fence. The chain dog listened attentively to the conversation from a distance.

"On Vavilov Street. He'll be there at 4:00 PM. His mistress lives there. She recently gave birth. He goes there almost every day to visit the child."

Berner imagined his wife Marina sitting in front of the mirror with her removed earrings, bracelet, and platinum watch with a diamond gleam on the table, carefully and sternly examining her belly. Down from her navel is a strip of dark pigment, like a tan, that appears more and more clearly.

"Who will get the job done?" asked Berner, peering over the fence onto the distant highway along which cars rolled by, disappeared, and then their lights reappeared again, as if someone were rolling golden apples through forests and fields.

"Why do you need to know this, Yakov Vladimirovich? Less knowledge, better sleep."

"Who is it?" Berner repeated his question demandingly. His nostrils, breathing in the forest air, caught the faint smell of smoke coming from a distant clearing, where at this hour, some intoxicated youths were burning a New Year's fire.

"A woman. An Olympic champion in the biathlon." Akhmet shrugged his shoulders, and Berner felt the warm smell of tobacco and cologne from under Akhmet's unbuttoned fur coat.

"A woman? They'll catch her!" Berner heard something in the house shatter, as if an icicle broke. He waited for the sound to continue, but there was silence.

"She won't be caught. Tomorrow evening she will be transferred to Chechnya. She signed a contract with the Chechens. She won't be in Moscow for a month."

"A Russian? Will a Russian woman kill Russian soldiers?" The night wind rushed over the tops of the black forest, as if someone invisible turned the page of a huge book and the breath flew into the tops of the fir trees, which then blew away and showered the snow.

"She'll be well paid. It's a sniper recruitment program."

"I want to look at her."

The world that surrounded him was represented by black peaks strewn with snow, golden lights on the distant highway, and an illuminated house, in the depths of which, in front of a mirror, his wife was sitting and felt how their baby was growing inside her. Berner could smell the tobacco and cologne emanating from Akhmet, and a deep longing and anxiety rose in his soul like acrid smoke from some ancient fire, where the remains of bygone civilizations, destroyed palaces and temples, and plundered cities decayed. This poisonous smoke of great losses and unfulfilled expectations seeped through generations and now surfaced with inexplicable longing and madness.

"Tomorrow afternoon in the gym," said Akhmet. "Look at her from afar before she is taken into position."

Akhmet bowed and went to the car. The tight, huge trunk of his Mercedes left the estate, and long amethyst rays could be seen streaming through the trees.

Berner stood on the dusty marble porch of his palace. The sky above him gaped like a huge black hole, in which the night dregs swirled. In his soul, like a volcano, melancholy oozed out through deep rifts and crevices. This poisonous haze stretched from his soul straight into the sky, as if it were a chimney through which the half-cooled smoke of an ancient underground inferno rose, which had swallowed up the biblical paradise, wondrous booths, virgin forests, birds, animals, and naive god-like people.

This feeling of a lost paradise and the inability to find it, to recreate it here on earth, visited him in the form of bouts of melancholy and despair, which were replaced by fury and madness. The only one who survived from that ancient, blooming time was a thick, glossy snake covered with scaly skin. Like a huge tapeworm, it crawled into him, conveniently curling up in his stomach, intestines, and esophagus. It tormented him, strangled him, and prompted him to act, driven from adventure to adventure. He multiplied his wealth, fame, and power, filling his inflamed womb with unquenchable thirst and hunger.

Sometimes it seemed to him that he, Yakov Berner, was the victim and heir of some ancient crime committed by his ancestors, the repository of the sins of his forefathers, fighting against God, or some other forgotten terrible act that was under a universal ban. The violation of this prohibition, the violation of the commandment, turned out to be a terrible punishment and retribution for his ancestors. Now this burden, flowing from generation to generation, crawled like a snake into his soul. It ate his soul up, disfigured it, and condemned it to crime and sacrilege. Now it already creeped into his unborn child, curled up in the blind, red embryo, barely noticeable among the mucus, maternal warmth, and flesh. It could be seen on the female belly by a faint strip of pigment.

The feeling was unbearable. His plans and designs, the pursuit of wealth and power, the desire to continue his family all turned into absurdity. Not coping with this absurdity, he wished himself death.

He gazed at the dark, pointed spruce covered with layers of snow. It seemed to him that the female sniper was hiding in the branches, looking like a fantastic bird with wings and a tail but a girl's head, and she was tracking him down. She clutched her claws into a branch, looking out for him with a night vision device, and through her scope he looked like a long, greenish bubble filled with fluorescent juices. The point will hit the bubble, the tight juices will sprinkle, and the shell will remain on the steps, empty, like cellophane.

"Well then, kill me!" he begged the bird-woman, looking at the dark fir tree.

Berner so intently gazed at the dark trees, so passionately waited to see the flash of a shot, and so fiercely sent his prayers and curses to the top that the air surrounding the branches trembled where snow fell from the spruce paws, and it seemed like a large owl had flown off.

He entered the bedroom with blue satin wallpaper, blue curtains, and a blue lacquered bed with some gold colors in the frame. Next to it was a blue bedside table with a huge, blue dressing table. Marina sat in front of the mirror in a spacious nightgown and combed her heavy, golden hair with a large comb. On the floor were shards of a split Mexican vase. It was her that made the sound, like an icicle falling, that Berner had heard from the porch.

"Is it broken?" he asked, not upset at the sight of the split vase, but glad that there was a reason for his caustic irritation. "You have an amazing ability to break everything!"

"Well, it's fine!" Marina tried to laugh it off. "It seemed tasteless in this room."

The vase, turned into a pile of purple shards, was purchased by Berner at a witchcraft bazaar in Mexico City. Among the skyscrapers were canvas sheds, tents, wooden stalls, and endless shopping galleries where nimble, dark-haired women sold witchcraft concoctions and potions, magic fruits and roots, talismans and amulets, and dried monkey legs and fish heads. The saleswomen immediately bewitched, conjured, spoke, and banished evil diseases. Once a year, this market turned into a feast of witches, where tambourines and maracas rattled, sweet dope was smoked, sorceresses danced, roots were thrown into the fire, and a huge crowd with ancient Indian faces glorified spirits and underground gods, performing their magic.

It was there, in these rows, that Berner bought the purple, glass vase into which the witch saleswoman blew a stream of magic smoke from her red lips.

There were now fragments of the vase, and Berner felt this poisonous, smoky trickle pouring into him.

"Did you find the vase tasteless? Does everything I love seem tasteless and vulgar to you? You are an aristocrat, and am I, in your opinion, a small-town plebeian?"

"I did not mean that at all!" Marina began to take offense, not understanding the nature of his irritation. Her eyes widened, starting to shine in response.

"Do you think I married you in order to hear about how I'm such a commoner?"

"Yes, leave me alone! If you start talking about being a commoner, it means that you are. Take note and get over it!"

"Maybe you've read a lot of anti-Semitic newspapers and magazines? Will you tell me about the Jewish-Masonic conspiracy? About the fact that the Jews destroyed Russia? Maybe you will call me 'rat-faced'? Well, say it! Say it!" he shouted and grimaced and felt hatred for her and attraction at the same time. He saw her beautiful face begin to distort and deteriorate into an unhappy expression that began to appear on her lips, on her trembling chin, and on her crooked eyebrows. "Go on, say it! Say it!"

"Why are you torturing me!?" she exclaimed in tears. "You know how

I feel about this! You know that I shouldn't get upset during pregnancy! Do you want us to have a freak child?"

She was crying, ugly, unhappy, and with swollen lips with dark powder rolling down her cheeks.

This unhappy, defenseless look of hers excited him. He hugged her and felt her heavy breasts under her nightgown. Then he took her by force, while she was fighting back and crying.

16

The soldiers, oppressed and exhausted, dozed off at their posts at the gloomy, half-shattered windows. In the attic, Kudryavtsev pushed the dormer open, laid the machine gun on the asbestos pipe, leaned the grenade launcher against the rafter, and looked at the square. Everything was calm. He was looking for a barely discernible shadow that would flicker in the darkness, followed by steps rustling in the entrance, where Krutoi, out of breath, exhausted, would appear before him. Kudryavtsev would hug him tightly and kiss him on the forehead, on his fluffy eyebrows and on his hot cheeks.

But it was deserted. The city was in total darkness, where danger and evil lurked behind every corner. The two recently destroyed tanks that had a slight dim from the glow finally went out, and the blackness in which the remnants of the brigade were hiding seemed dimensionless, shapeless, and chalky.

In the sky, among the clouds, gaps full of stars began to open like ice holes. The wind blew out evenly, carrying the clouds, and suddenly it became clear. Luscious, frosty stars flared up, close, white, with their ornaments and patterns, and distant, blurred, like clots of nebulae, like indistinguishable shimmering pollen. Endless worlds blossomed over the flat, colorless land, and there to infinity, his yearning gaze flew away.

He chose one star from the many constellations of the sky and stared at it steadily. As if feeling his gaze, the star, filled with brilliance, began to tremble faintly as it increased and swelled like a balloon. A nebula arose around it, as if the star was clothed in an atmosphere, fertilized by his gaze, and began to grow.

The star, like an egg of the universe, became the center of the spiritualized world. This world lived for a second until his eyes blinked, and then it died and disappeared. The star shrank and shrank until it was a weak but sharp point of light in a distant part of the sky.

Then he chose another star. Narrowing his eyes, he struggled to look for a specific star. The new star in his vision was at first white and dry, like a tiny shard of glass, until it suddenly gave off a greenish spark. Then it was blue and then red. It began to shimmer with all the colors of the rainbow. It signaled and called to him. From under the iron roof, from the skylight, he sent a return signal. The star accepted it, responded, and gave off a tiny multicolored flash. His eyes and the star were playing a sort of game with each other.

It seemed that the life he lived did not have an independent meaning, but served a mysterious purpose, beyond understanding.

His passions and aspirations, his suffering and hopes, drew him into a trap set by someone else. This carried him past the enormous truth that is present in the universe. If we were to reject suffering and passion through effort of reason by focusing all attention on breaking out of this trap, then the true structure and meaning of the universe will open. He would then understand why he was sitting under the roof of a cold house with his soldiers dozing off in anticipation of a battle through dirty windows, why a petrified Filya was stretched out on the staircase under a sheet, why shards of wedding glasses were scattered in the burnt old man's apartment, why in the square, under the inaudible radiation of the stars, laid the severed head of the brigade commander and the bones of soldiers picked by scavenger birds, among which you cannot find the burnt body of Krutoi.

He began to look at the sky again. He penetrated through the nearby ornaments of stars, as if looking through a silver filter into distant space. By willpower alone, he overcame it, plunging into the transcendental, mysterious fog. With the black of his pupils, like tiny jet nozzles, he conquered this space, hoping to find its contents and the core contained within it. But instead, a hole began to open into a black abyss. His mind, meeting with it, began to darken, and, fearing madness, he emerged back from the abyss. Frightened and shocked, he sat by the skylight, clutching at the wooden bulkheads.

He did not understand how the world works or how these stars and his scared heart were connected. He imagined his mother joyfully pulling him along the fluffy snow in his little childhood sleigh, flashing her felt boots past the killed old-timer with his bullet stuck somewhere in the man's pelvic bone. How was he, sitting in the attic, connected to the woman named Anna, who was silent somewhere below in a cold apartment, looking, as he was, at the misty stars?

He no longer looked at the stars individually, but all at once. He placed his tireless mind among the constellations, as if pressing his forehead against frozen glass. The images conjured in his consciousness were placed among the stars.

He suddenly remembered a railway neighbor, a long-dead, stooped old man, with a wrinkled, black face, dirty with coal, working on the steam locomotives, the coal-tar pervasive in his pores and folds. This neighbor coughed with illness and looked sadly from behind the fence with yellow squirrels, and only once a year, on the same day, he alone appeared in a ceremonial black uniform with silver braids, in a banded military cap, with many medals on his smoothed jacket.

Kudryavtsev did not think about his neighbor for many years, and now he suddenly remembered him. He placed the old man with his uniform full of medals among the stars.

He then remembered the duck he had once shot while hunting. He crept along the wet field, along the silvery stubble, to the blue spring pool among shallow potholes. He crawled on the sticky ground, dragging a single barrel shotgun behind him, until dark, chiseled heads glided over the arable land. He targeted them, worrying, and panting. He pulled the trigger, and through the smoke and the roar of the shot, noisy ducks flew up. Left in a shallow puddle, splashing the blue water was a duck, golden and emerald.

Now this duck with green fluff and pearly wing feathers occupied half of the sky where it was showered with stars.

He also remembered the old pocket watch left over from his father with a black and silver cover decorated in leaves and flowers attached to a silver chain. When he was sick and suffering, his mother would give him the pocket watch to play with. He would open the lid, and there, on the porcelain dial, was a fragile, dark, and as delicate as an eyelash arrow that ran the whole clock face.

Now this silver watch, huge, with monograms and leaves, hung on a chain directly from the stars, obscuring the constellations.

All this was done without his efforts. It resembled a game that he played with some unknown being, showing now the old man, then the duck, then the pocket watch, taking all of them out of a huge, mysterious chest filled with fogs and flickers.

It suddenly felt to him that it had already happened once before, not with him, but with someone else who had already lived long ago. Now these feelings were given to him so that he could survive, learning from other people's experiences that already happened. He suddenly imagined that in the infinite sky, at the other end of the universe, among other worlds, on an unknown planet, someone like him was sitting at a dormer window, looking at the stars, with the wreckage of cars and tanks laying on a town square in total darkness.

This sensation was real and at the same time fantastic, which made his head spin. In this dizziness, as in a huge, soft funnel, the shimmering veil was about to disappear and the structure of the universe, a single, fulfilling truth, was about to open.

But that didn't happen. The dizziness was over, but the darkness remained, which hid the inaccessible truth. He was to remain in ignorance until the end of his days. Fight, shoot, kill, run away from the faltering infantry lines, cover your killed comrades with a sheet. He would never know why he was given life, into which he was lured out of oblivion, endowed with a body, vision, and thought. Who is the one who takes advantage of his being, hiding in the craters and spirals of galaxies, until the time when he crumbles into dust?

He took the machine gun, stepped over the pipes and beams, and left the attic. He went out onto the stairs. Slowly, feeling for the steps, he went down. The door of the apartment opened, and the woman, pale, stood in the threshold. He discovered her appearance not by hearing her or seeing her, but by her cheeks and forehead, through the radiation of her heat.

"Are you asleep?" she asked.

He suddenly realized that he was expecting her to appear. He went down to her where he was sure that she was waiting for him in her cold apartment.

"Come in," she invited.

She stepped back, letting him pass. Passing, he accidentally touched her and felt her soft shoulder.

She closed the door. He found himself in the hallway near a black mirror filled with icy darkness. He left the damp, stone staircase outside the door, dozing soldiers, the deceased body of Filya, and the entire snow-covered square filled with rubble and craters.

"Come in."

He obeyed her, and each time following her quiet invitations, he took a few more timid steps until he went into the room. He saw the blurry outline of a bed, shelves with books, some kind of glass object flickering on the floor, an extinguished prickly chandelier, a table under the chandelier on a stool or nightstand stood a Christmas tree too pyramidal and thick to be real. Golden strings decorated its artificial branches.

"Sit down."

He obediently sat down at the empty table and put his hands on the tablecloth. His two heavy fingers turned black like stone on the light-colored tablecloth.

"I don't even have hot tea," she apologized. "Everything has been turned off. My flower began to freeze; I had to wrap it in a shawl."

He made out the dark dome of a wrapped flower on the floor. In this freezing flower, which she saved, her loneliness, along with something else, something sad and tender, was revealed hovering in the twilight of the room above the tree and above the bed covered with a bedspread.

"Now I will bring a candle..."

She closed the curtains. It became completely dark. Unseen, she walked past him, smelling fresh and again touched him with something warm and soft. Her light footsteps were heard in the kitchen. The slightest, most subtle light leaked in and began to get closer and stronger.

She appeared in the doorway carrying a candle and blocking the flame with a large, pink-transparent palm. Her face with the blue gleam of her eyes was illuminated by the golden candlelight, showing her parted hair. He was amazed at her transformation, by her strength, beauty, the white glow of her open neck, and the bulge of her breathing lips.

She brought over the candle, put it on the table, and removed her hand from the handle. Squinting his eyes from the sudden light, he looked at the yellowish, translucent cinder, at the restlessly vibrating tongue of fire, swelling with a liquid drop.

"It's light now," she said, and sat down opposite to him. Like him, she put her palms on the table. Kudryavtsev compared her large, soft, white hands with his black, dirty hands, hewn about with armor, stone, and a trigger. He did not remove them but seemed to be numb. He waited for her next orders.

"I was waiting for the New Year. I even decorated the tree..." He looked at the tree, entwined with a golden cobweb. Among the various ornaments, he saw a glass fish, faintly trembling on a thread, reflecting the light from the candle.

"Do you live here alone?" he asked, peering into the trembling glass fish.

"Yes," she said.

"The Christmas tree is beautiful." He was in a daze. Her presence, with the sight of her motionless hands, her brushed blonde hair, and her round, breathing neck hypnotized him and immersed him in contemplation. His frozen pupils gazed at the flame without blinking. The candle emitted a soft ball of light and many thin rays that went to the farthest corners of the room. It seemed like they were slowly rising, surrounded by fluffy, radiant light, and were then carried away by a high wind.

Like in a sunny autumn stream, a fluffy weightless seed hovered above the table, surrounded by a glass glow. It rolled and floated over the weeds, over the old fence, over the ridge of the dilapidated roof. In the very center of the flying seed, in the dark core, they sat. There was a candle between them. Their hands, without touching, rested on the cloth of the table.

She reached her hand across the table and covered his palm. His rough, black, bruised, and callused fingers disappeared under her white palm. He was afraid to move because he didn't want everything to disappear, for the candle to go out. As the wax stump swelled, the glass fish flickered on the tree, and her warm, large palm pressed his rough, numb fingers to the tablecloth.

She got up and walked around the table. She put out the candle and stood in front of him. She grabbed his head and hugged him. And he, sitting, hugged her. He immersed his face, closed his eyes, and breathed in her warmth and softness. Through closed eyelids he saw her breasts leaning heavily toward him, her rounded belly responding to his kisses, her smooth, rounded thighs, over which his palms slid. Kissing her, panting, hiding in her embrace, fleeing from the recent horror, from the premonition of death, he plunged into her, like into a dark, impenetrable forest, without a path, without any other living creature, which was impossible for his pursuers to invade, as in a dark river without banks, without lights, and without boats, which could pick him up and carry him away from this square, from the machine gun left in the hallway and the frozen peacoat standing stuck in the snow, through the dark mighty water, to where no one could find him.

"Wait," she said.

She moved away from him. Opening his eyes, he saw how with a strong wave she turned, pulled back the bedspread, and revealed the white sheets of the bed.

"Come here!"

He hugged her and did not let go. He tried to disappear into her, to become her, to flow into her, to transfer his existence to her. She seemed huge to him, larger than the earth and the sky, obscuring him from all sides, making him invisible, taking back his life, which she had once endowed him with.

It was like they were sailing on a boat, waves moving them from side to side, up and down, up and down, moving using red blades of oars. The wake of the water created a tight, elastic slap throwing the boat forward. Transparent, bluish dust blew off the wave from the wind...

He felt like he was skiing, running over the hills, up and then down, up and then down, red skis rushing, piercing the track. It was a long, sweet flight. It went from hot light to a cool, blue shadow, breaking the fragile elderberry branch as he rushed by...

He was swinging from heaven to earth, up and then down, up and then down. There was a cloud with a dark bird, then a lake in the glitter of water. As he pushed the swing forward, he could feel his weightlessness with such pleasure and happiness...

There was a small dot under his closed eyelids, a tiny spark in the distance. It got closer and closer, when suddenly it burst into the dark room. Bursting through like lightning, it exploded in his head, in the mirror, and in the chandelier. It illuminated the whole world, down to the darkest depths. Then it went out, but not before showering the room, the Christmas tree in the corner, and the glass fish hanging on the branch with a flickering dust.

They lay open in the dark, not feeling the cold air, as if they were surrounded by a warm cocoon. She bent over him and stroked his head with her palms, as if leveling, smoothing, and eliminating all the scratches, bumps, and growths, all the junk that had eaten into his rough skin. He put her soft, tight palms on him, and he felt hot waves roll off and penetrate him, where they softened tight, tense muscles, twisted knots, and numb joints. She removed her palms, and he saw them glow in the dark.

Carefully and gently, she ran her finger across his forehead, covered his eyes, ran along the bridge of his nose, and then left soft rings and curls of invisible patterns and designs on his shoulders, chest, and belly. She removed the thinnest, dark layers of soot from him, as a careful restorer removes layers of dull dust from an icon, revealing a luscious, pristine image. From her touch, he became younger. He transformed into a thin, slender, youthful teenager. From his closed eyes, he could envision forgotten wonderful memories from his childhood of walking through the forests, rivers, and meadows.

"How do you feel?" she asked.

"Good," Kudryavtsev couldn't tell if he had answered her out loud or in his thoughts.

Her hand was in front of his eyes. He envisioned a winter forest glade surrounded by snowy fir trees. A tall blue jay flew over the sharp edges of the forest and into the sun above the green, icy blue trees. He chased her through the snow, not wanting to be left behind as he left behind footprints in the illuminated glade.

She placed her hand on his shoulder, and he walked down the frosty street. The solar brick wall had a cast-iron water column. A woman was holding a bucket. A thick jet of water poured out of the tap where it hit the ground and sparkled. It scattered, splashed, and froze into precious glassy ice.

Then her hand was on his chest. He could see a snowy, clear field. There were silvery roads in the field. The wind blew the snow into drifts of long, foggy whirlwinds. On these roads, among transparent blizzards, a distant traveler was moving.

"Still good?" she asked.

"Still good," he said wordlessly. He fell asleep and slept for exactly a second, but in that second, he flew around the earth and woke up. She propped herself up on one elbow and stared at him in the darkness.

"We must go," he said.

He put on his clothes, put on his tough armor smelling of iron and sweat, and put on his dirty worn-out shoes. He reached out to her, but did not touch her, only the air around her. He stepped into the hallway, picked up his machine gun and went out, slightly closing the door.

He felt cheerful and fresh. He climbed into the attic where he nestled at the dormer. He groped in the darkness for the grenade launcher leaning against the wall. The stars were still sparkling. He gazed at their multicolored beads, at the colored dew, at the tiny spirals, at the silver curls and nebulae. The closed sky did not seem cruel with its ice bars. It did not contain a merciless secret. It resembled a night festive garden with lamps, flickering in the foliage, illuminating fruits and flowers. From this garden a disembodied creature fluttered, clouding the sky with its transparent wings. It then disappeared, leaving an enduring mark.

17

In the morning twilight, feeling icy streams pouring on him through the iron roof, Kudryavtsev went to check on the other soldiers.

Nozdra sat on the chair by the window, hunched over, with his head dropped to his knees. Kudryavtsev was worried that he went numb and froze and lost the ability to move.

"Are you sleeping?" he asked as he touched his shoulder.

"No." Nozdra slowly raised his thin, gray face, with sunken eyes. There was longing in those eyes. "I prayed for him. I thought it would help," said Nozdra, "but he didn't come back..."

"Come on, get up and stretch out."

He shook Nozdra lightly. He then took him by the shoulders from behind. He began to stretch and warm up the stiff muscles and push some living heat into them.

"Let's be strong!" Kudryavtsev slightly pushed him on the shoulder, encouraging him with this fraternal strike. Nozdra straightened up, fidgeted in his chair, and lifted his weapon. He began to peer into the gray haze that hovered over the square.

In the other entrance by the split window sat Tarakan and Chizh, who looked disheveled like winter sparrows. On the filthy windowsill lay Chizh's notebook and the stub of a pencil. God only knows what drawings have accumulated in this notebook overnight, drawn by Chizh's frozen and marred hand.

"What's the situation?" Kudryavtsev asked in a cheerful, commanding voice, while he gradually peered into the faded faces of the soldiers, on which shone the shadows of anxiety and suffering.

"I was waiting at night. Waiting for him to return," Chizh said quietly.

"At some point in the morning, I suddenly heard scratching and breathing! I thought, Krutoi! I looked out, and there was a dog!"

"We had a neighbor that died," said Tarakan. "His mother was so distraught, we thought she would die of grief. But the next morning after the funeral, a dog showed up at her house. She let the dog into the house, and they still live together. She said that it was the soul of Fedka, her son, who moved into the dog."

"When will the troops come?" asked Chizh, looking sad at Kudryavtsev, as if the commander was to blame for the absence of troops.

Kudryavtsev felt guilty. He gathered them all in this house. He inspired them, encouraged them, and put weapons in their hands. Now two of them are dead. One shot now lay in the stairwell. Another turned to ash remained in his tank. Who will be the third, the fourth? Isn't sitting in the house a disastrous call and a bad mistake? Isn't it his miscalculation that will be the death of them?

Tarakan looked with tired, understanding eyes. "Oh, come on," he said to Chizh, "the troops will arrive. Are we not troops? I'll go, Comrade Captain. I'll place a banner at the entrance. These bitches will definitely attempt to break through."

He got up and went upstairs to the attic, where there were grenades and a bundle of thin wire. Kudryavtsev looked at him gratefully. The soldier helped him in a moment of despondency. He handed over the crumbs of strength he had saved amid the dangers that killed Krutoi. Kudryavtsev watched the worn-out soles of the soldier slap down on the steps and thought of the butterflies in his glazed collection.

Submachine guns struck from the square with a dense, jagged rumble, from different distances, at different angles. Kudryavtsev jumped away from the window, dragging Chizh along with him. He heard glass crumbling all over the facade and bullets hammering into the brick. The submachine guns fired at random, without intention, and prevented anyone from looking out of the windows.

"They're running along the house! To the entrance!" Tarakan shouted from above, announcing from the staircase a simple request. "Don't let that bitch get to the entrance!"

Chechens crept up to the house at dusk. Once in the dead zone, they ran along the facade, pressing against the wall. They were covered by dense fire. Kudryavtsev felt the spearhead of the attack aimed at the entrance. He put the barrel of his gun through the railing and aimed it down toward the opening of the door.

"Chizh, step back!" he managed to shout, but failed to discharge the machine gun. Punching through a dilapidated tree, a grenade flew into the entrance, hit the apartment door, plunged inside, and from there it exploded, creating chips, molecules of burnt air, and a wave of elastic heat that pervaded everywhere.

Kudryavtsev dropped his gun, which was slipping through the railing. Stunned, through tears and fumes, he saw a Chechen burst into the entrance. Ismail's face, with his inky, red-hot eyes, carrying a grenade launcher, was looking for Kudryavtsev.

"Chizh, go upstairs!" Kudryavtsev shouted weakly, trying to push sulfuric fumes, sour blood, and soft stuffy dust out of his mouth. Unarmed, having lost his gun, he backed up to the stairs, pushing Chizh back to where Tarakan's gun was firing.

There were three of them on the upper platform.

The Chechens were eager to rush in through the entrance. They fired blindly, filling the staircase with bullets that ricocheted, clanked, and sparked against the railing supports.

Through the railing in the narrow gap, Kudryavtsev saw Ismail aim a grenade launcher, pull the trigger, and release a ball of fire. The explosion was like a huge, blunt log that struck his forehead and threw him against the wall on the back of his head. He sank into the stone, into its darkness. Gradually the darkness disappeared and turned into a transparent ice. Kudryavtsev sat there motionless, without breath, frozen into the ice. He sat on the floor sealed in the block of ice that was in his ears and eyes and freezing his tongue to his lips.

Kudryavtsev saw through the transparent thickness of ice that Ismail was running silently onto the platform with bloodshot eyes.

He slowly turned to aim his machine gun at Kudryavtsev, where his triumphant, frenzied eyes groped through the ice block and looked into Kudryavtsev's eyes, which were bloodshot and looked like crushed cranberries. The barrel turned toward him, and he could see a tiny recess of the muzzle that was ready to open fire.

Then the white flame was blocked by Tarakan, who extinguished it with his dirty clothes and arms outstretched. He rushed at the Chechen, grabbing and leaning on the gun, and Kudryavtsev, from within his glacier, saw how Tarakan's ribs filled with fire, inflated by bullets shot into his body.

Leaning on the end of the gun, the soldier looked like a quivering butterfly. The Chechen with all his strength pushed through the dying soldier, trying to get to Kudryavtsev.

In Kudryavtsev's flattened, paralyzed body, among the icy convulsions, a surviving joint trembled. Then a thin muscle stretched. From this trembling muscle, sick waves of life rolled through his body.

He sprung up, tore apart the ice block, showered the ground with its transparent fragments, and broke free. He slammed the Chechen with all his revived, hatful rage and knocked him to the ground. They rolled down the steps, as Kudryavtsev pulled black handfuls of hair from his shaggy mane. His gnarled, iron fingers reached the sweaty body of the Chechen, penetrated under his ribs, and pried off cartilage and veins. He pulled them out, feeling a piece of torn flesh in his palm.

The Chechen howled and then twisted and gnawed his teeth into Kudryavtsev's shoulder, biting through his deltoid muscle. Kudryavtsev, feeling no pain, pushed his long finger like a bent nail through the Chechen's lips and tore his mouth apart.

The Chechen opened his bloody, torn mouth, flailing his wet tongue. Kudryavtsev grabbed a bunch of his black hair, took hold of his shaggy head from the steps, and then struck it against the stairs with force. He did it again and again. He beat, grunted, and squelched, while hearing the nape of the Chechen's bone split as the skull shattered into fragments and softened. A black liquid poured through the cracks.

He kept smashing the head into the steps until it became flat in the back and leaked on the steps, like a broken pumpkin.

He threw away the Chechen. Panting, on all fours, like a wounded dog, he crawled onto the landing where Tarakan lay.

The soldier's eyes were open and shiny. It was the metallic sheen of death that overtook him.

"Tarakan!" called Kudryavtsev, grabbing his wrist. "Tarakan!" He felt his wrists, trying to catch a pulse as weak as the ticking of a clock. "Tarakan!" Kudryavtsev howled and coughed up blood and red saliva.

Chizh threw grenades down the stairs one after the other. They exploded and compressed the air. Chechens rolled out of the entrance, and ran along the wall, burying themselves in the dead zone. Nozdra, from above through the window, drove them away by firing long bursts.

Kudryavtsev sat on the steps, half naked. Anna was holding a bowl with water. She used a clean rag and dipped it in the water. She then touched the icy pulp to his burns, scratches, and long lacerations and to the swollen, red and blue bite mark on his shoulder. He washed his eyes that were stuck together with blood, his nostrils clogged with debris, and his mouth pitted with poisonous saliva.

They covered Tarakan with a sheet, with his shoes sticking out from under the fabric, and laid him on the landing. Filya lay on the floor below. Kudryavtsev felt the touch of the cold, freezing pain of the rag and could not get rid of his hiccups. It was the remnant of something terrible that had awakened within him during the battle, some sort of shaggy, red animal that won the fight against another black, shaggy animal that was now lying on the stairwell.

He got up. The woman helped him put on a shirt and a woolen jacket over his shoulder. She fastened the buttons, looking on with large, tearful eyes. He walked around her and went down a few steps, where Ismail lay long and listlessly, exuding a dark slurry from his now disfigured head. Kudryavtsev grabbed the Chechen by the hair like a sack of potatoes and dragged him down past the debris that littered the building from the explosion and past the blown-up apartments. Ismail's feet thudded down the steps, and something inside him was gurgling, like in a half-empty canister.

Kudryavtsev brought the corpse to the front door. He threw it among the splintered wood, spent cartridges, and bits of dirty rags.

He picked up his gun and, moving his legs as if inserting them into stone holes, went up the stairs. He passed Filya with his white nose sticking out from under the sheet. He walked past Tarakan, whose dirty shoe was tucked up and peeking out from under the white cloth. He approached the window, behind which, in the light of a new day, lay the square with the remains of the exterminated brigade. The city was foggy with roofs, pipes, and box-like buildings. He looked at the city where he had lived for a day, this city that ate the juiciest chunk of his life, chewed it, and spit out death and abomination. He cursed this city.

He wanted a force to arise, a vengeful lightning or a red incinerating fire that would be thrown down from the sky and destroy all the houses, bridges, buildings, and products of human labor in the city. Along with them, he wished death upon all the people, young and old, smart and foolish, noble and mean, all the damned people inhabiting this city. He cursed his tongue, facial features, graves, utensils, sounds of his songs, books, prayers, and commands. He wished that his leaders would die and never be resurrected, that the wombs of their women be sealed and burned, and that the seed of their men be baked and dried.

He cursed this city and demanded retribution. He invested all the remaining reserves of his life into his curses and was ready to lose his life, if only his curses were heard and retribution fell on the city. In his passionate curse of this city there was something ancient, inevitable, and destructive for himself.

He heard a distant explosion. The quake first swept underground, along the foundations of buildings and through the buried iron pipes. Then, with a lag, it traveled through the foggy, frosty air. Both tremors met in the eardrum of his sensitive ear, and he defined the impact as the explosion of a heavy, high-explosive shell burrowing into the ground, which then created a huge hole into some asphalt and stone.

Following the first explosion, and slightly displaced in space, followed a second explosion with the same deep and long tremor. The vibration of the explosion rolled through the city, rocking the houses. It reached his eardrums, and Kudryavtsev realized that his prayer was heard. The curse had fallen on the city. Heavy bombs from long-range howitzers were now falling on him from the sky, and a cloud of smoke would soon appear.

Two clouds, lazy and lethargic, began to rise above the distant rooftops. They didn't seem like smoke, but steam. They looked like cows grazing peacefully. But then the animals had other heads, and they began to resemble multi-headed, slow monsters that rose above the city buildings.

"Have they arrived?!" Chizh looked on with excitement from the distant explosions and then looked at Kudryavtsev's face, demanding confirmation. "Did the troops arrive?"

Kudryavtsev did not answer. He couldn't answer. His throat, with a trembling Adam's apple, gurgled with a scream. The breath that had just pushed out the words of curses now stopped, unable to force its way out to shout out words of gratitude, not to the troops who launched the offensive, not to the batteries of tracked howitzers that threw shells at the city, but to the sky, to the formidable and just power who hovered above him, who heard his prayers and began to destroy the city.

The explosions rolled around the city, coming in from different sides, as if a giant stepped over roofs with thick legs that broke, crushed, and tore out roots. Already in several places among the pale, vaporous clouds, black smoke was growing. It was as if a huge, unkempt crow sat on the city as on a nest, spreading its wings over it.

"Is that our guys?" Chizh barked to Kudryavtsev and, without waiting for an answer, looked at the city with joyfully shining eyes. "Hammer this godforsaken place to the ground!"

Kudryavtsev peered sharply into the panorama of the tormented city.

By the roar of the bombs, by the frequency and accuracy of the smoky clouds, he determined the direction of the blows. There were two of them. One was aimed at the center, in the wake of the lost brigade. Another bypassed in an arc, through the outskirts, perhaps by rail with access to the station square.

Clairvoyance returned to him.

He saw how the chains of special forces, hiding behind the corners of houses, diving into the gateways, under the cover of hammering machines, suppressed the cells of snipers. Tanks with direct fire blew up houses, showered facades, and drove blunt explosions into porches and windows. Spetsnaz ran into the gaps, falling on hot bricks, covering the advance of the tanks. A steel colossus, crushing rubble with their tracks, entered the ruins, unfolded a heavy cannon, and took aim at a close sniper.

The explosions fell into the city. Fire and smoke were swept up in the tiled gardens. They fell into high boxes, and then a smoky ear grew on the wall, spread out, and turned into a languid, dirty mane.

Kudryavtsev rejoiced at every explosion, breathing violently, trying to catch and deeply breathe in the stench of burning, TNT, and poisonous combustion gases. A furious creature, summoned from the sky by his call, tossed and turned over the city.

Tanks were driving through and aiming at firing points to cut corridors for the infantry. Self-propelled howitzers Hyacinths and jet Hurricanes fired, hitting the squares, cutting off escape routes for the Chechens, and destroying reserves.

Kudryavtsev saw an explosion on the square in the white snow. A bloody eye blinked under black eyelashes. The blow rained down on the glass, and cold, hard air rushed into his face. The smoke from the explosion carried away to the station and to the side, where the gardens and houses were crowded, cracked, and exploded, as the tiles flew up into the air. Kudryavtsev shouted joyfully, thinking that perhaps the shell hit the house where the platoon commander was killed. Now in place of the garden, barbecue, wooden table, bricks, and multi-colored curtains of the house, a black hole gaped.

"That's a hit! Amazing job!"

The third shell fell among the remains of the brigade. Together with fire and smoke, pieces of metal, wheels, and shafts flew upward. The roar rolled metal among the wrecked vehicles and the warped tanks. A gray, steel dust hung over the square.

Another blow overturned the tanker, tore apart the cistern, and set fire to the remnants of the fuel, blazing yellow and bright.

The shells fell on the brigade, killing it a second time. They tore off the turrets from the tanks, threw up twisted cannons, tossed about the tanks, and overturned the trucks, as if looking for something among the wreckage, something they had dropped. They were looking for it with every explosion and rumble.

Kudryavtsev watched as the brigade was killed again before his eyes. Among the iron dust, metal splashes, and soot of burning tires, the disturbed souls of the dead were worn. The yellow mustard smoke was the smoke of re-burnt bones.

Chizh and Nozdra listened to the roar of explosions. Anna lurked, listening. The dead, Filya and Tarakan, covered by sheets, were listening. The head of the brigade commander was listening under the peacoat. Only Krutoi, having come under attack for a second time, found himself among the burnt tanks as a swirling cloud of incandescent ash.

"Excellent, guys! Another hit!" shouted Kudryavtsev, standing tall at the window, exposing himself to blows of rushing air. "I'm going to start an attack as a distraction."

The shell fell not far from the truck where the set of Bumblebees lay, the tarp over the body of the truck shook, and a thought flashed in their minds that in case the three-story house was hit, they would be swept away by a vacuum explosion and not survive.

"Attack them, men, without regret! Start a diversion!"

The heavy shell of the Hurricane landed on the edge of the square, where it plunged into the ground and exploded with a metallic howl. It tore apart the gas pipe hidden in the depths, and from the black gap a red flame hit, whistled, and fluttered. It became joyfully excited, as if the wind blew the red cloth and it trembled and tore.

"That's another hit!" Kudryavtsev repeated like a madman. He looked at the roaring flame that ripped from the ground by his will, the eternal fire that flew from the center of the earth, lit in honor of the fallen brigade.

The shells shook up the square like a heavy, damp featherbed and blew it away. They exploded on the outskirts, setting fire to warehouses and oil storage facilities. The city was on fire from all sides. It seemed that slow giants were rising from their couches and stretching out their hands to each other, dressed in puffy sleeves.

Militants ran across the square, disturbed by the shelling and knocked out of cover. They rolled out in small groups, then froze and rushed forward fast, cautious and nimble, like mice leaving their nests. They clung to the facades, disappearing into the buildings near the station. There was no panic in their strides, but the meaningful movement of combat units leaving one line and occupying a new one.

"Chizh, it's our turn!" Kudryavtsev seemed to emerge from under a muddy, hot shower. Instantly calming down, he watched the rush of the Chechens. "We cut them off from the station! We do not allow them to gain a foothold on the tracks! From there, the Marines will arrive!"

He grabbed the grenade launcher under his arm and picked up the machine gun with his free hand. Hitting the railing, he moved into the smashed, wide-open apartment and shouted to the whole house, giving the command to Nozdra, who was sitting in the attic, "We're cutting these bitches off from the station!"

He threw the loaded grenade launcher onto a pile of burnt rags. He poked the machine gun through the window, where a red tablecloth was wrapped on a stick. He rested the machine-gun bipod on the windowsill, which was crunchy from the splinters. He looked through the sight at the square, at the crimson gas torch, and at the snow pitted with funnels.

The second wave of Chechens rolled along the square. Their grayish faces, dark caps, and submachine guns pressed to their chests were visible. The commander waved his hand to determine the direction. Obeying his command, the insurgents changed their trajectory and rushed directly to the station. Kudryavtsev's machine gun hit their pulsing chain through the foggy air. A round flame bubbled from the gun, greedily chewing on the ammunition, pushing out the empty cartridges in a ringing arc. In the square, snow ripped open by bullets began to smoke. The Chechens stopped as if a headwind had blown in their faces. They turned and fell back, clumsily overtaking each other. They were followed by three points from Kudryavtsev's, Chizh's, and Nozdra's machine guns. The militants jumped, wagged, and disappeared into the gateways from where they had just jumped out.

"Not sweet enough? Here's some shashlik for you! Here's some ribs!" Kudryavtsev fired at random into a cluster of houses where the Chechens took refuge.

It became quiet, and in this near silence the distant explosions continued to whine, the flag flew outside the window, and the gas flame roared from the underground hole with a jet whistle.

Several bursts hit the wall of the house, showered with dry hits and the juicy clink of broken glass. Kudryavtsev pulled away, hiding behind the ledge, sensitive and keen-sighted with the impatience of a successful hunter, forgetting about his wounds and abrasions. Through thought, persuasion, and deceitful decoy, he was calling his game out of hiding.

Again, the Chechens ran in short rolls toward the station under the cover of indiscriminate lines. They threw themselves into the snow. They jumped up and continued to make their way to the station. Kudryavtsev took out their round, falling lumps with a machine gun. He felt them through the roar and flying glimpses as he received continuous painful shocks to his shoulder.

Two were lying in the snow and did not get to their feet. The other two from the running chain returned to the fallen ones, trying to help them up. Kudryavtsev caught them in his sights with a prancing eye and circled his sights on the group, sending long, sparkling bursts. Kudryavtsev knew he hit his target. Their muscles and tissues were torn apart by his bullets, and they bled, shaking from unbearable pain. He was bound to them by this pain, by the fiery fibers of the lines and by his hatred.

"Taste my shish kebab! For the friendship of nations!"

It was the fight for which he stayed in the house, for why he gathered a handful of fighters and took up the defensive as he followed orders from command. The battle was preceded by sheer fear, the defeat of the brigade, and the loss of reason and will.

It was a battle that Filya, Tarakan, and Krutoi did not live to see, nor did the brigade commander, whose head with sleepy eyes full of ice was covered with a dirty peacoat, listening to Kudryavtsev's machine gun. It was a battle that followed the destruction of the brigade, whose tanks and charred armored cars littered the square and whose souls were silently groaning over the battlefield.

Kudryavtsev heard their voices and saw their thousand-eyed crowd. He sent thundering bursts and then stopped firing for a second when the red flag fluttered in the wind, covering the window.

"They will not pass, Comrade Brigade Commander!" he cried, pressing onto the jolting stock. "Men, they will not fucking pass!"

It was quiet when he stopped shooting. He watched through the evaporation of snow as the motionless worms of the Chechens he had shot darkened.

He heard a sound like the clanging of metal nails and nuts in a tin can. This was the sound of a BMP going at full speed.

The combat vehicle slid into an area that looked like sharpened sails, sliding on runners in a long arc. It turned, directing the thin rod of its weapon toward the house. On the armor, a blinding light flickered and sparkled, like a short circuit. Bullets of a large-caliber machine gun hit the wall of the house at different heights, and one pierced in the area of the window, releasing a cloud of brick dust in the air.

"Have you decided to play? Let's play!" Kudryavtsev grabbed a grenade launcher, as if grabbing a club with both hands, preparing to crush the advancing enemies. "We are well trained!"

He could not distinguish the tail number and did not know whether it was a brigade vehicle captured by the Chechens, or their own that was in service. He rested the pipe against the windowsill, aiming at the vehicle. He addressed the flag outside the window as if it were a living creature, persuading them not to sway or obscure the sight. He silently persuaded Chizh and Nozdra not to show themselves from their hiding places. He persuaded himself not to rush, nor breathe, but to slowly put pressure on the trigger. He made a shot, splitting the instant into tiny particles of time. He managed to aim it and fire. The grenade flew through the air and hit under the bottom of a car, making a blaze and short explosion with a small, blinding sun. At the same time, a flash from the tip of the enemy cannon, followed by a rumble in the apartment, plunged Kudryavtsev into blindness.

18

Berner started his morning at his corporation by walking through a stately granite portal. Guards in uniforms with silver security patches rose to meet him and gave a salute. The clerk, with a bow, smiled softly as he pressed the elevator button. A high-speed, illuminated capsule, smelling of delicious varnishes and splashing with light music lifted him to the top of the building. Walking briskly through the waiting room, he nodded lightly and gracefully to his secretary. Berner then found himself in his office, in his cockpit, as he called it, which was a glass prism cut like a crystal into the stone top of an old-fashioned Stalinist house.

From this glazed crystal cockpit, like a pilot, he controlled the flight of the corporation, inscribing it into the mighty turbulent currents of the world. Behind the thick, transparent walls, a huge panorama of Moscow curled into pink morning steam, shaggy chimneys, countless mica roofs, golden churches, dim bridges over the frozen loop of the river, and squares with a shimmering carousel of cars in long lines, like incisions on the road along radial avenues, shrouded in bluish smoke and blurry plasma.

He sat down snugly and comfortably in his chair. It creaked obediently, responding to the pressure of the back of his head and spine. Copper watch cases with enameled dials were cut into the oak panel of the wall. The clock showed the time in different time zones around the world, which made it easier to track the circulation of financial ebbs and flows from the nighttime half of the planet to the daytime. On the wall, screens shone like moonlight, providing an entrance to the Internet, to databases describing the activities of the corporation, to the world broadcasting network, and to the Ostankino studio, which he controlled.

In a smart control room with many keys and buttons, telephones connected him with the Kremlin and with government services in Moscow and the provinces.

The cockpit in which he was housed was comfortable, equipped with high-speed systems that guided the corporation's colossus in the foggy sky filled with danger and threats. As a loaded Boeing changes altitude and speed and turns, so the corporation responded to the slightest manifestation of his will.

Every morning he began with a series of short telephone conversations with the most important and influential people. These conversations did not contain anything significant. They were devoid of any business context. They were merely check-ins, a reminder that he still watches over them. He appears and interacts in the sphere of political and business interests. This is how the birds in the forest call out and whistle, how the wolves howl in the steppes. They send signals from radio beacons installed along the edges of the mined field.

He called two deputy prime ministers and wished them Happy New Year. To one of them he even recounted his horoscope in a funny way, recommending the most favorable days for a trip to America to meet with the director of the International Monetary Fund. To the other, he shared a short, funny anecdote about Jews with two sawed-off shotguns, the same one that he had heard at the New Year's Eve party.

He called the country's chief customs officer and mentioned not a word about the large batch of German limousines, property of the corporation, which was supposed to cross the border without inspection and reach Moscow. He only reminded the customs officer of the next day's tennis rematch, which he hoped to win after his recent defeat and beat such a brilliant tennis player as the customs officer.

He phoned the chairman of the Security Council, a hostile man close to a group of "Sovereigns" from which a threat came. In his New Year's greeting, Berner mentioned how highly the American ambassador spoke of the chairman at a recent reception at Spas House.

Then he hesitated, smoothed the hair at his temples, straightened his wide silk tie, and called the president's daughter.

Her sweet, simple voice with a mocking tint excited him. Talking to her, he exchanged some banter, and he experienced a slight dizzying excitement. He apologized for not calling on New Year's Eve, since he knew that the family was celebrating in a close-knit circle and decided not to disturb them. He said that they discussed the current political situation and the problems of the election campaign with his banker friends. He said that everyone, unanimously, decided that she, the president's daughter, who knows her father's psychology better than others, should become the brand of her father's new campaign, creating a new, unexpected, and attractive image of the president for the people. He also said that on the TV channel he controlled, a special group had been created to prepare videos where the president appears as a kind family man, a lover of Russian nature, a physically strong person, an athlete, a fisherman, and a hunter. In the end, he praised the president's New Year's message and saw that he had not forgotten his promises and had already phoned the Barclay Bank branch in Paris.

The conversation turned out to be extremely successful. It was light-hearted and ended with an agreement to meet the next day at the theater for the premiere with Mark Zakharov.

Berner leaned back in his chair, performing his morning ritual of phone calls. He notified his friends and enemies that he took his place in the glazed cockpit within the corporation, controlled by his will and mind, breathing softly and powerfully with engines, as it continued to fly horizontally. He was already ready to invite in deputies and listen to their reports, but he suddenly felt a painful desire to hear the voice of his friend, Vershatsky, who would be killed that day. He wanted to remember a phrase so that he could later remember it after his friend's death. He could not explain this painful need and decided that it was a modified desire to receive a souvenir from a departing friend. Instead of something physical, he just wanted to hear his voice. Instead of a conversation, he just wanted to hear a phrase with intonation.

He dialed the number.

"Yasha, my friend," he heard Vershatsky's voice. This voice was usually ironic and caustic but now seemed moved and agitated. "I was just about to call you. Must be some kind of telepathy!"

"No doubt," Berner said. "We can sense each other from any distance, like twins!"

"It seemed on New Year's Eve that I had somehow upset you. I could not understand what it was, so I decided to call."

"You have such a kind heart, Lyovushka! You were, as always, flawless. Like an English aristocrat!"

"We must not upset each other. There are so few of us true friends! It will also likely dwindle. I want us to remain friends under any circumstances!"

"I could not agree more! This year promises to be difficult, and in many respects, decisive. I want to be seen together more often. Let our enemies know that we are indomitable and therefore invincible!" Berner said as he listened attentively to Vershatsky's words and searched for everything among them that would be remembered forever.

"And I, oddly enough, expect a lot from this year!" continued Vershatsky. "I have a good feeling. Yesterday we had a fortune teller at home and they foretold much success this year! Would you like to hear a fortune?"

"Nah! I'd rather use the forecasts of my think tank," Berner laughed. "I will then put this forecast, if it is favorable, in the mouth of my television astrologer and reporter!"

"Listen, Yasha, let's meet up! We should have dinner together. Come to the Imperial. Nobody else, just you and me!"

"I'm busy today."

"Put it all aside! Come on! I'll tell you a funny story that I heard yesterday from our great, little, plump mockingbird."

"What's the story?"

"A small masterpiece! A precious study! About both of us! Please come!"

Here it is! thought Berner. *A small masterpiece! A precious study!* This is what he was looking for. So, he spliced the words in his memory and kept it in his mind to preserve it.

He etched these words into his memory, like a stone fossil imprint of a patterned fern leaf. They will remain there for the rest of his life, which will continue for many more long years after Vershatsky's life ends.

"Okay, I'll come," he promised. "At seven o'clock!"

Putting down the receiver, looking into the foggy Moscow distance, he thought that tonight, when it got dark and the crimson advertisement for Smirnov vodka would light up over the rooftops, Vershatsky would be gone.

He pressed a button on his desk, inviting in his deputy.

Deputy Feofanov was a young man who had an internship at Columbia University. He was involved in a securities placement in Germany, with experience working on privatization committees. Berner saw him among his friends and watched him during negotiations on the corporatization of an aviation company. He offered a large salary and put him on the board of the corporation. He was pleased with Feofanov, but lately there have been signals through his security service. According to them, Feofanov was meeting with competitors. He was twice seen at dinner in the company of the director of an arms company, at a time when a sharp conflict was brewing with his own company. There was no recording of the conversation, but the very fact that he was communicating with the enemy was alarming and dangerous.

Now, looking at this young, polite man with an impeccable hairdo, in a snow-white collar and a dark blue jacket, Berner peered at him and wondered, *He'll betray me, won't he?* He waited for confirmation of his suspicions when Akhmet finally brought the tape with Feofanov's overheard conversation.

Looking into a dark, gold-edged notebook, Feofanov reported to the chief the situation in Berner's corporation, in all its branches from Barcelona to Vladivostok.

He reported about an explosion on a Siberian gas pipeline near Khanty-Mansiysk, the destruction of a pumping station, and a small forest fire caused by the accident. He talked about the flak he received from the Saratov criminal group on one of the directors of the Volga branch and about the suspicion that the aforementioned flak involved the regional administration, dissatisfied with the activities of the branch. He talked about an unpleasant incident on the Polish-Belarusian border, where a batch of Mercedes were detained. The agreement on its unhindered passage turned out to be violated, and in this, according to Feofanov, the president of Belarus was involved. In conclusion, knowing Berner's special interest in this topic, he reported on the construction of a guest villa near Nice on the Cote d'Azur and that one of the best designers in France had been invited for its interior design.

"Okay," Berner said. "Please mark yourself. Contact the Ministry of Defense and agree on the supply of our gifts to Chechnya, to the active army. Soldiers will receive canned food. Officers will get our signature bottle of vodka. And please, do not hesitate on this. Let them fly there!"

He waited until Feofanov made a note in his notebook, examining his beautiful hairstyle and pleasant face. He thought, *Will he betray me? Or will he not betray me?*

"I was told you like lobster soup," Berner said with a smile. "Are you really going to split their shells with these plumbing tools?"

"Don't be lazy," answered Feofanov. "I've always wanted to understand what the creature is, surrounded from the outside by such a dense shell."

He will betray me! Berner decided firmly and laughed amiably.

"Has the messenger from Dudayev arrived?"

"He is waiting."

"Call him in!"

The Chechen was broad-shouldered and narrow at the waist with flexible joints, which concealed the possibility of a sudden jerk or throw. A thin suit and a silk shirt with a standing collar hugged the muscular body of the rifleman and rider. He extended a warm, strong hand to Berner, and pressed it to his chest after shaking hands. Berner sat him down at a low, inlaid table, where there was a hot teapot with a red pattern that matched the nearby cups. There was also a dish with sugar cubes, a Turkish delight, nuts, and oriental sweets waiting for them. The Chechen noted with a grateful smile the oriental style of tea drinking and fixed his yellowish lynx eyes on Berner.

"Did you get an appointment with the deputy prime minister?" Berner asked, picking up a heavy, round teapot. He filled the guest's cup, feeling the hot aroma of black and gold tea.

"I'll meet with him tomorrow," the Chechen replied, waiting for Berner to fill his cup, and only after that he stretched out his thin, pointed fingers to the platter with nuts. "Thank you for your support and help."

"Any news from Grozny? I'm sorry about what happened," Berner tried to give his voice an intonation of compassion and guilt.

The Chechen felt it. Confidentially, not as an enemy, but as a friend, he answered, "You know, the Russian troops made a mistake. They underestimated Dzhokhar's tactics. Now their advanced units are completely destroyed. The reserves are at a halt, and a large number are killed or captured."

"Tell Dzhokhar to give special attention to Russian prisoners. I would like to be given the opportunity to return at least a small group of soldiers and officers from captivity. These humanitarian actions will facilitate negotiations and bring us closer to our goals."

"Dzhokhar understands this. You will of course be given such an opportunity."

Berner caught the energy emanating from the Chechen. A mysterious combination of strength, courtesy, treachery, refined contempt, and willingness to give in, showing the highest honor and stabbing him right away, while holding the blade down his throat.

"How does Dzhokhar feel?" Berner was catching this complex explosive mixture, like a rush of a breeze merged with common breathing. This is how the wind blows from the mountain, carrying the smell of hot slopes, delicate flowers, and an invisible corpse hidden in a crevice. "It is a pity that we could not keep the process in the realm of peaceful talks in light of economic interests."

"I know that today Dzhokhar spoke on the phone with Moscow. He, too, regrets the start of hostilities. He hopes for an early end to the war, for a return to peace and the sphere of economic interests. He believes that this conflict is amenable to regulation on both sides. He should not go beyond the limits marked by politicians."

"We understand that very well. I will raise this topic in my conversation with the prime minister. The war should not obscure economic interaction between us. The level of military operations must be controlled by both sides.

"You promised to take our money to your bank." the Chechen said as he carefully took a bite of a Turkish delight, and Berner caught sight of his white teeth sinking into the pinkish, glassy molasses.

"I'll keep my promise. My financiers are slightly confused by the nature of this money. Interpol notes the increase in drug flows into Russia. There is information that your people are sitting at the borders in Nakhodka, Tajikistan, and Azerbaijan."

"War requires money. We did not start the war," the Chechen replied, quietly putting down his cup and looking at Berner with red eyes.

"Stopping the war requires money too," Berner said.

"You must be sure that any slowdown or suspension of the war by Russia will be paid for by us."

"The main payment that we expect from you is the agreement to keep the entire oil complex intact. Our troops, at any intensity of hostilities, will not touch the pipes or factories. You must do the same on the Russian side."

The Chechen bowed his hand to his heart, making it clear that their agreement was not just an agreement between partners, but an oath and promise.

"We Chechens keep our word. As a sign of his respect, Dzhokhar sends you a modest New Year's gift." He pulled a tiny box out of his pocket, opened it, took out a gold ring from Morocco, and handed it to Berner.

Berner accepted the heavy, shining ring on which their prophet's sayings were written in Arabic script. He put it on his finger. He felt a cruel, killing force strike from the ring, as if it were a golden, sharpened tooth of a merciless beast.

The ring hastened to shine. Pale and frightened, he accompanied the guest to the door. He then looked at his finger, where a pink, inflamed burn was visible.

He summoned Akhmet to him and said, "Well, let's see your Olympic maiden."

"I would not recommend it, Yakov Vladimirovich. But if you insist, let's look at a distance, in a dash."

They rushed across Moscow in two cars. At the front, streamlined and swift, like a predatory fish, was Berner with Akhmet. In the second car, heavy and muzzled like a bulldog, were the guards. They raced, pulsing with an evil flashing light, turning on a siren, and running red lights.

Berner looked at the snow-covered Moscow facades and could not understand what sick, perverse passion made him rush to look at Vershatsky's killer. What an insatiable, vicious curiosity that prompted him to look at a woman who, in an hour, will put a bullet in his long-time friend. In this curiosity was the excruciating interest in the cause of any death. There was a double interest in the instrument of death, not to mention in himself, who had condemned this friend to death, paying to put a rifle in the hands of a hired killer. There was an attraction to the woman-killer, a secret desire to possess her and through this possession to consecrate the forthcoming action, to turn it into a sacrifice, into a ritual, into an erotic cult. Of course, there was an attraction to Vershatsky, who naively assumes to live, love women, increase his wealth, and see Berner at a cozy table tonight, indulging in sentimental memories. There was also Vershatsky's mistress, who gave birth and was waiting for the young father to spend time with their new baby.

His attraction was passion, vice, and inexplicable deep anguish mixed with sweetness, and something else that was no longer hidden within him, but next to him or over him, hanging like a nameless, formidable force controlling him. All of them—Berner, Vershatsky, his mistress and baby, a woman sniper, Ingush Akhmet, the minister of defense, the president's daughter, unknown soldiers dying at that moment on the streets of Grozny—all were points at which the lines of a geometric figure converged. This figure was a flat projection, a shadow of another unrecognizable, volumetric figure, consisting of many faces, angles, and ledges inaccessible to earthly thinking. This figure was like a huge meteorite floating in the blackness of the universe, a deadly, gray rock that flew in from boundless space and hung over their earthly lives. This earthly life of people, including the life of Berner, was covered by the shadow of this nameless, cosmic rock.

They arrived at the sports complex. Berner, accompanied by Akhmet, walked through the cool, light entrance, where tennis and volleyball were being played on green fields in glass rooms separated from the snow and blizzards. Here, the people swam in emerald pools and raised multi-colored barbells.

They got to the shooting range. Akhmet asked him to wait and then disappeared in the doorway. Berner absentmindedly looked at the tall, skinny athletes in their picturesque workout gear and wondered at his lack of freedom. He didn't make himself come here. It was not he who forced this unknown woman to become an instrument of death. It is not he, the head of the corporation, who negotiates, makes money, appoints and overthrows ministers, creates global projects, and engages in exciting and dangerous espionage. It is not him standing on a soft green carpet under a glass dome, watching a handsome athlete with wet hair, who had just come from the showers, throwing a light jacket over his strong shoulders.

This strange split of losing himself in these thoughts resembled dizziness. Life fell out of focus and split in two, like in a badly tuned binocular. In the interval between the two images there was something else, something dark, undrawn, hidden under the imaginary reality, which appeared as a black blur leading to infinity. He was afraid of it, and felt a formidable, incarnate will emanating from this spot, which ruled over him and moved his actions and desires, where at any moment, it was ready to drag him into the abyss. It felt like madness and ended when Akhmet appeared at the door with a tall, young woman.

She had blonde, short-cropped hair, a small, handsome face, and calm, gray eyes. A sports bag hung over her shoulder. Low, strong breasts protruded under her sweater, and a silk scarf was tied around her neck. Faint wrinkles gathered around her eyes. *She has wrinkles due to aiming through the scope of the sniper*, thought Berner.

"Sir," said Akhmet, "this is Lena, a member of the Olympic team. Lena, this is Yakov Vladimirovich Berner. He knows how difficult it can be for Olympians, and he will be funding the team's training."

"Thank you," the woman said. "We do have many difficulties finding funding. Help us, and we will meet your expectations."

She said it kindly and calmly. Her gray eyes slowly and carefully examined Berner's face and stopped at the bridge of his nose. Berner suddenly felt like a target.

He would never understand what motivated this young, attractive woman to shoot her compatriot in the head that evening and then fly to Chechnya, where, among the ruins, wearing woolen, tight-fitting gloves, she will patiently wait for a Russian soldier to appear in the distance, carrying a bowler hat, or an officer, holding the scope to her eyes, and with accurate shots send them to the next world. She smelled faintly of perfume. Her lips were in translucent lipstick. She adjusted her silk scarf with dry, white fingers.

Berner suddenly thought that it was not too late, that he could cancel his order, disrupt the operation. He could tell her not to dare go to Vavilov Street, where a position is equipped in the attic and a sniper rifle is waiting for her in a case, disassembled into base components, nor go to the airfield, where the military plane was preparing for her flight to Mozdok.

He wanted to tell her this, but an unknown, forbidding force emanating from a dark spot, as if from a dungeon, prevented him. A huge, strangely shaped rock, flown in from other worlds, consisting of unknown substances and metals, with the imprints of alien life, hung over him, and he felt its gravity overcoming him in the shadow of this asteroid.

"Well, I'm off. Goodbye!" the woman said. She shook Berner's hand, and he watched how gracefully and easily she walked away, flickering her silk scarf.

He was on his way to the business club for lunch. Passing Pushkin Square, near the monument he saw a crowd, red banners, and flags, and he heard the metal waves of the loudspeaker hitting the car windows.

"What's going on?" he asked Akhmet.

"The reds are rallying against the war in Chechnya."

"Stop!" he ordered the driver. They stood at the sidewalk. Berner rolled down the window, and the shrill, saw-like moans and screams of the speaker burst into the velvety warmth of the cabin along with the hard, cold air. On the podium a small, well-known man made into a caricature by the news on TV, the leader of the Communists, jerked his thin fist into the air, shrugged up his shoulder, and shouted words furiously like scraps of burning cloth. The crowd caught and grabbed them on the fly, eagerly swallowing them. The steam from the many mouths seemed to be the smoke of these eaten wads of fire.

"Comrades! We appeal to our soldiers and officers! Fraternize with the Chechen soldiers! Turn your weapons together against the bourgeoisie and bankers who have unleashed this fratricidal slaughter!"

The crowd was roaring, flapping red flags and paper banners. Berner suddenly felt a fierce, burning hatred for this crowd, for its orator, for his twitching fist, and for the red, paper banners and paper posters.

In all his recent reflections and bewilderments, his metaphysical doubts associated with the mysteriousness and futility of being alive gave way to a blinding hatred for these worn, black coats, ridiculous hats and caps, and these sullen, frowning faces and clenched fists, in which roughly made banners were clasped.

This crowd wished him, Berner, death. They wished death to his wife and unborn child. It was ready to burn down his house, trample on his flower beds, and destroy his vases and statues. A black, foul-smelling, hate-fueled crowd wanted to break into his library and study, into his greenhouse and azure pool to destroy, desecrate, and leave vile ashes.

He paid them back with hatred. He did not let them out of the putrid gateways. He tricked them with his TV programs and fooled them with television games, where he teased and tamed, cut into chunks, and then turned these chunks against each other, ridiculing their idols and leaders, desecrating their dreams and ideals, and turning their desires, doubts, and fears into an idiotic theater.

If these actions did not help break up the crowd, which were stupefied by hunger and animal instincts, as it happened once before, they would storm the Kremlin or mayor's office and attack with machine guns and tanks, crush with their bulldozers, burn napalm like rats, and drive everything back into the slums in damp barracks and communal apartments.

"Let them eat their own shit! And we will order soup with sturgeon! Let's go!" he ordered the driver.

After lunch, time began to move in painful jerks, from one television news program to another. In about sixteen or seventeen hours, a message about the murder of Vershatsky was supposed to sound. Berner was nervous and became restless. He constantly looked at his watch. Struggling with the slow passage of time, he decided to go to an art gallery, where his money was used to present an exhibition that attracted modernists.

The gallery was full of people, and when he entered, he immediately asked the gatekeeper, "Where is the TV in this place?"

He was shown a shoddy TV set in a cramped dressing room.

"Check if it works well," he ordered Akhmet and walked into the crowd.

In the spacious hall, an incomprehensible action took place. Spectators crowded the walls. These were fashion critics, famous artists, reporters with television cameras, and fancifully dressed visitors.

In the middle of the hall on the wooden, patterned floor, a yaranga was built, made of poles pasted over with pieces of paper that resembled a shaggy hide. The yaranga glowed faintly from the inside, where a barely discernible creature resided within. It was either a man covered with the same ragged features or an animal in shaggy fur. Right there, near the yaranga, in the light coming from the structure resembled something like a sled. On this sled sat a shaman, wearing a mask, carrying a tambourine, and glued from head to toe in the same paper rags. Something loud and guttural cried out in some mysterious, apparently non-existent language. Among the rumble and gurgling, like flashes of light in the endless wavy snows of the tundra, there were obscene words that disappeared again among the barking along with the howling and thumping of a tambourine.

Berner listened irritably to the dog barking mixed with obscenities. He did not understand the meaning of what was happening. He was annoyed at the sight of the yaranga with a hidden, lurking creature and damp, chewed paper scattered on the floor. He believed all this was quackery, paid for by his wallet and that he should reduce the costs of these mediocre fools who consider themselves the salt of the earth.

The shaman stopped shuddering and shouting. He hit the tambourine hard. Silence fell, and there was a grunt with heavy puffing from within the yaranga. Forcing his way through the stakes, a strange, humpbacked creature with a molded, paper muzzle and a long, sharpened horn crawled out. On four legs, its back humped, swinging its rope tail, the moaning creature moved across the floor. It approached the crowd, resting its horn on the knees and crotches of the men, thrusting a paper snout under the women's skirts, while moaning and grunting like a porcupine.

The shaman began to groan and curse again. He brought out a makeshift bag and carried it to the audience. He stomped and danced. He began to remove bright, colorful masks from the bag and presented them to the audience. Anyone who pressed a painted red-yellow, blue-gold, or green-black mask to his face suddenly seemed to lose his mind. They started jumping, squatting, and spinning around, making inarticulate sounds.

The shaman, peering through the slits of his visor with laughing eyes, handed Berner a black and gold mask with a red pattern, resembling the head of a Chinese dragon. Berner took it and pressed it to his face. He felt the mask stick to his forehead, the bridge of his nose, and his cheekbones. It had grown along with his skin, saturated with his blood and juices. It had become his face. And he, as if they had brought him a cup with a laughing potion, felt a surge of insane fun, energy, and freedom, a desire to jump and wave his arms. They jumped and danced around him. They pushed and tugged at his sleeves, pinched his chest and buttocks. Obeying the general madness and obeying the mask that became his face and essence, he started shaking, turned like a loach, howled like an animal, and snapped like a bird. He began to grab neighbors, hug women, shamelessly wagging his hips, depicting a frantic dance that was born of absurd and random movements.

Akhmet found him in the raging crowd. He pulled out Berner with force and took off the mask. Berner, breathless, with a burnt face, as if he had kissed a hot frying pan, looked with incomprehensible eyes.

"What's...?"

"Seventeen hours... News..."

Berner was absentmindedly staring at the TV, still feeling the unknown creature that had flown into him, unwilling to leave his body where it had clung to his bones and muscles from the inside.

There was some kind of strike. Some ministerial meetings.

"Crime chronicle," the announcer said excitedly. "We have just received a message that the famous banker Lev Vershatsky was shot in the head at the entrance of his house on Vavilov Street. Apparently the sniper was firing from an attic opening on the roof of the opposite house. Law enforcement officials refused to provide details of the incident in the interests of the ongoing investigation..."

"Let's go!" Berner said, sober. "Specify which morgue, probably the main morgue of the city."

At the entrance to the morgue, journalists crowded the area with television cameras. The policemen did not let them in. Berner stood aside, waiting for Akhmet to call the authorities and receive permission to enter.

"How do you feel about what happened?" a young, gambling reporter ran up to him, beckoning the operator with a wave. "After all, you were friends with Mr. Vershatsky..."

"I can't believe it... I want to see it with my own eyes..." Berner replied, seeing the TV cameras approaching him.

Akhmet came out with the chief of police, where they were led through the entrance to the morgue building.

In the middle of the tiled, brightly lit hall stood a gurney. On it, under some covers, was Vershatsky with his head opened up. Berner's eyes were struck by the white, illuminated forehead. On it, above his left eyebrow, there was a black bullet hole full of glassy, half-frozen blood. Vershatsky's lips, still pink, were tightly and angrily pressed together, as if he had given a vow of silence. But his eyes were open, where under long lashes were two moist, bluish slits through which he peeped at those who surrounded his body.

His wife was there, looking shocked and sick, with a tear-stained handkerchief crumpled in her hands. A doctor in green surgical scrubs stood at a distance, for he had nothing to do, and he remained away from the group either out of decency or out of curiosity for the eminent visitors. There were also several investigators, quietly whispering about something.

Berner looked at his friend's beautiful, clear face, blue and white as moonlight. He felt a strange desire to insert his finger into the round wound and feel inside the sharp bone edges. He looked at Vershatsky's proud, crooked nose and clearly heard his voice from their morning call, "A small masterpiece… A precious study…"

Berner will never know the true content of this sketch, but he will remember the voice, the white, illuminated forehead, and the red wound, clogged with a large, glossy cranberry.

He went up to Vershatsky's wife and, bending over, kissed her hand. He noticed that the scarf was trimmed with circles with an embossed pattern.

He then went to the doctor and asked, "Was he still alive when he got in? Could he have been saved?"

"No. He was dead on arrival. All bodily functions had already stopped."

Berner stood under the lamps that illuminated the white tiles, the marble relief of Vershatsky's face, and the red hole in his forehead.

Somewhere far away, in the blazing Chechen capital of Grozny, troops were advancing. The cylinders and spheres of oil refineries that now belonged solely to him, Berner, were now shining in his mind. A car raced through the city, carrying a woman sniper from Moscow. In his soul, instead of feeling triumph, confusion arose. Something sticky and viscous accumulated in his throat. Under his heart, like a restless embryo, something began to throb and twitch. He smelled a faint whiff of formaldehyde, just like that time in Mexico City among witchcraft potions, dried monkey legs, and furry skins.

He bowed to everyone at once, Vershatsky, his widow, the doctor, and the investigators, and then headed for the exit.

On the street, journalists surrounded him.

"What is your assessment of what happened? In your opinion, who is the killer? When was the last time you saw Mr. Vershatsky?"

"I can't speak now," Berner answered, but then forced, "We were very close. He was a wonderful friend, a wonderful family man, a talented financier, and an impeccable citizen. In our desire to make Russia great, they wanted to stop us. I give my word over the body of my murdered friend that the killer will be found and punished."

He left without looking back, knowing that the cameras were watching him and looking at his back, seeing him off with keen, greedy pupils.

He got into his car. "Home!" he ordered to the driver.

They raced, overtaking cars, raising a blizzard in their tracks, scattering frantic, purple flashes on the sides of the car. They passed the Triumphal Arch with sculptures of horses and armor as empty as chitinous beetles. They drove through Poklonnaya Hill with a small church resembling a gilded kiosk and the Victory Monument, sharp as a prickly knitting needle. They turned onto Rublevskoye Highway, slipping through Krylatskoye, which held the presidential house, which looked like a sealed ark where goats, roosters, hippos, and other strange and noisy creatures come to from the Kremlin corridors in case of a flood. They got out onto the Uspenskoe Highway.

Berner felt his insides shake. The embryo within him swelled and bubbled. It pushed his intestines apart and pushed outward and upward, through his esophagus and larynx.

"Stop!" he ordered the driver. Both cars came to a halt. The guards rushed out onto the road, where they surrounded him in a semi-circle, and he, covering his mouth with his palm, went to the side of the road, through the ditch, into a nearby forest. Knee-deep in the snow, pressing his forehead to the trunk of a pine tree, he bent down. He began to vomit. He gasped and spit out a foul foam, as he emanated tears and blood. Shrimp and blood clots flew outward, and with his bulging eyes, half-blinded with tears, he saw a red, naked, skinned, squirrel-like creature fall out of him and, twitching like a carcass, looking at him with a sharp muzzle, it fled into the forest.

He returned to the car.

"Are you alright, Yakov Vladimirovich?" Akhmet asked carefully.

"I'm fine," Berner replied barely audible as he plunged back into the car. "Home!" he ordered the chauffeur, feeling how he was pressed into the seat by speed, as the pine trees flashed, merging into green-white whirlwinds.

19

Kudryavtsev woke up from a tremor that shook his entire body. It was as if someone was shaking him and trying to shake out his eyes, teeth, entrails, and all his bones and veins, like he was a sack of potatoes. He was lying on the floor, on top of a pile of rags. A layer of ash was floating in the air, and Nozdra was holding a full glass of water over him as Anna was bandaging his chest. She gasped, as if every coil of the white fabric caused her own suffering.

"What are you doing?" he whispered.

"Oh, my dear!"

"Where was I wounded?"

"You were wounded everywhere..."

"Nozdra, where is the BMP?"

"The damned thing is knocked out and on fire..."

"Where is Chizh?"

"He's dead..."

He tried to get up, but he began to shake again, and it seemed like someone was trying to knock his eyes out from their sockets and his teeth from his jaw. He eagerly grabbed a glass of icy water, spilling it on his chest.

"Help me up..."

Anna and Nozdra obediently grabbed him from both sides, and with good effort lifted his loose, shaken body, where he felt not pain, but a dull stupor. He tried to keep focus on a small static point in his mind, making his way through this tiny hole, like a spider moving along a thin, luminous web. In this widening gap, not allowing it to close, he saw the windowsill with an overturned machine gun, a grenade launcher with its last grenade, and a snow-covered, gray square. In the snow in the distance, the BMP smoldered and burned.

"There," he turned his eyes and nodded to the exit. Obeying his command, they led him to the door to the landing.

Chizh's face was resting on the windowsill, with his forehead touching his weapon. His hands continued to grip the gun, but his body was disheveled and it could easily be seen that he was lifeless. On the windowsill, among the shells and shards of glass, lay a dusty notebook. Kudryavtsev, holding on to the doorframe, looked at Chizh. It seemed to him that from the square, out of the dim light, a huge, black, and slimy log had approached the window. This log stupidly and senselessly hit the house and killed Chizh. Before that it had killed Filya, Krutoi, and smashed Tarakan's chest, but had only stunned Kudryavtsev. It froze for a moment where it stopped swinging, but it would move again and would certainly kill Nozdra, the woman with an expressionless face, and he himself, who had put them all at risk of being brutally killed by the swinging log.

He lost consciousness again but woke up in the apartment sitting on a pile of rags, leaning against the wall. Anna threw a coat on his shoulders and buttoned it up to his neck. He sat, bandaged, clothed in an overcoat on his naked body, and slowly, by an enormous amount of will, gathered the pieces of his personality that had been blown apart, like when they collect a broken cup from the shards, put it on the table, and fill in cracks with beads of glue. While the container is almost intact and regained its shape and color, it still lacks several important fragments.

Through the window into the house, the same inanimate force pressed down, flattening people's lives. The battering log aimed its black, blunt butt at them. From this end, from the fossilized tree rings, a helicopter took off with a crack in the glitter of propellers.

Humpbacked, spotted, and with a narrow fish tail, carrying tight bundles of missiles on its underbelly, the helicopter passed over the square. It then made a turn and, flashing an elliptical of its blades, disappeared from sight while continuing to emit a whistling, dying sound.

Another flying vehicle with a red star appeared in the view of the window. Kudryavtsev tried to get up, seeing how the helicopter turned over the station, and from there, from the roofs and windows, he could see the smoke trails fly to the helicopter. Two rocket-propelled grenades, fired from launchers, which looked similar to lumps of burning wool, were thrown toward the helicopter. They missed their target but instead hit and exploded on the arcs on the square.

The appearance of helicopters meant the approach of troops. Somewhere nearby, troops were gathering and preparing for an assault, and the helicopters were probing the enemy's front line, preparing for the infantry.

Kudryavtsev, with his hastily restored and scrappy consciousness, explained the appearance of these helicopters as a close end to the suffering he had endured. But the complete picture of the world did not add up, because something was missing. He stood at the window, trying to figure out what he should do and what should be done with the appearance of these helicopters.

The flying vehicle, which had disappeared behind houses and roofs, returned again. Close, noisy, and fluttering with screws, it rolled down in a straight line, like a pike that had spotted its prey. From under its belly, it stretched out its fins, from which rockets spun, scratched the sky, and landed among the houses. More bombs landed in the square, throwing all the debris and smoke up into the air. The earth caught fire. Chechens ran out of the smoke, scattering out like a fan, under the pressure of the blast wave, as if a splinter was stuck in each of them that drove them forward with pain and sharpened, ragged edges.

Kudryavtsev saw the shells hit, but this did not cause him joy. The tiny shard missing in his mind was lost. He looked out of the window at the world, and though this world had many meanings, he was at a loss for any understanding.

The second helicopter took the place of the first, where it stopped for a moment, leaning against the air with sparkling blades. It spat out a sharp, black spray. It drove long spindles, and on the square the missiles curled through the air before leaving cuts in the snow.

These cuts pointed toward the house. A truck stood in the way of those ragged scratches. In the back of the truck, neatly arranged, lay flamethrowers filled with aerosol. The poisonous dew of the flamethrowers sprayed in the air and exploded and burned the atmosphere, creating a void, into which, like a black hole, rushed the walls of buildings. It tore off tank turrets and uprooted trees that did not have time to burn particles of flesh; everything turned into a blast furnace.

Kudryavtsev knew the destructive power of a vacuum explosion. He looked at the black scratches directed toward the truck, but in his confusion did not understand what to do.

The world was crushing and twitching like an image on a split-screen.

Each separate fragment had its own meaning and plot. It was its own picture and truth.

He, a boy in red boots, runs along a spring stream and whips at the air with a twig, driving a small chip of wood into the stream with such joy, such a sparkle, under such a wonderful, warm sun...

He, a cadet, buries himself into the sticky mud, listening to the tremors of the earth. A tank is advancing on him, crushing crunchy tracks into the rut. He wants to jump up, run away, and hide in a nearby ravine. But he remains, and lets a heavy, black carcass drive over him...

He and his mother go out into the evening fog. The pond glistens dimly with cold dew underfoot. He squeezes his weak mother's hand, feeling a cooling touch. Such pain and love arise in him, the desire to convey to her his ardent strength and tenderness, to prolong her stay on this earth...

He's in the officer's dorm room with drunken faces and bottles of vodka. Someone is shouting, using foul language. Opposite is a tattered, drunk girl, her lips in bright red lipstick. Her blue, watery eyes, look like those of a caught fish...

He stands on a street in Moscow with a damp blizzard and a neon bank sign. The fat rear of a Mercedes drives away with a ruby fire. There are some well-fed, dark-haired people in long, warm coats...

He steps in the snow, holding the dead body of Filya, feeling how faintly his frail body flickers and ripples, when the wall of a brick house is approaching...

The world was crushing and twitching, as if on a split-screen, and Kudryavtsev could not focus back on the image or grasp the main meaning in any of the manifestations of his visions.

He heard the roar and whistle of a helicopter. The machine was not yet visible, but its sound, the whistle of its blades, indicated the attack vector.

"Anna! Nozdra! To me!" he called out.

They approached, he put his hands on their shoulders. Obeying his silent instructions, they took him to the far corner of the room, where they sat him on a pile of the old man's blankets. They too sat down next to him, and he did not let go of them as he hugged them, keeping them close to him.

The helicopter approached, carving a glittering, narrow cut in the sky. Kudryavtsev was drawn to this sound. In his stunned state and his shaken will, he pulled together the torn world with the last of his strength. He slipped up, as he was surrounded by fragments of images, but he did not allow everything to burst into countless fractional sets. Suddenly, he succeeded.

With the world brought together, a distinct meaning had appeared, a wonderful truth that had no expression, as if a huge, winged wonder rose and stood, blocking the window. It looked into their room with shining eyes. It covered him and the woman and the exhausted soldier with a heap of noisy wings, which screened them from death.

A fire support helicopter fired a pack of S-8 rockets from its drum and hit the truck. A curly fireball boiled over the square. The explosion broke off half of the house and scattered brick dust and debris from the torn rooftop with many small and shapeless scraps, which burned like fuses.

Kudryavtsev was sitting on the floor, hugging the soldier and the woman, as if he saw how a space devoid of walls opened before him. Through the swinging ceilings and beams, there was flying dust with a stifling whirlwind of burnt aerosol, a snowy square, the greenish stucco molding of the train station, a dark platform, and a string of steel tracks. On the rails, waving a white and blue flag with a low "hurrah" were the Marines, dressed in black and wearing berets, running and firing their machine guns.

Kudryavtsev looked at the Marines, and his lips soundlessly uttered something he could not pronounce, some inexplicable word.

20

On the edge of the Smolensk village stood a brick-built church with five domes and a bell tower tent. There was a worn-out road covered with tractor scars and strewn with manure. A yellow flock of birds flew past, landing on the nearby fields. Behind the church was a blue, snow-covered garden that was full of hare tracks and snowdrifts. Under the walls there was a small cemetery full of red and white crosses and silver fences, in which were settled wreaths of paper flowers that had been crushed by the snow.

The village was dark with humpbacked huts, smoke from fireplaces, and bristling fences. Fields were spread out around them. They looked glazed, as if worn by the wind. Transparent drifts wandered through them, and in the distance there were sleighs and the frozen forest, which looked like a blue fin, stuck out on the hill.

The church's liturgy ended. The people, who over time had become more and more old men and women, slowly dispersed. They lingered at the door, signing the cross and letting in the cold. From the window, they could be seen flickering their scarves and hats as they made their way home.

The priest, Father Dmitry Nozdratenkov, tired of the liturgy, felt unwell and patiently waited for the parishioners to disperse in order to retire to the sacristy, take off his heavy, stiff vestments sewn with golden thread, and, after locking up the church, go home. At home, his mother will treat him with hot tea and viburnum, lay him on a warm couch, and throw blankets and sheepskin coats on top of him, and in the light heat he will doze off and think about his son Gavryusha, who had gone to serve in the Chechen War. It was more than a week since they had heard from him. His mother, listening to the radio, sighed heavily and cried secretly.

The church was heated. The light from the windows illuminated the Christmas decorations and the striped and elegant rugs. There were also white, handmade towels on the icons and green spruce branches, on which Christmas ornaments were hung with the delight of the parishioners.

Where the light of the windows did not reach, in a gloomy corner, near a dark oak crucifix on the icon case, there were lamps shining. The largest lamp, made of ancient crimson glass and in golden plumage, burned in front of the icon of the Archangel Gabriel, depicted in full-length on a long board at the moment when he was scattering his blue cloak and folding his wings strained from flight as he stood at the threshold in front of the Virgin Mary, reporting to her the Good News.

The archangel was the patron saint of his son, Gavryusha. Father Dmitry was waiting to be alone to appear before the angel and pray for his son.

Old Marfusha, a pilgrim and a traveler, who had disappeared all her life in distant monasteries and parishes, began to shuffle toward him, shuffling with old, felt boots. She was small, with a slight hump, clothed in a checkered cloth shawl, from under which the blue eyes of a child looked out. She bowed, held out her hands for the blessing, and gnarled like a trough hollowed out of a tree.

"Father, bless me to go to Pskov-Pechory after Christmas. There, they say, Father John Krestiankin has become very ill. I want to visit him once more, to confess."

"Go if your soul compels you." Father Dmitry blessed her bowed head. "You're too old, Grandma Marfusha. Don't get too cold on the way home."

"By your prayers, Father, by your prayers..."

Bowing, she trotted and shuffled to the exit with the heavy doors. The light and snow flashed once more, surrounded by pink steam.

A tall, thin man with a boney face belonging to the blacksmith Styopa approached, who had injured his hand while working. His gray hair stuck out like a crest, as he held his hat in his good hand. His damaged hand was hidden under his coat.

"Pray for me, Father Dmitry. Pray that my hand heals. How will I work? We'll die of hunger. You must pray. I have given fifty thousand to the church."

"God will help, Styopa. I pray for you, and you are recorded. But go to my mother. She will pour motherwort into your bottle, and your bones will grow better from it."

The blacksmith bowed, covering his suffering eyes. Serious and strict, he walked to the exit while rearranging his legs straight, like poles. His uncovered head flashed through the sun and snow, becoming enveloped in steam.

The last person to arrive was the church elder Elena Andreevna, all in black, like a nun. She was sharp-nosed and nimble, like a jackdaw. She accepted the blessing and immediately began to pronounce strictly, "Father, it hurts that a lot of firewood goes to the furnace in the church! There doesn't seem to be enough! They don't come here to bask, but to pray to God. Let's pray that there will be enough to warm the houses! Please, Father, tell Afanasi not to use too much wood. We used the tithing money to pay for wood!"

She was displeased while looking around the church with her last probing gaze, checking whether all the candle stubs were extinguished and thrown into the wax box and whether all the icons and books were tidied up and locked in the office. She then trotted to the exit and made the sign of the cross at the door. Outside, jackdaws flew over the road in the winter sun. She jumped up, mingled with them, and sank.

Father Dmitry was finally alone. He rejoiced at the silence and loneliness in the empty, spacious church, where the shadows of the parishioners still hovered along with the smoke from the censer, chants, and prayers. This prayer was kept under the vaults and among the paintings, icons, and copper chandeliers like a living, disembodied cloud, like a warm breath.

He picked up a spruce twig that had been dropped on the floor and, smelling its delicate, resinous scent, went to the window. It was in that hour of the short winter day when the sun loses its silvery and white brightness, begins to turn red, increases in size, and descends below the fields. Due to the darkness, they ignited long mica fibers on the road, which made the tracks from the sleighs look like golden foil in the snow.

From the semicircular church window he could see hills, lowlands, a frozen river, bushy dark willows, and remote villages covered in snow in the spacious distance, in which they lived, indulged in labor, stoked stoves, grew old, and gave birth to new people. Here they sinned, suffered, grumbled about their unbearable lives, drank vodka, saw off the recruits, and, in short hours of rest, sang stringy songs at feasts or dozed on the stoves among blizzards and starry nights.

Father Dmitry, a simple-minded village priest, loved the people of his village, and he tried to help them in every possible way. He did not understand why Russian life felt so sad, century after century. Sometimes he secretly murmured that God, having saved other peoples, rewarding them with a comfortable life and prosperity, sent such misfortunes to the Russian people, who are hardworking, patient, and kind. He went through the events of their native history in his memory and did not find sin and seduction among the people for which it was possible to punish. Not understanding the reasons for his people's suffering, he prayed in front of the brown icon of the Virgin Mary.

He approached the iconostasis, holding a spruce twig in his hands. The archangel before whom he stood was in deep shadow, barely glowing with a halo and golden wing tips. The lamp before him burned gloomily and preciously. In its rays, on the face of the archangel, a small, tar tear shimmered, suddenly emerging from the old board.

Father Dmitry knelt and submitted before the beginning of his prayer. He directed this prayer upward, into the distance, into infinity, to the place where angel wings splashed in the eternal azure. While praying, he tried to open his heart like a flower so that prayer would come not only from his mind, his whispering lips, and his gazing eyes, but also from the essence of his wordless soul.

He prayed for the Russian army, for the ancient warriors who went on campaigns to Constantinople and later to the Don and Nepryadva, who fought on the ice lake. He prayed for those who came later, who fought with the Lyakhs near Smolensk and Pskov, carrying icons to the fortress walls, and for those who stood in the face of death near Borodino and then festively entered Paris. He prayed for the regiments that went on the Balkan campaign under the banners of the White General, and for those heroes who perished in the Masurian swamps. He prayed for the army of the Great War, which repelled the Germans in the great fields and rivers and hung their red banners on the palaces of European capitals.

He prayed, trying to imagine their myriad of ranks in helmets and armor and the fluttering of their spears, bayonets, banners, flags, and standards. But the prayer felt weak, and he did not believe it reached to angelic heights. There was no desired warmth in his heart.

He prayed for the Russian commanders and warriors, for the generals and militias, and for the privates. He prayed for Russian princes and warriors who shined among the saints, and for all the unknown German, Japanese, and Soviet soldiers. He prayed for everyone who fought in small wars where Russia had sent them and where they won or suffered losses. He prayed for the most ancient beings, as well as for the living, and for those who will never die. He wished them victory, endurance, and spiritual achievement. He wished them a brotherhood equal to that of the elder and the apprentice, or of the weak and the strong. He prayed for the soldiers who found themselves in the dangerous and hostile Chechnya and asked the Lord not to harden the hearts of Chechens and Russians, as to not divide peoples with blood and hatred, to not destroy cities, to not kill nor torture, but to throw a veil on hating eyes, to hide them from each other.

He was praying and pushing aside with his call, feeling the solid barriers that separated his heart from the endless azure. But his heart glowed faintly like an impenetrable vault that did not let a ray of azure pass through.

Then he turned to the archangel, to his bowed head shaded by a halo, with his wings, in which the wind of heaven had not yet calmed down, with his blue cloak, in which the curl of the sky swirled, and with his light feet touching the ground. He prayed that the archangel, who brought the Holy Virgin the wonderful, unspeakable message, would with his prayer remind the Mother of God about her son Gavryusha and put in his angelic word for him. He prayed that the Mother of God, in her endless love, would save her son from all possible and impossible troubles and take him through every space and land, through trenches and battlefields to here, to his native village, to his father's house, where there is still a wooden horse on the shelf, with which Gavryusha played in his childhood, and where on the shrine near the icon lay an onion-dyed egg made last Pascha before he entered the army, when they were all together.

He prayed for his son, remembering him as a baby in his cramped, white crib, as a boy picking a basket of green onions in the garden, as a boy laughing and floating in the river, and as a young man, looking stern and sad with a shaved head, among other recruits, who were loaded into a military transport.

He prayed for his son and for his companions, with whom it fell to him to endure and serve, for the commanders so that they would not abandon him and would rescue him in difficult times, for the army that defeated its camp in the winter steppe, for all the Russian people, who in their cities and villages languished in labor and hardship, in an eternal expectation of a miracle, and for Russia, beloved and adored, which is endless, gracious, and guarded by the prayers of all saints, intercessors, angels, the Queen of Heaven, and everyone who was allowed to be born in it for great joys and great trials.

He felt his heart suddenly expand hot, as if rays of light were shining through his chest, and he ascended through the church vaults. It was the archangel who raised him on his mighty wings. From there, with his all-seeing eye, he saw his son. He was alive, sitting on the floor of a smoky and dilapidated house. Next to him was a fellow soldier in bandages, hugging him with his arm. Above them was a woman in a torn dress with a wondrous face, as on an icon, shading them from the smoky wind.

It lasted but a moment. He sank to the ground under the arches of the evening church. It was gloomy. The angel was barely visible. In the light of the red lamp, a tear shimmered on the face of the icon.

www.ingramcontent.com/pod-product-compliance
Lightning Source LLC
Chambersburg PA
CBHW031458120626
46545CB00005B/1666